Politics in Land and Water Use Management

Politics in Land and Water Use Management

Fred Simon Lerise

University College of Lands and Architectural Studies (UCLAS)

Dar es Salaam - Tanzania

Mkuki na Nyota Publishers,

P. O. Box 4246,

Dar es Salaam, Tanzania

www.mkukinanyota.com

Published by Mkuki na Nyota Publishers Ltd,
6 Muhonda St., Mission Quarter, Kariakoo
P. O. Box 4246, Dar es Salaam,
Tanzania

www.mkukinanyota.com

ISBN 9987 417 29 9

Printed and bound in India at Rakesh Press, New Delhi-110 028.

Table of Contents

CHAPTER TWELVE: WATER-USERS' ASSEMBLY AT WORK 121

CHAPTER THIRTEEN: IRRIGATORS' ASSOCIATION AND THE VILLAGE COUNCIL TAKE OVER THE MANAGEMENT OF THE PROJECT 131

CHAPTER FOURTEEN: LESSONS FOR POLICY MAKERS AND PRACTISING PLANNERS 153

AKNOWLEDGEMENTS

I wish to express my special gratitude to all individuals, friends and organisations that supported me with encouragement, knowledge and funds that enabled me to carry out the research and write the thesis on which this book is based.

Foremost appreciation is due to the people of Kilimanjaro, especially the villagers of Chekereni and other villagers in the Lower Moshi Plains. Special thanks go to those I interviewed. They were patient with me and my questions, and carefully narrated their experiences to me, without which I would have no stories to tell.

I am also grateful to various people in different offices in Moshi Town, in Dar es Salaam and Chekereni village. The people I met made me feel welcome and provided me with information, most of which is presented in this book.

I owe much to the supervisors of my doctoral research, who helped me with knowledge of how to acquire information and what to do with it, during and after fieldwork. I am greatly indebted to Annelise Bramsnaes, of the Institute of Town and Landscape Planning at the Royal Danish Academy of Fine Arts, Copenhagen, for her tolerance with several readings and comments on endless drafts of my work and her continuous efforts to keep the study focused on the right course.

Bent Flyvbjerg at Aalborg University introduced me to the case method and narratology and made me able to build the Chekereni case. I will always be grateful to him, not only for his attention to detail and precision, but also for his way of arguing by showing examples. I benefited from continuous comments from Jorgen Andreasen at the Department of Human Settlements at the Royal Danish Academy of Fine Arts, Copenhagen, and from Esbern Friis Hansen at the Centre for Development Research, Copenhagen.

Special thanks go to all my friends in this profession, who read and made useful comments on drafts of various chapters. I can only mention a few here; especially, Volker Kreibich at Universitat Dortmund, Jens Muller at Aalborg University, Finn Barnow at the Royal Danish Academy of Fine Arts, Copenhagen, Hans Bjonness at Norwegian University for Science and Technology, Jackson Kombe, Shaban Mgana and Tumsifu Nnkya at the University College of Lands and Architectural Studies in Dar es Salaam.

Thanks also go to librarians at the Centre for Development Research, Copenhagen, the University College of Lands and Architectural Studies in Dar es Salaam, and the Regional Documentation Centre in Moshi, for their invaluable assistance in making available the documents, plans, books, articles and reports on which this book has drawn considerably.

I must also express special acknowledgements to ENRECA-DANIDA for a generous grant which not only financed the research and its publication but also made it possible to practice the case method research protocol.

At the foot of these acknowledgements is my family; Paulina, Mashingo, Seenga, Maria and Filomena, for it is their tolerance, care, patience and support that have enabled me to finish this work and still have a home to go to.

Fred Simon Lerise

October, 2004

Dar es Salaam, Tanzania

Dedication

I wish to dedicate this book to my parents: Mzee Simon and the Late Mama Maria. They shed a lot of sweat so that they could buy me my first exercise books and a pencil, and made tireless efforts to send me to my first classes, thus, setting the foundation on which this book has been placed.

Chapter One

Introduction

The Issue

This is an account of village land use planning and its influence on land use intensification process in rural Tanzania. It shows how smallholder cultivators, government agencies and representatives of international donor agencies, pursue their interests in managing land and water use in Chekereni village, on the slopes of Kilimanjaro. Among the findings from the investigation is that, the belief that structures in terms of policies, legislation, procedures and plans will condition actors and therefore guarantee a certain behavior is questioned. Disputes over access to water are still common, to the extent that issues such as land-use intensification options and environmental conservation find no place on the village-level land-development agenda.

Despite the three and half decades of policies, plans and attempts by the actors, land productivity has not been improved, and instead the efforts have basically brought the small holder cultivators in the village back to where they were before making the attempts.

Tanzania is famous for its post-independence attempts towards rural development. It is one of the few African countries that nationalized and centralized the control of access and use of land, water and other natural resources. It has committed substantial resources in terms of legislation, by-laws and guidelines and plans to intensify land use on a fair and equal basis in the rural areas.

In reality, the aims of the different policies, legislation and plans have not been achieved. Land-use intensification in the rural areas is still very low. Equity and fairness in access to land and in the use of water and other natural resources has not been enhanced. Disputes over property rights in land and natural resources are increasing, while environmental degradation is still a key issue in rural land use. In short, the fame of the multitude of Tanzania's plans and policies for better rural land use is not matched by actual developments on rural lands. Questions addressed in this book are; first, why are the aims declared in the different policies and plans not achieved and secondly, why do attempts by smallholders,

1

government agencies and representatives of international donors achieve so little in the way of land-use intensification?

To find answers to these questions, we shall first have to be clear on what happens when attempts are made to execute policies and plans. How and in what situations do the different institutions use the available policies and plans, and what are the results? These questions are answered by investigating an example where policies, legislation, by-laws and plans have been formulated and used. I would argue that if we know how the current legislation and plans are used (or not used), we shall be in a position to address the other questions and probably develop a better understanding of the plan-reality problem facing rural land-use intensification initiatives in Tanzania. In pursuing these issues, this book will take readers on a journey of three and half decades of rural development in Tanzania, tracing the course of land-use intensification processes in Chekereni village on the slopes of Kilimanjaro.

In the Tanzanian institutional set up a village is the lowest administrative unit and at the same time the lowest unit for rural land-use planning. Village councils are local-level government institutions responsible for carrying out national as well as local-level policy decisions. In Tanzania, a village comprises a vast area of land, including housing, farming and in some areas grazing grounds and forests. The lowest number of households is officially set at 250 households for a registered village. Chekereni village covers 2578 ha. According to the village council records, the population was estimated at 1054 households in 1994. About 50 per cent of village land is owned and used by farmers living outside the village.

By examining the details of the decision-making process in specific land-use change events in Chekereni village, we shall be able to experience the interaction between local institutions, donor agencies and central government policies, plans, laws and procedures and how they work on the ground.

Such knowledge is intended to contribute to making the actors in rural land-use planning more aware of the level of performance of the different policies and plans for achieving the stated purposes. With that awareness, it is possible for decision-makers to re-assess their faith in laws, procedures and plans. Today, little or no concern is given to whether or not the purposes of laws and plans are achieved. As we are concerned with the plan-reality problem in rural land-use, we need to focus as closely as possible on reality in order to understand it.

The intention is to carry out a deep investigation which will focus on the context, process and nature of the strategies used by individual smallholders, community leaders, government officials, politicians and experts when they make land-use change decisions.

The case method and narratology provides the best approach to carry out such a study and produce in-depth knowledge of rural land-use planning in Tanzania. In this research the village council is the main social actor, while the village land is that which the land use intensification is being tried out on. In concentrating on Chekereni, it has been possible to make an intensive follow-up of issues and processes and also maximize proximity to the phenomenon observed. The approach not only provided deep knowledge but also made it possible to nurture greater trust and hopefully to improve the validity of the narratives presented in the subsequent chapters.

Before detailing the land-use intensification process in Chekereni village we shall briefly look at the background to the issue.

Tanzania entered the 1980s with an economic as well as an environmental crisis. After the implementation of the resettlement programmes based on socialist beliefs, or "Ujamaa" in rural areas, problems of land-degradation, losses in agricultural production and disputes over land rights increased. In 1987, the Director for Urban Planning in the Ministry of Lands Housing and Urban Development, who is responsible for village land-use planning, approached the Department of Urban and Rural Planning, for advice on how to improve the performance of village land-use planning in dealing with the crisis. The advice given focused on how to produce better land-use plans. Two years later, in 1989, the Director General for the National Land-Use Planning Commission within the same ministry, organized a workshop for regional town planning officers. The low rate of plan production and implementation was perceived as the main problem. The workshop recommended formulating guidelines for village land-use planning and implementation.[1]

Towards the end of the 1980s, disputes in land rights and in access to water use and other natural resources increased. The institutions formally handling the disputes could not cope. Instead villagers queued for assistance from the President. The President was overwhelmed. In 1990, a Presidential Commission was created to study the sources of conflicts and advise the President. Parallel to the Commission, an inter-ministerial committee to draft a land policy was formed.

The attention given to rural land use in Tanzania derives from its contribution to the food and income of the people of Tanzania and to the national economy. The leading land use in rural Tanzania is agriculture, which is mostly carried out by smallholders. More than 85 per cent of the people in Tanzania are involved in agriculture and are responsible for about 50 per cent of GDP. This is among the reasons for the government's interest in improving the productivity of rural lands so that their potential contribution towards national development can be realized.

The pre-Ujamaa period, 1880s to 1967, is a relevant developmental stage for understanding rural development issues in Tanzania and for understanding the land-use intensification process in Chekereni village. It is the period during which the country was colonized and at the same time an independent native government took over the administration of the country. Important national policies like the introduction of a one-party state, the abolition of traditional leadership in 1963, the 1967 Arusha Declaration and the 1968 Villagization Directive were enacted in this period. These changes were mainly to facilitate a smooth transition from the capitalist state under the British colonial administration to a socialist state or Ujamaa. These were national-level decisions, which had a direct impact on land-use planning in rural Tanzania and in Chekereni in particular, as shown in the next chapter.

Chapter Two
The Formation of Chekereni Settlement

Don't ask, 'What's the problem? ' Ask, 'What's the story?' - That way you'll find out what the problem really is.[1]

Chekereni becomes an Important Place

The Moshi-Tanga-Dar es Salaam railway branches off to Kenya at Kahe at the foot of Mount Kilimanjaro. After taking Tanzania from the Germans, the British restored the railway, extended it to Mombassa and made Kahe an important junction. The road linking Moshi to Kahe crosses the railway six kilometres north of Kahe. At this crossing, as at many others, the British put up a sign warning road users to 'check the train'. To the natives the railway crossing became a landmark referred to in Swahili as *Chekereni*, a softer version of the English warning. Eventually the landmark, fifteen kilometres south of Moshi Town, developed into an important place and became a famous Ujamaa village in Kilimanjaro region, known as Chekereni.

The location was also favored in respect of its proximity to employment opportunities. Of the six estates established south of Moshi Town after the construction of the railway, Gynja sisal estate, overlooking Chekereni, attracted most of the migrants who later settled in the village. Land for the estates was acquired from native authorities under the Imperial Ordinance enacted by the German Colonial Government in 1885.[2] The Ordinance shifted ultimate control over the land from traditional institutions to the colonial government. Land already acquired and used by the natives was left under the control of traditional leaders known as Mangi[3] in the Chagga language. Thus the 610 ha. of the Gynja estate were acquired through the Ordinance and held under 'statutory rights', while the land around Chekereni was under customary or 'deemed rights' which are also recognized by Tanzanian land law.

By 1932, Gynja estate had about 6,500 employees drawn from the different regions in Tanzania and from Kenya. Migrants secured employment first, and after becoming familiar with the surrounding area, acquired land and started farming.

Mzee Mbindyo is one of the migrants who obtained land without direct consent from the Mangi. He describes how he identified and

5

acquired land and eventually decided to settle in Chekereni.

> I came by train, (from Kenya) in 1944.... I was employed to weed. Four years
> later, I decided to look for land across the railway, in the present Chekereni
> area.... I went into the bush and moved around looking for a suitable area to
> clear and settle. As I was moving around I came across a house belonging to
> Mzee Alois, a clerk in Gynja estate.... I went back to the camp and asked Mzee
> Alois for permission to clear a piece of land close to his house. He agreed
> and even allowed me to stay in his house and maintain it, as it was almost
> falling down. I moved from the camp and lived in Mzee Alois's house after
> improving it.... I cleared trees such as *vikwata* and *migongo mwitu*, until I was
> satisfied with the amount of land cleared. The first crop was maize. [4]

Most people who settled in Chekereni before or during 1960s, when
sisal was the country's main agricultural export, followed Mbindyo's
approach: first employment in one of the estates, and later, land and a
home. In general, this is how the land-use intensification process in the
southern part of Chekereni started.

Administratively, Chekereni was located on the border between Uru
in the north and Kahe settlements in the south, under Mangi Sabas and
Mangoto respectively. The Kilimanjaro Paramount Chief or *Mangi Mkuu*[5]
subdivided the land between the sub-chiefdoms according to river
catchment areas, thus matching water resource areas with traditional
institutions. (See Map No. 1)

Mangi Mangoto and Mangi Sabas managed their lands differently.
Land in the Kahe part was acquired and developed spontaneously by
smallholders with either direct or indirect consent from Mangi Mangoto,
mainly following procedures similar to Mbindyo's. Unlike Mangi Sabas,
Mangoto allowed many migrants from outside the district to settle in
Kahe, probably because most of the earlier migrants in Kahe were
pastoralists who were not yet attached to land like their counterparts from
the highlands in Uru north of Moshi town and closer to the slopes of the
mountain.

The northern part of Chekereni, which was held by the Uru people
under the authority of Mangi Sabas, was acquired in a more controlled
manner. Spontaneous occupation was very limited because the acquisition
process closely followed indigenous Chagga land-tenure practices, which
are common in most parts of Kilimanjaro region. Mangi Sabas and his
Wachili ensured that most of the beneficiaries were people from his
jurisdiction.

Map 1: Sub-Chiefdom Administrative Boundaries: Moshi Rural District

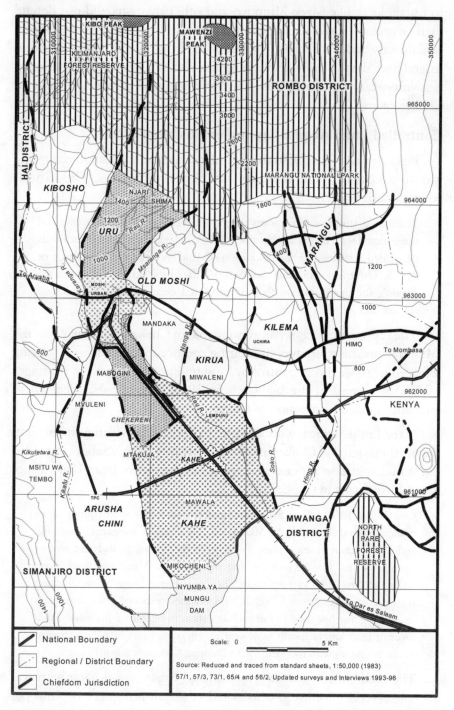

	National Boundary
	Regional / District Boundary
	Chiefdom Jurisdiction

Scale: 0   5 Km

Source: Reduced and traced from standard sheets, 1:50,000 (1983)
57/1, 57/3, 73/1, 65/4 and 56/2, Updated surveys and Interviews 1993-96

As we shall see later, the differences in access to land seem to determine land-owners attachment to the land. Those who found it easier to obtain land, like Mzee Mbindyo and other migrants, did not defend their customary rights with the same vigour as those who were allocated land directly by Mangi Sabas. To understand how the differences in access to land have shaped land-use planning and land development in Chekereni, it is important to clarify how land was acquired in the Uru part of Chekereni.

Controlled Land Acquisition under Customary Rules

Figgis noted in the 1950s that spontaneous land acquisition was giving way to access through allocation by native authorities. This British administrator wrote:

> Traditional land-tenure customs date from the period of patriarchal and unrestricted settlements and became adjusted in later times to meet the needs of guided settlement where allocation of land was made by the Mangi or Mchili. There is no common date between the (different) chiefdoms (in the region), for this transition from unrestricted clearing of land to guided settlement.[6]

The report supports what we were told in Chekereni, namely that the 'Mbindyo era' of spontaneous clearing and occupation was slowly being replaced by more direct control by local traditional leaders. As shortages of land increased in the highlands in 1960s, Mangi Sabas decided to introduce guided occupation in Chekereni.

Mzee Linus Ngowi, who was one of those who cleared the bush in the northern part of Chekereni, remembers how Mangi Sabas controlled the land-acquisition process and encouraged farmers from Uru villages to establish farms in Chekereni:

> One day, (in 1960), Mangi Sabas announced to us (Uru residents) his plan to reduce the land shortage. Our Mangi said, 'the threat of hunger is increasing, and our children have no place to set up home. Let us go to Uru Chini to open up farms.' On the next day, together with our Mangi and Wachili, we walked to Uru Chini in the present Chekereni area.... Mangi Sabas allocated large pieces of land to each Mchili, who was then responsible for organising its clearing, further subdivision and allocation to people of his *mtaa*.[7] Each piece of land, known locally as *soroveya* (survey) runs from the railway straight to the boundary with the Tanganyika Planting Company Sugar Estate.[8]

The land shortage issue which Mangi Sabas was dealing with was also observed by Johnsen, who noted: 'the half-acre piece of land per head (in the highlands) was rather low compared to the minimum land requirement of slightly less than two acres'.[9] Thus pressure on land in the villages in the more fertile lands of Kilimanjaro compelled Mangi Sabas to establish farms in the less fertile dry lowlands.

The decision nevertheless added more people to the growing settlement of Chekereni.

Villagers interviewed, like Mzee Linus Ngowi, remember two allocation incidences made by Mangi Sabas. The first allocation that was carried out in the 1950s did not cover Chekereni. It ended up in the neighbouring village of Mabogini. The second and last allocation took place ten years later and covered all the land under the administration of Mangi Sabas in the plains as shown in Map 1.

According to Mzee Ngowi-who was supported in this by other respondents, Mangi Sabas was concerned with the broad as well as detailed aspects of the subdivision by allocating a block of 100 acres to each Mchili, who was later responsible for the detailed sharing out:

> Subdivision into individual farm plots and allocation to families was done by respective Mchili. Each plot was demarcated by putting marks on standing trees. Four tree marks were sufficient to identify a single farm plot. The next task was to clear the bush. The land allotee did that. With the help of my five children, it took me two years to clear my plot, which measured fourteen acres. Not every farmer cleared his land as soon as I did. Some did not return after the allocation.[10]

Clearing the land meant replacing charcoal burning and free grazing with crop production. That was an initial step towards land use intensification in the area. Among those who immediately cleared their farms like Mzee Linus, very few moved to the new lands. Homes in Uru are well established. The settlement is served with more community services than those available in Chekereni. The highlands, lying at between 800 and 1800 metres above sea level, experience a more conducive climate compared to the almost semi-arid plains. Fear of malaria, which respondents referred to as *isemu*, was another limiting factor. The land was thus being managed by commuting farmers. The main use was rain-fed cultivation and fodder supply for livestock in the highlands, twenty kilometres away. To date, that farming system has not changed.

Another important detail in the allocation was its spatial organisation. Each Mchili apportioned land to his people according to clans in a *mtaa*, in such a way that neighbours in Uru were also neighbours in the plains.

As we shall see later, this pattern contributed significantly in maintaining community feeling among Uru people and thus in building social cohesion at the grassroots. As well as maintaining social and clan ties in the new lands, the pattern was also functional in respect of agricultural production.

Blocks of land allocated to each *mtaa* were carved out starting from the railway line, crossing the Moshi-Kahe road and continuing eastwards. This alignment was designed to ease irrigation by drawing water from the Rau river which runs parallel to the railway line. To separate the blocks, footpaths were established perpendicular to the railway line. They later developed into roads with individual farms on either side, thus ensuring that each farm had direct access to the Moshi-Kahe road, an important link to homes in Uru and markets.

It appears that Mchili could not and did not finalise the acquisition process. According to Mzee Ngowi's story, Mchili was responsible for supervising the clearing, subdivision and allocation to individual families. In order to make the allocation conform to Chagga tradition, the Mangi's authority was needed. Mzee Ngowi added:

> After a substantial part of the area was cleared Mangi Sabas visited us and confirmed the allocation in a big celebration. Several goats were offered by the allottees as appreciation to the Mangi, especially after the first harvest.[11]

According to Chagga custom, once the Mangi confirms land rights, tenure is secured. It becomes difficult for either Mangi or Mchili to reallocate the land. It is no wonder that Mzee Ngowi talks of there being a big celebration during the reconfirmation, because in my analysis, such ceremonies are what enhanced the security of tenure among landowners from Uru. The importance of having the Mangi authenticate allocation was also confirmed during feedback discussions.[12] A ceremony of this sort was held in 1961 to confirm the last customary allocation in the area.

The high security of tenure, combined with community feeling, are probably among the factors which later encouraged Uru people with land in Chekereni to prevent the strong Ujamaa village council from acquiring their land. Lands allocated by the Mangi were thus managed under those Chagga customary rights, which are also recognized by the Tanzania Land Ordinance of 1923, as 'deemed land rights'.[13]

Following the same custom, if a piece of land has not been cultivated for three consecutive seasons and the respective Mchili becomes aware of it, he may request the Mangi to consider reallocating it. The requirement within Chagga custom that land should not be left unused for a considerable period corresponds to provisions made in the 1948 Land Regulations[14], a government notice issued by the British Government and adopted by the independence government to deal with land use in lands held under statutory rights.

In short, the important lesson to be drawn from this account of land allocation by Mangi Sabas is that in Chagga custom access to land involves four stages:

1) broad allocation by the Mangi;
2) detailed land subdivision organized by the Mchili;
3) clearing by allottees; and
4) confirmation by the Mangi.

Revocation may take place if the land is not in use for a considerable period or a result of other problematic situations.

While most of the migrants who settled in the Kahe sector were content with dry cultivation, those who came from Uru had a background in irrigated farming and were therefore not satisfied with only rain-fed, single cropping season. They decided to enhance the intensification of land use through traditional irrigation.

The story of this local initiative in introducing mixed irrigated cultivation in Chekereni is important from a land-use planning point of view, because it shows how a group of smallholders came together to improve land productivity, but, lacking support from the district, saw the initiative fail.

Villagers Attempt to Introduce Traditional Irrigation

The low and unreliable rainfall,[15] proximity to the Rau river and the farmers' experience of irrigation were among the factors which encouraged the decision to introduce irrigated cultivation in Chekereni. As the traditional form of irrigation was an important resource in the process, let us briefly consider its main characteristics.

In traditional Chagga irrigation, a given river is controlled by the Mangi:

> Canals or irrigation furrows were cut from an intake high up on mountain stream...following the contours of the land. From each furrow were cut branches and then sub-branches that fed fields and people's homesteads. The need to keep the irrigation furrows in top condition means people have to co-operate and co-ordinate and that was done by the 'elders of the furrow'-in Chagga *Wameeku wa Mfongo,* in a clan or for the whole community. And that

system which has been so successful was recorded in full operation in the mid-1850s and has contributed to the increased carrying capacity and therefore intensive agriculture on the slopes of Kilimanjaro.[16]

The migrants from Uru were therefore convinced that they had a well-established institution and decided to introduce it on the new lands to manage irrigation practice. Thus from an institutional point of view, it was a question of extending the *Wameeku wa Mfongo* concept to Chekereni.

The fact that the Rau River from which the migrants proposed to draw their water, was largely under the jurisdiction of Mangi Sabas and that most of the migrants in Chekereni were his subjects, justified their request for access to it. In addition, the well-established, irrigated coffee and banana farms in Rau village and other parts of the plains attracted the migrants. They were therefore convinced that if water were made available, that could transform the open vegetation into mixed thick vegetation, including trees, bananas, maize, etc., like the vegetation in the highlands. A decision was therefore made to draw water from Rau River applying gravity as a delivery system.

The farmers considered several options. First they thought of constructing a canal direct from the Rau River to their farms. They gave up that option because of the distance involved, the likelihood of high water loss due to evaporation, and the high labour requirement for excavating the five kilometers trench. In addition, the work would have been rather complicated and difficult as the trench had to cross other existing canals. They therefore pursued a second alternative, which involved extending one of the existing canals.

The farmers and their Mchili approached Usagara Farms Ltd.[17] for permission to extend the Rau canal and for access to water from it. Their request was granted. Digging proceeded smoothly until the trench reached the Kahe Moshi railway line, which it had to cross. A strong culvert had to be constructed under the railway. The farmers could not cope with that alone, either financially or technologically. They therefore approached the Moshi District Council and the Railway Authority for assistance. Promises to assist were made but not honoured. As the farmers could not buy or construct the required culvert, they painfully abandoned the alternative.

Although failing in this first attempt, they did not despair but approached their neighbours in Mabogini village, to the north, and requested their permission to extend one of the canals. In this second attempt, they managed to avoid both the road and the railway. But since the Manosa canal which they were allowed to extend was already being used almost to full capacity, the amount of water which reached the farms in Chekereni was too little, only enough to be able to irrigate a few farms.

Thus the farmers' objective of irrigating their farms in Chekereni could not be fully realized, partly because of Chekereni's location close to the end of the Rau River and the need to cross the international railway line. With the exception of the small area, which could be irrigated, the smallholdings in Chekereni and further south had to depend on scarce, unreliable rainfall.

The dominant land use in Chekereni therefore remained dry farming, with free grazing after harvesting. A notable difference between the south and the north was that absentee farmers managed most of the farms in the north, while the farmers in the south occupied the land they cultivated.

Free grazing was practiced in both areas, but mostly by families living in the south. Seen from a land-use planning point of view, the failure to introduce irrigation and therefore mixed permanent cultivation on land which had already been cleared might have exposed the soils to erosion and also made the area vulnerable to flooding. From the social point of view, the two groups of migrants developed a social system in which they co-existed. Since the migrants were from different cultures, they brought with them different customs with respect to land rights. However, since most people were from Kilimanjaro, Chagga custom dominated.

In terms of boundary and land-ownership conflicts, the Uru farmers are said to have co-existed peacefully with the other migrants. According to Mzee Mhoja, a migrant from Mwanza northern Tanzania, who shared boundaries with farmers from Uru, the social system worked:

> We were not used to having land conflicts. When a farmer arrived, he acquired sufficient land while recognising and respecting the rights of other, earlier settlers. For example, we shared boundaries with Chagga farmers. They came from Uru with *masale*[18] and planted them along the boundaries. If you do not cross the *masale*, there will be no conflict. We had no conflicts (with our neighbours).[19]

Other respondents supported Mzee Mhoja's explanation and added that neighbours, with or without the involvement of the Mchili, dealt with conflicts. When the Mchili could not solve a conflict, the Mangi was informed, and his judgement was final. Land-use management by the Mangi system was, however, confined to lands owned by natives under customary rules while lands held under statutory right were administered by the central government through relevant legislation.

While the land held under the customary system in Chekereni was being cleared and occupied by smallholders, the government was keen to acquire the same land and convert it to more intensive use. Because of its extensive land-use practice, involving charcoal burning and free grazing with limited cultivation, the land in Kahe was more attractive to the government's plans than the land in the Uru area.

However, the government's perception that the Kahe part was vacant and that its use should be intensified through large-scale farming was not accepted by some of the migrants with land rights in that area. Although both individuals and government shared the same objective of intensifying land use in Chekereni, the government in this case wanted to carry out its own land-use intensification project on lands held by smallholders by replacing them with a large-scale farm. As we shall see, conflicts between the government and landowners did not so much involve disagreements over land use but rather how to compensate the already established rights and interests. It is at this point that we notice the origin of conflicts over land rights caused by a practice of decision-making which ignores the smallholders' knowledge and rights over their land even if such rights are fully recognized by the law. The following chapter focuses on the government's interactions with smallholder cultivators and how the consequential conflict was dealt with. Who won or lost and why?

Chapter Three
Government versus Smallholder Farmers

Government Plan to Replace the Traditional Farming System Fails

During the early 1960s, government intervention on lands held under customary rights took the form of prescribing and enforcing agricultural management practices including conservation measures. However, in instances where the government was convinced that a given piece of land was not utilized in such a way as to exploit fully its productive potential, the government used the powers of the Land Ordinance[1]to acquire such land for public interest. Part of the land in Chekereni was subject to such acquisitions. The first attempt to acquire the land was made by Moshi District Council.

A year after independence, in 1962, the District Commissioner in Moshi, acting on the advice of the district agricultural officer, decided that the land in Chekereni would be more intensively utilized if the smallholders and pastoralists using that land were replaced by a large-scale farm. According to an interview with Mzee Mbindyo and Mzee Mpangalala, who were among the early settlers in Chekereni, the Kahe agricultural extension officer recommended a sisal estate to be established on the land owned and used by Mzee Mbindyo. The District Commissioner agreed to the suggestion, and presumably allowed preparations to start.

Technically the decision may have been correct. The site selected was accessible from Moshi Town and close to Gynja Sisal Estate. From a topographical point of view, irrigation could be made possible by extending Gynja canal. But the site-selection process ignored existing use and ownership rights and was bound to lead into conflicts.

Mzee Mbindyo became aware of the district council's decision when land preparations started. He narrates:

> One morning, some years after independence,[2] I saw the ward extension officer for Kahe on a big tractor, approaching my compound. The tractor driver, under instructions from the extension officer, started to clear the bushes around my compound. The tractor made several rounds without the extension officer saying anything to me. Later the officer and the tractor left. The next morning, the officer came and told me that I was required to demolish my house to make way for a large-scale farm which had been decided upon. The

land was thus being cleared by the district council which was setting up that farm. I was not ready for that order. I told the officer, 'I will not demolish my house or move from this land. Why should I move?' I asked. After hearing these words, the officer ordered the tractor to stop clearing and they left. He did not answer my questions.[3]

Two days later, Mangi Mangoto of Kahe and Mzee Hosenieli, the TANU[4] Chairman for Kahe, visited Mzee Mbindyo and summoned him to the District Commissioner's office. Mzee Mbindyo accompanied the team of leaders to the Commissioner's office. Here is his account of what transpired:

The District Commissioner asked me, 'Why did you refuse to move?'. I stood up to answer, but he said, 'You can sit down and talk, because we have conquered colonialism. Still seated, I replied: 'When they say I have refused to move, I do not understand why I should be chased off of my land. I have not committed any crime since I came to Tanzania...they should give reasons as to why I should move.' The extension officer replied: '(The district authorities) want to open up a big farm in Chekereni. One person cannot stop the development of many. We would like to have many people start farming in the area to increase production to make citizens happy.' I said: 'I am also a citizen.... I will not shift unless my wishes are met. I shall identify another site where another house should be built for me. And the right type of trees, *vikwata*, should be used.... While constructing the new house, they should dig a well into the ground to make the house strong. If you agree to this, then I am ready to move.' The Commissioner accepted, and we went back home.[5]

Let us briefly examine and interpret this story. The officer who wanted to acquire Mbindyo's land did not take into account customary claims and rights held by the land user. Nor was there any intention to involve Mzee Mbindyo in the decision before the land was cleared. It was only after his resistance that it became necessary to involve him, as rights holder, in the decision. On the other hand, it was an opportunity for Mzee Mbindyo to be heard and influence the decision, an opportunity he took advantage of.

Mzee Mbindyo, like all other landowners who had cleared the bush in Chekereni, scared away wild animals and used the land for a long period, felt secure and regarded the land he cleared as his own. This feeling was supported by customary rules: whoever clears the original vegetation and occupies the land for a reasonable number of seasons becomes the owner. The 1961 Land Ordinance also recognizes such customary rights, according to which one of the ways through which they may be extinguished and the land lawfully alienated is by compensation.[6] Also traditional leaders, for instance the Mangi, could re-acquire land rights held under customary regulations if the rights holder committed a crime. From the story it is clear that Mzee Mbindyo was aware of these provisions, which is why he said that he had not committed any crime. Mzee Mbindyo justified his reason by referring to customary regulations.

The extension officer supported the district council's decision by referring to the public interest and to modernization, or rather the 'development of many'.

All in all, the meeting between Mzee Mbindyo, representing local traditional institutions under customary rules, and the District Commissioner, representing central government and statutory rights, provided room for a dialogue between the two institutions. It was resolved by the decision that the land clearance should continue in order to achieve the intended objectives, while Mzee Mbindyo should be compensated.

As Mzee Mbindyo was aware that he could easily clear another piece of land and establish a new farm, he was not very concerned about the land he was to release to the district. Rather, he was concerned about his houses and wanted to be sure that the compensation matched the quality he was expecting. He was able to have the type and level of compensation agreed in front of the Commissioner and other local leaders in the meeting and to him, it seems, acceptance by the Commissioner was equivalent to a written agreement.

A day after the meeting, the extension officer went to Mzee Mbindyo's compound. The officer showed him some alternative land for a new compound. Mzee Mbindyo accepted the proposed site, but also asked in which direction he could start clearing a new farm to avoid future conflicts with the district. Instead of showing him the location of the farm and the direction in which clearing could start, the officer told him, 'First you get a house, and later we will give you a farm, which we will clear for you.'

Mzee Mbindyo agreed and told the officer to start acquiring building materials such as poles; he said that, he was willing to assist in the construction in order to ensure good quality. He was also ready to accept one house if it was roofed with corrugated iron sheets and to forgo his four huts and chicken shed roofed with thatch. According to Mzee Mbindyo, the officer seemed to agree to all this, but after leaving the compound that day he never came back. The land clearance did not continue.

Letter from the Regional Lands Officer giving guidelines for survey of Ujamaa villages:

MINISTRY OF LANDS, HOUSING & URBAN DEVELOPMENT
LAND DIVISION,
P.O.BOX 97,
MOSHI

Ref No. MS/5165/21   17th March, 1971

Administrative Secretary
Kilimanjaro

Re: Survey of Ujamaa Villages in
Kilimanjaro Region

I refer to your letter No. R:20/9/III/106 dated 26th February, 1971 and to the Regional Surveyor's letter No. S/52/29 of 16th February, 1971 on the above subject.

I have fully discussed this matter with yourself and the Regional Surveyor separately and we have more or less agreed on the procedure to be followed in this exercise and which I undertake to detail below.

In the first instance Regional Administration who are Project leaders will select a suitable area required for an Ujamaa Village as and when requests arise from wananchi. In this exercise no doubt the assistance of certain experts will be sought eg. where the Kijiji wants to establish itself as a small Scale Industry the help of the Ministry concerned will be enlisted, or where farming and livestock projects are to be preformed the help of the Land Use Planning Section of the Ministry of Agriculture and Co-operatives will be sought.

When Regional Administration are satisfied as regards both size and suitability of the land they will apply to this office for the land in the usual manner forwarding along with the application a suitable sketch plan showing estimated dimensions and area. Then the Land Office together with the Office of the Area Commissioner will ascertain as to whether third party interests exist on the land or not. If there are third party interests on the land the team will record the nature of the interests and their value. This report will be sent to Regional Administration, the applicants. Then Regional Administration will decide as to how the third party interests will be relinquished.

At this stage a request may then be sent to Surveys for surveying the land as directed by the President. Furthermore I venture to suggest that after survey is complete the land should be allocated to Regional Administration for Kijiji cha Ujamaa. The latter is subject to agreement by the authorities concerned.

/HM.

Z.W.Haule
REGIONAL LAND OFFICER
KILIMANJARO

Copy to: Commissioner for Surveys and Mapping, Dar es Salaam

"   " : Commissioner for Lands, Dar es Salaam
"   " : Director of Agriculture & Co-operative, Kilimanjaro.
"   " : Regional Surveyor, Moshi
"   " : Area Commissioner, Moshi
"   " : "   " Same
"   " : District Land Officer, Same
"   " : O i/o Vijiji vya Ujamaa Moshi
"   " : K.D.C.Moshi, c.c.Pare District Council, Same

It has not been possible for the author to establish clearly the reasons why the project was stopped, as neither the extension officer nor the District Commissioner could be found for interview.

But the story was accepted in feedback sessions in Chekereni, and there was no extra information as to why the clearing was stopped. Whatever the reason, Mzee Mbindyo believes it was because of the conditions he made.

However, the government's wish to develop the area into a large-scale farm did not end there.

In 1966 the government announced its intention to support sisal cultivation ventures in order to promote exports. Under the policy, individual farmers and private companies were encouraged to acquire large parcels of land, preferably close to well-established estates, and to start sisal cultivation. Following the announcement of the policy, in the same year, a private company based in Moshi became interested in establishing a farm in Chekereni. The company identified two hundred acres of land in Chekereni close to Gynja, anticipating that they would obtain support in the form of services such as tractors, fertilizer, advice etc. from the already established Gynja Estate. The company made an application for the land to the Moshi District Commissioner. The Commissioner directed the application to the Provincial Commissioner, probably because of the first experience and secondly because the amount of land applied for was too large for the district to approve.

Mzee Hamisi Mpangalala, once a manager for the Gynja Sisal Estate, was present when the Provincial Commissioner visited Chekereni to inspect the land in question. He remembers how the land was allocated:

> The Commissioner came to Chekereni to inspect the land before the allocation. It was a bush with wild animals. He saw the land and told the applicant, 'Now you will be allocated 100 acres. You clear it first, and I will come to inspect and, if satisfied I will then allow you to have the other 100 acres.' I remember the Commissioner standing on the bonnet of the Land Rover, which had brought him to Chekereni, filling in forms and stamping the papers with a stamp taken from his handbag. The allocation was done right in the field, after which he left. (...) The company hired a tractor from Gynja and cleared the first allocation. The commissioner was satisfied, and the second allocation was made. [7]

The site visit enabled the Commissioner to see the land and probably to carry out some form of pre-allocation site investigation. In making a second visit to finalize the allocation, the Commissioner was keen to ensure that the allotee was a genuine farmer. Withholding the allocation for a period corresponded to the Right of Occupancy (Development Conditions) Act of 1963,[8] which requires that at least 50 per cent of the allocated land be cleared during the first year of the acquisition.

According to Mzee Mpangalala, the land clearance went on well after the final allocation. However, before the Company had finished the clearing, the Mangi of Kahe intervened. Mzee Mpangalala tells us how Mangi Mangoto managed to get the allocation revoked:

> Mangi Mangoto reported the case to the Kilimanjaro Paramount Chief and requested his assistance. The Paramount Chief and Mangi Mangoto came to Chekereni. They accused the Private Company of being a trespasser on Kahe land. The two traditional leaders pointed out that procedures require that the local Mangi be consulted before any allocation of native land is finalized. The farm preparations stopped. The company representatives went to Arusha to inform the Provincial Commissioner about the objections of the two local leaders. They did not return. [9]

In my view, Mangi Mangoto's decision to involve the Paramount Chief was strategic and effective. He might have thought that challenging a decision by the Provincial Commissioner required an equally powerful authority. They both played a game in which neither consulted the other. From a legal point of view, Mangi Mangoto was right to claim powers over the land, even though the Commissioner allocated it. His claims were supported by the 1950 amendments to the 1923 Land Ordinance, which required the native authority of the area to be consulted before native land is allocated.[10]

It is interesting to note, nonetheless, that although the political, legal and administrative powers of traditional leaders, including the Mangi, had already been abolished in 1963 by the independence government,[11] Mangi Mangoto still felt responsible for the land within Kahe. It could also be argued that the Provincial Commissioner did not see any need to consult Mangoto, as he had no formal powers. On the other hand, it was inevitable that the company had to stop clearing and developing the land in order to clarify its tenure first. As the Company representatives did not return to Chekereni, neither Mangi Mangoto nor Mzee Mpangalala was aware of what they were told by the Commissioner. We have not been able to establish whether or not the revocation was formalized. If not, then it constitutes a potential conflict, as the company that cleared the land may claim compensation.

This story illustrates the unclear status of lands held under customary rights. It also demonstrates the potential conflict of authority between the central government and traditional leadership. Even where landowners were able to argue and get their claims respected, the unclear situation was not beneficial to land developers. Although such conflicts were much more pronounced before independence, the situation is still the same in this period, with a native government in power.

The next section will bring us to a new period of significance in the socio-political context in Tanzania. This is the period following the 1967 Arusha Declaration,[12] when TANU also became active in land allocation matters, including in Chekereni. In the following story, local TANU leaders acting on the advice of the Mangi of Kahe enabled a group of smallholders to settle in Chekereni after their settlement was flooded. As well as introducing TANU as a new actor in the land-use intensification process, the story shows how a small community of flood victims organized themselves and was able to cope with the disaster. The story is also contextual in two ways. First, there was unclaimed land, which the Mangi was eager to allocate to his people, and secondly there was a national interest in resettling smallholders into compact settlements-in other words, it was the inception stage of the villagization resettlement policy.

Floods Justify Resettlement in Chekereni

On 29th April 1968, heavy rains poured down on the Kahe area. The rain continued for three days, and on 1st of May Lemduru, one of the villages in the area, was severely flooded. Forty-three families lost their houses, and farms were completely destroyed. The victims held a meeting and asked their leader to report the disaster to the Kahe Ward Secretary [13] and petition for an alternative and safe piece of land.

Mzee Wetundwa, who was chairman of the Village Development Committee,[14] reported the disaster. At the office in Kahe, he met the TANU chairman, who received the request and worked on it. First, the TANU chairman consulted Mangi Joas, who had inherited the position from Mangi Mangoto. Mangi Joas advised the chairman to consider the land in Chekereni which had once been cleared for sisal cultivation but abandoned. He told the TANU chairman:

To my knowledge the land has not been allocated to anybody and is free and could be acquired without problems.[15]

The three leaders agreed to Mangi Joas's suggestion. The TANU chairman then wrote a letter to Mzee Chateka, the local leader of the settlement close to the area.

He gave the letter to Mzee Wetundwa and told him to inform the flood victims that they were allowed to cross the Rau river and establish new homes and farms in Chekereni under supervision of Mzee Chateka. Mzee Wetundwa left for Lemduru and organized the flood victims as directed.

On 15th May 1968, forty-three families started to move. Mzee Wetundwa recounts how they were received:

> We came to Chekereni and found Mzee Mbindyo and Mzee Chateka. I gave them the letter…they received us and allocated land to all of us. We were 43 families, and each obtained four to five acres…. We cleared the bush and established new homes and farms. [16]

Mzee Wetundwa's account of the resettlement is not different from that of other flood victims who moved in Chekereni in 1968, though it is less detailed. According to Mzee Mbindyo, the TANU chairman's letter urged Mzee Chateka to organise the land allocation in such a way that a particular pattern would be achieved. Mzee Mbindyo begins his account by citing the letter.

> (The letter[17]) read: 'Mzee Mbindyo and Chateka…these people are running away from floods, which have occurred in Mkonga. Allocate them homestead plots- starting from where the railway crosses the road (at Chekereni point), then moving southwards, towards Kahe, until you reach Mbindyo's farm. They should build their houses in such a way that they overlook the road and the railway. Farms should be established behind the homesteads, towards Mtakuja village.' We received them and allocated a one-acre homestead plot for each family so that those with livestock could have the space to build a cowshed within the compound. Because there was a bush to clear behind the plots, we told each family to clear farms but not more than five acres.[18]

The land, which had once been cleared for sisal cultivation, was thus subdivided and allocated to the flood victims. A homestead area known locally as Chekereni was thus established, making a second cluster in addition to Kwa Mbindyo further south. To date the names of the two residential clusters have been maintained, but the spatial as well as social structures were drastically changed during the implementation of Ujamaa in Chekereni in the 1970s.

Nevertheless, after the 1968 resettlement, the land in Chekereni was mostly claimed and owned in accordance with customary land rights. Access to land through 'clearing and occupation' or through allocation by the Mangi was no longer possible without conflict.

Access to land was thus through inheritance, buying, renting or simply borrowing for a given season without cash, but with other forms of payment. We shall therefore enter the year 1969, in which Ujamaa was introduced in Chekereni, with a situation in which all the land had already been claimed. Encouraging further migration into the area, the main aim of Ujamaa, would certainly lead to conflicts with the original migrants.

Local Institutions Performed better than Central Government in the Pre-Ujamaa Chekereni

In producing the land-use changes described above, different strategies were applied. Individual initiatives by migrants were among the decisive tools through which their plans were realized. Similarly, the power and capacity of traditional leaders in organizing their community members was another useful resource in land-use change processes. For instance, the Mangi institution, with its clear line of responsibilities, contributed significantly in implementing the plan to establish farms in Chekereni. In general, most people knew which procedures and authority to use. The type of democracy practiced by the traditional leaders may be questioned, as only the Paramount Chief was elected.[19] Whether that type of democracy is good or bad, the chiefs had the final say. There was more legitimacy between the leaders and the grassroots, and social sanctions worked. In my view, the situation in which central government officials replaced the local traditional institutions provided fertile ground on which national level policies like the villagization programme could be implemented with little or no resistance at the local level.

The performance of central government agents in the story did not match that of local traditional institutions. The locally based central-government intention to establish sisal estates in Chekereni and the national programme to transform Chekereni were not realized, partly because of resistance from local traditional institutions, and partly because of the limited capacity of the central government, especially in respect of funds.

One of the questions guiding our research was whether land-use planning goals were achieved. At this stage of the story, we try to answer this question on the basis of the results of land-use changes in pre-Ujamaa Chekereni. Improved land productivity, long-term resource conservation and an effective conflict resolution mechanism are the main goals we focus on. Improved land productivity was a concern of all actors.

Cultivation and seasonal grazing replaced hunting and charcoal making, the main economic activities in Chekereni. Crop cultivators shared land-use rights within a resource management system where they all agreed on when and where cultivation or grazing should be allowed.

By that period, resources, especially grazing lands, were already scarce, and pastoralists had to obtain such resources outside the settlement. Because of the failure of the Uru migrants' attempt to introduce irrigation in Chekereni, their wish to intensify land-use through irrigation could not be realized. Thus smallholders' dry cultivation remained the dominant land use.

From a conservation point of view, environmental degradation was not yet an issue in Chekereni or in lower Moshi in general. There is no evidence from the villagers interviewed to suggest that overgrazing, soil erosion or loss of land fertility was problems facing cultivators in the pre-Ujamaa Chekereni. Neither is there any indication in the literature that the Moshi plains were among the target areas of the 1927 National Conservation bylaws and land-use schemes.[20] An important point with respect to environmental conservation, was the government's concern with the management of river valleys and catchments areas.[21] Although there were no interventions in respect of land in Chekereni, they had direct benefits in terms of ensuring a steady supply of water to the settlements in the plains.

Rural land-use planning in Tanzania is supposed to be guided by the 1961 town and country planning legislation. In reality, there is no strong evidence to suggest that the law has had significant influence over land-use change in rural Tanzania, partly because the provisions relevant in land-use planning did not focus on agriculture as an important land use.[22] Instead, rural land-use planning was mainly dealt with through agricultural development policies.

The government's intentions to improve crop production and raise the standard of living of the rural population were announced through the first Three-year National Development Plan (1961 to 1964). The Plan adopted the World Bank's suggestion that 'Intensive advice and inputs to settled farmers, i.e. 'improvements', and resettlement of selected farmers or 'transformation', would make them modern and better producers'.

The government considered the scattered pattern of land use to be inefficient in service provision and believed that it would be less costly to provide schools, dispensaries, improved water supplies and extension services to a community of farmers living in compact settlements. [23]

Within the transformation approach, it was also argued that when peasants settle in new environments (lands), they become receptive to new ideas and keener in following instructions from agricultural officers and thus in adopting new land-use practices. It was thus proposed to establish rural settlements in areas with low population densities. We can at this stage interpret the World Bank idea of 'transformation' as the origin of the villagization resettlement programme in Tanzania.

To facilitate the transformation programme, the Land (Village Settlement) Act of 1965 empowered the Minister for Lands, Settlements and Water Development to acquire land and allocate it to the Commissioner for Village Settlements in the Ministry of Agriculture. The Commissioner was then responsible for managing such settlements and granting subsidiary titles to cultivators. Once land had been allocated to a particular scheme, the Commissioner, together with respective scheme managers, was to carry out the following duties:

1) To make rules for the development of the settlement;

2) To control cultivation, harvesting and marketing of cash crops; and

3) To ensure conservation and protection of natural resources, water catchment areas, forests etc.[24]

The Chekereni land was among the sites that were earmarked for the schemes. However, due to a lack of funds and the poor performance of the earlier pilot projects, which had led to increased social, economic and environmental problems, the transformation programme was abandoned in 1965. Thus the government objective in establishing a planned village in Chekereni could not be realized. Related to the abolition of the programme are two decisions, which are important to the Chekereni investigation.

First, the government made the 1967 Arusha Declaration, in which it renewed its commitment to rural development, including the revival of the transformation programme. In 1968, as a follow up, the villagization directive was issued. This required rural families living in scattered homesteads to establish compact settlements similar to those proposed under the transformation programme.

Unlike in the World Bank financed resettlement, families will move into the new settlements on a voluntary basis, with little or no support from the government. District authorities were therefore required to persuade their people to join the villages, using the argument of the free land and community facilities available.

The second decision was the transfer of village land-use planning activities and responsibilities from the Ministry of Agriculture to the Department of Town Planning in the Ministry of Lands, Settlements and Water Development. This transfer placed village land-use planning under the Town-Planning Department, but without clear terms of reference and procedures in rural settlement planning.

In addition, the practice of village land-use planning had very weak or at least unclear institutional as well as professional back up, because the Land (Village Settlement) Act of 1965 was abolished along with the Rural Settlements Commission. The town-planning director therefore had to start a new task from scratch at a time when rural land-use planning expertise was needed more than ever before, to support the implementation of the nation wide villagization programme under Ujamaa.

Chapter Four

Chekereni Becomes an Ujamaa Village

The First Ujamaa Migrants Arrive in Chekereni

"Land-seekers became 'socialists' in order to fulfill their cultural obligations: Obtaining land for free to allocate to their children."

In the early days of September 1969, a land rover belonging to Moshi District Council stopped at the place where the Moshi-Kahe road crosses the railway. Twelve men got out and camped under the large baobab tree located near the crossing.

Mzee Masanja Mhoja, one of the flood victims who had moved to Chekereni in 1968, had a home nearby and saw the people arriving. He describes how the group was received:

The group had a letter from the district council, which said: 'These people have decided to establish a village in Chekereni and would like to form an Ujamaa village, 'We received the people as our visitors. We did not harass them at all. We organized a meeting of the people who were already living in and had land in Chekereni. The main issue for the meeting was 'where to let these people settle'. As we did not want a stranger to decide for us, we elected Mzee Stephen Wetundwa, who had land and was living here, to lead us in that meeting. Under the leadership of Mzee Wetundwa, the group was shown part of the present residential area, the primary school plot and un-cleared land south of the residential area. The land we allocated to them was partly unclaimed, as the owner had run away from the village. One Mzee Tumbo, who had a lot of land in different locations in the village and was willing to set some aside for the poor migrants contributed another piece of land.[1]

The story suggests that, the villagers were sympathetic and could allow the Ujamaa migrants to occupy land in their village. Mzee Makishingo was the leader of the first Ujamaa migrants. We shall use his story to illustrate how the group was formed, how they decided to come to Chekereni and how they acquired land. We shall also have an opportunity to see the role of the district council and the early migrants in Chekereni in that process.

Among the questions put to Mzee Makishingo was how he decided to come to Chekereni. He replied:

Before I came to Chekereni, together with my friend, Modest Mchau, I was running a retail shop in Marangu, in the highlands, where I lived. As our children grew up, we realized that the land we had would not be sufficient to meet their future requirements under Chagga practices of inheritance. From June 1969, we started to look for additional land. We tried in several places. We made the first attempt in two separate locations in Marangu but neither was successful. Another attempt was made during August 1969, in a village located forty kilometres away in West Kilimanjaro in the present Hai district. We made several visits to Naibili and Kikuletwa area and identified several acres of land which we were able to buy at Tshs. 200/= per acre. We got an offer of three acres for Tshs 600/=, but the landowner did not turn up on the day payment was due. We were therefore not able to buy land in West Kilimanjaro.[2]

Mzee Makishingo is referring to a Chagga custom which requires parents to have or acquire sufficient land for inheritance to children, especially sons upon marriage, the same cultural reason that was given by Mangi Sabas when he decided to open up his land in the plains back in the 1960s. So Mzee Makishingo was doing what other parents were also doing, seeking land for his children. After failing to buy the land they had chosen, they heard that it was possible for the district council to assist them. They approached the council and were informed of the possibility of obtaining land in Chekereni:

> At the council, we met the administrative officer, who told us to consult the Ward Executive Officer in Marangu, which we did. In the ward office, we were told of a vast area in Chekereni, which was **underutilized by pastoralists** through grazing. The officer added that, it was likely that the district council would allow people to acquire farms and settle in that area. He outlined a strategy to us in order to succeed: form a group of at least ten people and make a joint request to the district council. The officer also told us that such a request would certainly receive a positive consideration because of the new policy of villagization. (emphasis by the author) [3]

With that information and virtual confirmation that it was possible to acquire land in Chekereni, they left the ward office very happy, with only a simple task ahead: to convince people to join their search for land. Here is what they did.

> We went back to Marangu. We told our friends and relatives, 'There is a possibility of getting land in Chekereni, close to Moshi town. If we get that land we may cultivate tomatoes, onions, vegetables and sell them in Moshi town.' I managed to get ten names and informed the ward executive officer that we were ready. The officer then told us about another condition, namely that the area in Chekereni was too big, and that people from all over Kilimanjaro

region were supposed to be informed so that they could also list their names, as long as they were ready to live together in an Ujamaa village. He said, however: 'The council will announce the intention to all the districts in the region and will give a date on which people interested in land should come and they will be shown the land'. [4]

After the first visit to the ward office, Mzee Makishingo became the contact person between the group and the officer. From the officer's talk with Mzee Makishingo, it was clear that the district council had decided to established an Ujamaa village in Chekereni and in other settlements in the plains, where grazing was the main land use. The decision must already have been made in 1968, because in July of that year the District Executive Officer had written to the local TANU leaders in the settlements in the plains about plans to establish settlements in their areas. We quote the letter:

> Plans to establish new settlements in the Lower Moshi area were proceeding very well, and about 6,000 people have been listed. The district has also made an estimate that each family has been earmarked for a plot and four acres farm, in addition to community facilities: centre, roads, school, office, and hospital and open spaces. The 6,000 people would therefore require 3,250 acres. As establishing new settlement is a serious endeavor, it is important that we involve various committees and experts from respective departments in addition to the nearby sugar estate. Local leaders should be patient while the implementation arrangements were being finalized. [5]

The letter indicates that the district council was aware that the exercise needed land-use planning inputs. Land subdivision standards had already been established to guide the resettlement. Thus the letter warned the local TANU leaders to be patient and not to allocate land to migrants before the planning procedures were completed, so that the 6,000 people listed could be allocated land in the plains without creating disputes. Therefore the local TANU leaders and Mzee Makishingo and his group waited until September 1969, when the announcement was officially made:

> We arrived at the Moshi Town Council office very early in the morning. A lot of people (at least 800) had listed their names, but few were selected as pioneers. We were selected and got into a Land Rover, which brought us to Chekereni. We were dropped at the baobab tree overlooking the railway crossing. We were allocated about twenty acres, which we subsequently realized had already been surveyed by surveyors from Dar es Salaam, as we discovered the beacons later. [6]

The last sentence in this extract suggests that the land shown to the first Ujamaa migrants had already been surveyed and demarcated. This contradicts what we had heard earlier from Mzee Mhoja, that the early migrants gave the first Ujamaa migrants land. Apparently there is no agreement between the early migrants and the first Ujamaa group over this issue, which is both understandable and interesting.

The disagreement became evident in one of the feedback sessions in which Mzee Makishingo did not accept Mzee Mhoja's views. Mzee Makishingo supported his argument by drawing our attention to a map made by the district council. He told the feedback session that the land, which was allocated to the first Ujamaa migrants, was indicated on the map. The map referred to is a plan made by the Regional Water Engineer's office in June 1970, a year after Mzee Makishingo and his group had settled in Chekereni. The plan, showed the alignment of a proposed village canal as well as a sub-division plan for part of the village residential area. The feedback team also mentioned that they were aware of surveys of the village canal made in Chekereni in 1969, possibly the same time when the subdivision was made and the plots demarcated on the ground.

All in all, the plan shows that the government was keen to have a planned Ujamaa village in Chekereni. The water engineer's plan was used in aligning the village canal and with it the location of the irrigated lands in Chekereni. Both the canal alignment and the detailed land subdivision proposal for the residential area were followed closely by the Ujamaa migrants, thus shaping the physical structure of the village to this day. The layout shows a grid pattern with parallel roads providing easy circulation and accessibility within and outside the cluster. Because of its flexible layout, it has become a pattern of reference for residential development in the village. From a physical planning point of view, that was a significant input.

From a land-rights point of view, the story points to a situation in which both groups were trying to justify their tenure positions by simply telling a story, which supported their claims. While we may have to accept the two stories as presented, we should also note that once the flood victims had been resettled in Chekereni in 1968, it would not have been possible to have land which was free and unclaimed. To address the land rights issue, meetings were held, resulting in guidelines issued by the Regional Lands Officer[7] to the Regional Administrative Officer, who was responsible for the implementation of Ujamaa in the region.

1) Before a site is considered suitable for an Ujamaa village, land-use planning

experts should carry out a land-suitability assessment and determine the
size of the village to be established.

2) Regional Administrator to make an application to the Regional Lands Office
   for the land. The Regional Lands Office, together with the office of the
   Area/District Commissioner, would determine the nature of land rights
   existing in the area. And then it will be up to the Regional Administrator to
   decide how to relinquish third-party interests.[8]

As a matter of principle, the guidelines addressed central issues in
the overall process of establishing Ujamaa villages, but they came out
late for Chekereni. In my analysis, if the Land Officers advice had been
followed, some of the conflicts in land rights, which emerged during and
after the implementation of Ujamaa, would not have surfaced.

So far, we have described three events in which the district council's
involvement in the implementation of Ujamaa in Chekereni is noted.
The events are deciding on suitable settlements, assisting in organizing
the Ujamaa migrants and in facilitating their acceptance by the earlier
migrants, and detailed planning, at least at the beginning. These activities
were important, but not sufficient to make Chekereni a full fledged Ujamaa
village. Thus the next step was to replace the local institution in Chekereni
with an Ujamaa village council, which would introduce and manage the
village accordingly.

Electing the First Village Council: An Institution to implement Ujamaa in Chekereni Is Born

By 1971, the first Ujamaa migrants were fairly well established in
Chekereni. They had brought in their first harvest of maize, but they had
not yet managed to build their houses, being accommodated instead on
the Gynja estate camp. Other migrants arrived as individuals or in groups
and were received by the first Ujamaa migrants. They all worked on the
same farm on a communal basis, as that was the Ujamaa way. For some
migrants, working communally was not acceptable and they left.
Nevertheless, the group was slowly growing. In the same period, the district
council increased its involvement in Chekereni.

In February 1971, the district water department started to construct
the irrigation canal, which had been planned in 1970. The four-kilometre
canal drew water from Rau River at an intake close to that of the Gynja
canal. Obviously the volume of water in the Gynja canal was affected,
but since the estate had been abandoned due to the low price of sisal,
there was no conflict over water. The canal was operational by the end of
1971, and most of the land occupied by the 1968 flood victims could be
irrigated, another successful piece of assistance from the district.

During the same period, the district council declared Chekereni as an Ujamaa village. From a land-use planning point of view the declaration, which was mainly administrative, had the following potential implications. First, the guidelines outlined by the 1969 Presidential Circular, which became the blueprint for Ujamaa and villagization, had to apply. They included the following:

1) Individual ownership of land was against socialist principles and should be rejected.

2) Rights to land were only rights to use, not to own, and each member of an Ujamaa village was entitled to a piece of land on condition that he or she uses it.

3) Each village should have at least 250 households before it can be registered.

Thus, following the declaration, individual land rights in Chekereni were under threat. Most of the earlier migrants had to fight to protect them. Some lost and left Chekereni.

Six days after the declaration, the district Ujamaa and Co-operatives Officer[9] organized a meeting to elect the first village council. According to the minutes, the meeting was attended by 48 villagers and presided over by nine officers and politicians from the district and ward offices. By any standards, that was over-representation from the institutions above the village, which, in my view, may have been a strategy to support the Ujamaa migrants. There were two candidates for the chairmanship. Mzee Wetundwa, who led the resettlement for the flood victims and organized the first meeting to receive the first Ujamaa migrants, represented the original settlers. Mzee Makishing, who organized the first Ujamaa migrants, was the other contestant.

As few original settlers had registered themselves as members of the village and even fewer recognized the importance of the meeting and the elections at that time, their attendance was very low. Mzee Wetundwa lost. Below is his story of how the meeting was conducted:

> In the meeting 48 people were eligible voters. Only eighteen were among the original settlers; the rest were from the first Ujamaa migrants. Mzee Andrea, a former Mchili, wanted to be the first chairman, without being voted in. But the meeting insisted that he had to be elected by those present. The meeting went very well. Mzee Makishingo was elected chairman and I became his deputy. We also elected a secretary, works leader and eight councilors. [10]

After the meeting, power shifted from the original settlers to the 'strangers', as Mzee Mhoja referred to them. Most of the original settlers whom I interviewed regret, though not openly, not attending the meeting and casting their votes, since later they came to realize the importance of the change of power. On the other hand, the Ujamaa migrants knew that success in their goal of obtaining land for their children in Chekereni depended on the power they acquired from the election. They have therefore been keen to maintain such powers, and for over 25 years of Ujamaa in Chekereni the 'strangers' have monopolized important leadership posts, for instance the chairmanship.

Two months after the elections, the new village administration was keen to attract more migrants into Chekereni. They thus formulated procedures on how migrants should be received and how they can acquire land. Thus on 24th September 1971, a village assembly[11] was held to draft and then approve what the leaders refer to as a 'village constitution.'

Among the important provisions for the new comers were:

1) They should write a letter to the village chairman, declaring their intentions and reasons for wishing to join the village.

2) The application to be discussed in a village council meeting.

3) If accepted, the applicant to pay a sum of Tshs. 52/=.[12]

4) For original settlers wishing to join the village, an application was also needed, after which the applicant should surrender all his or her land to the village council for re-allocation.

5) Equivalent plots of land to be allocated to each person, whether a new or an original settler.

6) Each registered villager to be entitled to only two private farms in different locations in the village.

Given the opportunity to obtain land, almost for free, obviously a reasonable number of Chagga people were attracted to Chekereni. As we shall see later they were ready to meet the qualifying conditions and become "socialists" as long as they could acquire land.

From the land-use perspective, not much had changed. Only a small portion of land had been transferred from smallholder ownership and cultivation to communal management under the Ujamaa migrants. The village canal was operational, and irrigation farming had just started suggesting some form of land-use intensification. Obviously the lands, which could be irrigated, became valuable and would become a point of attraction and water management a potential area of conflict.

So far, we have identified at least five main groups of actors in the land development process in Chekereni. The first, the early settlers who acquired land in Chekereni, as a group, through allocation by their traditional leaders. The second, flood victims who came in as a group and were also allocated land by traditional leaders and third, the group who moved to Chekereni individually and negotiated with previous owners. The fourth group is made up of the Ujamaa migrants who came in as a group but later increased in numbers, as individuals joined them. In addition to land, the group secured political powers through the election.

The district authority forms the fifth actor. As a part of central government, they achieved their goal of establishing an Ujamaa village in Chekerein. They registered success in implementing an important national policy. The point is will the government be able to transform the area from the "underutilization by pastoralists through grazing" to a more intensive land-use? Will the Ujamaa migrants forget their real intentions in coming to Chekereni? The other landowners have lost their political powers, are they ready to loose more of their land as well? These are among the issues we follow up in the next chapters.

Chapter Five

Allocating Land to Consolidate Leaders' Political Powers

The 1971 village constitution spelt out procedures by which migrants could obtain land in Chekereni. In Kilimanjaro by that period, it was only in Ujamaa villages like Chekereni that one could acquire land by making an application and paying less than Tshs.100.00. In addition, by the end of 1971 irrigation had become possible, making land in Chekereni even more valuable. The good performance of the first Ujamaa migrants in communal activities also contributed indirectly to making the village attractive to migrants. How?

After the first election, the attention of the village council was directed towards the principles of socialist production. To start with, the land they obtained from the original settlers and used in common was declared to be a village communal farm, which is, village property belonging to all registered villagers. Under Ujamaa principles, members were therefore required to work together and share the harvest. This was based on the central philosophy in socialism that if villagers worked together instead of individually, they could produce more and therefore have more to share. The funds generated by common projects would be used to finance village administration and meet the costs of establishing and running community facilities such as primary schools and dispensaries. The first Ujamaa/communal farm was therefore established in Chekereni on the basis of these assumptions.

The early success of communal farming was of interest to leaders at district, regional and national levels. Political leaders at different levels needed a successful experiment to show that Ujamaa could work. On 3rd June 1972, the late President Nyerere and the then Kilimanjaro Regional Commissioner visited Chekereni to inaugurate the village canal. They were impressed by the well-managed 56 acres of the village communal farm. The President directed the Commissioner to assist the village, as it had the potential to become a good model for a Ujamaa village in Kilimanjaro.

Impressed by the achievements recorded by the voluntary Ujamaa villagization, the 1973 TANU annual meeting resolved that living together in villages was the concern of all regions.

The meeting declared that: It is compulsory that, by 1976, all rural families living in scattered homes should settle in nucleated villages and carry out communal farming. To facilitate implementation of the declaration, the Rural Lands (Planning and Utilization) Act number 4 of 1973 was passed. Within the provisions of the Act, the President had unrestricted discretionary powers to declare any land a 'specified area', after which the Minister for Regional Administration (by then part of the Prime Minister's Office) could make regulations and control land use in that area. The Act transferred powers to regulate land use in Ujamaa villages from the Minister for Lands, Housing and Urban Development, to the Prime Minister's Office. That transfer might have resulted in administrative conflicts if the new law were closely followed. But it was not.

The two central government decisions re-activated the Moshi District authorities towards the Ujamaa villagization programme. The same year, Chekereni village was fully registered through efforts made by the district council. In land-use planning terms, registration amounted to official confirmation that the village council had administrative powers over the land area which fell within its jurisdiction, and that the village council was legally recognized. In addition to the registration, the district authorities declared Chekereni the best Ujamaa village for 1973, after the village council had expanded the village communal farm from 56 to 72 acres. The village council received Tshs. 50,000.00 as a prize for that achievement. The money was used to finance a dairy project and a poultry farm as village communal projects.

Using the status conferred to the village through the registration certificate, the council applied for a housing loan from the Tanzania Housing Bank. The registration certificate and accounts approved by the District Ujamaa and Co-operatives Officer were a sufficient collateral for the loan amounting to Tshs. 1,400,000.00. The money financed construction of fifteen mud and pole houses, roofed with corrugated iron sheets, which were mainly for the first Ujamaa migrants. Most of them have not been able to repay the loan to-date.[1] It is however worth noting that, the 1973 Chekereni Ujamaa village offered land, irrigated farms, a share in communal projects and a housing loan to the Ujamaa migrants.

With Ujamaa in Place, Land was Plenty in Chekereni

'I agreed to the conditions of Ujamaa and the village constitution, as I came to Chekereni with a genuine land problem'[2]

Mzee Justin Ngowi is one of the migrants who joined Chekereni in 1973 after being persuaded by the first migrants. In the following sections he describes how:

> During that time (in 1973) I was employed as a waiter in a hotel in Moshi town. Mzee Makishingo used to frequent the hotel, and I also knew him before in Marangu, where I come from. One day, Mzee Makishingo and his friend visited the hotel to eat. We had a chat. They told me, ' Now you are employed, and you are old, but what will happen if this or another job will not be available? Where will you go? It is better you join us in Chekereni. You will be allocated land.... Your land will be there for ever but this job will not.' I was convinced, and after a few days I moved to Chekereni and decided to live here. I was allocated this plot for housing and later a farm that is now under irrigated paddy cultivation. By that time bushes and a lot of wild animals occupied most of the village land. The village was not yet established. We **worked very hard to clear** and establish this village.[3] (Author's emphasis)

Most of the Ujamaa migrants who came after 1973 have a similar story. They all used connections, either through the village leaders directly, like Mzee Ngowi, or through friends or relatives, who then introduced them to the appropriate councilor. Few people came on their own initiative after hearing about Chekereni from friends. But they needed and used a link person to obtain approval as required by the *'Village Constitution'*. Although there was not much bush left in Chekereni by 1973, the Ujamaa migrants still claim to have expended energy in clearing the land. This is because, under customary land rights, tenure is more secure if one is the first to clear the land.

A significant point here is that the Ujamaa migrants do not think it is sufficient to base their claims on village allocation alone. In my view, claims by landowners that they cleared their land themselves, which we shall continue to come across, should be taken as a way of justifying their rights.

However, this type of justification is dubious, because, as we have seen already, all the land in Chekereni had already been acquired. In reality, Mzee Ngowi was allocated land that must have been owned by one of the earlier migrants.

While Mzee Ngowi is one of the group of Ujamaa migrants who decided to migrate after being persuaded by the leaders, there are others who had more serious land problems and who struggled on alone.

Mama Ontoneta Kahumba, for instance, is one of the women who joined the village after 1973, as a single parent with three children living with her. When her husband died, she had been left with four children. One of them was already married and, according to Chagga custom, he was entitled to inherit part of the family land. Mama Kahumba realized that if the family land were subdivided, the remaining portion would not be sufficient to support the rest of her children. To make matters worse, the other three children would also require land in the future. Mama Ontoneta was compelled to ignore Chagga customs and assume the role of her late husband. She moved out of her village, in search of land for the family. She then learned about the possibility of moving to Chekereni from a relative, whose daughter had successfully moved and was willing to help. Mama Kahumba describes how she acquired land through the aid of her relative.

> When I first came to Chekereni, I was received by Mama Atanasia Juma, who came from Marangu and was a relative of mine. She told me to write an application. I wrote a letter and went back home in Rombo to wait for a reply. After two weeks, I came back and I was told that I have been accepted. I was shown this plot in the housing area. I was required to build a hut on my plot first before I could become a full member of the village and officially registered to qualify for a private piece of land for farming. I agreed to these conditions, since I had come to Chekereni with a genuine land problem. [4]

The condition to build a hut before becoming a fully registered member was probably incorporated into the *Village Constitution* in order to check out migrants who were interested in acquiring land but not ready to develop it and live in the village. It was the strictness of the village council in enforcing the condition of building before registration that ensured that first housing cluster was built fairly fast. The number of registered villagers increased rather quickly, from 46 in 1972 to 250 in 1976. By attracting more Ujamaa migrants to the village, the Ujamaa village council was behaving strategically. Since more people were registered, the number of votes for Ujamaa increased. In addition, the increase in village members increased the labour available for village communal projects, upon which the village council relied both financially and politically. In pursuing this objective, balancing land and the number of people in the village was put aside.

For the village council, it was important to check absentee landowners. They wanted people to reside in the village and contribute their labour to village projects, which earned the village council money, fame and power. Since most migrants were desperate for land, the condition did not matter very much. On the other hand, it achieved the strategic objective of the village leaders, namely, to obtain virtually free' labour and to secure the votes necessary to continue marginalizing the original settlers. That in turn facilitated the process of acquiring additional land from the earlier settlers for allocation to new migrants in the name of 'Ujamaa'.

The stories from the two Ujamaa migrants, described above, show us the role of the village leaders in facilitating access to land for new migrants. The stories suggest that the land acquisition process was a peaceful one. Both migrants wished to show that land was available, plentiful, unclaimed and capable of being allocated without conflict. They tell such a story to justify their claims but in reality; the process was not so harmonious.

Mzee Chami's story may illustrate this point. Through the story, we are able to see the *Village Constitution* in real conflict with the earlier migrants and also with the Ujamaa migrants. Finally, the story also illustrates the power and strictness of the village leaders in land allocation, especially in enforcing equal plots-size standards and land-use conditions. Mzee Chami's story starts with how he got the information that he could obtain land in Chekereni.

> My friend living in Chekereni told me that I might get free land. I visited Chekereni in October 1976, met the village chairman and told him about my wish to join the village. He told me to write an application. I wrote a very brief letter saying: 'I request permission to join Chekereni village so that I can get land for farming'. There was no need for many words.... I came back in January 1977 and found my application already approved. But there were a few questions, which I had to answer. I was called in by the village chairman and asked, 'Do you have a wife?' I said, 'Yes'. It seems it was a necessary condition to have a wife in order to be accepted, because a person with a wife will be freer to work in the communal farm while the wife attends to private family farms. I told him I had a wife and two children. I became a member of Chekereni village in January 1977. I was given another condition: to work in the village communal farm for four days a week for free, totally free. Without any payment. Like the others, I was promised some money after the harvest was sold and the costs of the village office and other expenses met. The remaining amount would be shared among the villagers according to the number of days they had contributed to the communal farm. After joining the village, I started to work in the communal farm.[5]

The issue of land allocation and having a wife is worth commenting upon. During the Ujamaa period, land was not allocated to families, as it had been in the pre-Ujamaa period under the Mangi system. The Ujamaa village council allocated land to those who presented applications and qualified to join the village. A man and his wife could therefore qualify and were considered to be two different individuals if they made separate applications and were willing to participate as individuals in the village communal farm. One of the results of that practice was that, women owned slightly more than a quarter of the 1007 residential plots in Chekereni in 1994[6] through allocation by the village council. This would have been unlikely under the customary allocation system.

Mzee Chami did not favour the idea of his wife making a separate application as he wanted her to work in their private family farms. Thus Mzee Chami was the only member of his household who offered to work in the village communal farm.

Focusing on the early non-Ujamaa migrants, it is clear that they had more difficult choices to make, first to surrender their land to the village council, and secondly to work for four days in the communal farm for 'free'. For them, joining the village meant losing a substantial part of their land and change from customary rights holders to village council allottees.

Not all the earlier migrants accepted these conditions. Some decided to sell their land and leave. Mzee Chami is one of the Ujamaa migrants who benefited from such decisions. Like most migrants who joined in 1977, Mzee Chami was allocated a half-acre plot for residential use in the residential cluster where cattle sheds were not allowed. He wanted to keep a few cows and goats as he had done in his small plot in the highlands, but that was not accepted in the housing area in which he was given a plot. By that time there was only one residential cluster where livestock sheds were allowed. In 1975 the village council decided to confine cowsheds to that cluster in order to minimize conflict over crop damage. The village council observed the land-use restriction so closely that, Mzee Chami was unable to violate it and keep livestock in his plot. But he could not do without keeping a cow or two, in order to supply his household with manure for the farm. He was used to keeping cattle for manure as part and parcel of the coffee-banana farming system, which he wanted to introduce in Chekereni. He therefore was keen to obtain a housing plot in the cluster, which would suit his requirements.

In the following account, Mzee Chami narrates how he managed to buy land very cheaply in the residential area of his choice, where he lived until 1995 when he died:

> You see, the village council had made a land-use plan (a verbal land-use zoning restriction). Livestock keepers were supposed to reside only in one cluster, where they were allocated a one-acre plot instead of half an acre, which was

the standard plot size in the other clusters. I then decided to acquire a plot in that residential area. I got an offer and on February 1977, I bought a three-acre farm including a house for only Tshs. 150/=.... The farm was owned by (an original settler) who did not like Ujamaa. He refused to pay the Tshs. 52/ = required by the *Village Constitution*. He moved out of the village. He said 'Slavery has come to Chekereni; I have to leave.' I cannot remember his name. He used to sell fish and was nicknamed in Swahili 'Mjomba Mjomba', meaning 'uncle'. I was able to buy the land and the house so cheaply because the owner was running away. There were other villagers who ran away before they could find someone to buy their land. So he was lucky.

The farm I bought was big, more than three acres, but then because of village restrictions (on land use and size) I was only allowed to keep one acre. I managed to use the three acres for two years until 1979, when the Village Land Allocation Committee discovered it and subdivided the land for other villagers. I could not stop them. Since then I have been left with one acre, which I have been using till now. The Committee used to go around searching for vacant lands for allocation. By then the village was empty, with very few houses, they could easily find a vacant plot. In addition there were people still sending applications to join the village and asking for residential plots. The committee moved around in the whole residential area, subdividing and allocating land according to planned size.... Even if you had ten acres, it was either one acre in Mwamko cluster or half an acre in other clusters. And that was the procedure. If you did not accept the size you simply left. I stayed.... There was nowhere to go to make complaints. You were told that this was an Ujamaa village and all people in the village had to have equal pieces of land.[7]

A number of important land-use planning issues are raised in Mzee Chami's story.

If we think of Mzee Chami as a person looking for land in the market sense, then we see that Ujamaa created conditions which made *Mjomba Mjomba* ready to sell and thus made cheap land accessible to Mzee Chami.

The idea of having equal plots of land may be a good one, but it does not take into account the land rights of the earlier migrants.The original settlers who were interviewed argued that having to share their land with the Ujamaa migrants was not fair. The Ujamaa migrants had their lands in the highlands, which was not available for sharing, so why should the principle of sharing be applied to land in the plains only? We also learn from Mzee Chami's story of the village council' eagerness to have their land-use plan followed. They were able to achieve this, at least at the beginning. Since the plan was used as a tool in guiding and regulating land use, we should examine it a little further.

The village council was also aware that families keeping livestock within their homesteads needed a larger plot-twice the size-to provide extra space for cowsheds and related activities. A larger plot would also attain certain health standards. Most crop-farming activities were confined to the land south of the village. The village canal was also aligned in such a way that it could only irrigate the communal farm and the nearby private farms, all of which were located in the southern part of the village. The village council was then convinced that if keeping livestock were restricted to the northern part, they would have protected their crops.

From the village council's perspective, farming activities north of the village did not matter, even if farmers were in conflict with cattle. Since there was no possibility of irrigation in that area, the farms were available for grazing after harvesting, from early August to late November. Also, the customary landowners in the area had only established a few homes. Most landowners were still living in villages in the highlands, as absentee land users. They were not registered as members of Chekereni village and thus were not represented in village meetings.

One could also interpret the decision to confine the livestock problem to the northern part of the village as a retaliatory measure against the landowners there. The latter had managed to defend their land rights against acquisition by the village. Mzee Wetundwa describes how they managed while the other earlier migrants could not.

> Those people (allocated land by Mangi in the northern part of the villager) are lions.... They stood up strongly and defended their land. They said, 'There is no dog (meaning village leaders wishing to acquire their land) which will enter our land'. They fought very hard. Some went as far as Dar es Salaam (to the Ministry of Lands). But in our area (southern clusters) they found us who came from far away. We came here, we are not united. When the people in our area were told about Ujamaa, they were afraid. The people from Uru fought until they got their land. They were not afraid. [8]

Given the resistance of the customary owners, conflicts with other migrants did not end; indeed, they will continue to surface now and then as the story unfolds.

Viewed from a functional relations point of view, the plan was not well thought out. The area beyond the communal farm was mainly used for free grazing. The village council's idea to zone the northern part for families keeping livestock meant livestock had to cross the village communal and private farms. Conflicts were inevitable.

Although the separation of livestock from crops was technically necessary and politically feasible as an idea, it did not last long. The homestead plots which could be made available in the northern cluster became fewer than the number of villagers wishing to keep livestock.

It was not possible to carry out further subdivision in the cluster designated for livestock keepers in order to accommodate all the people who wished to keep livestock. On the other hand, the village council could not just stop people owning a goat or two. After all, keeping livestock within the homestead is part of the culture of most of the tribes found in Chekereni, especially the Chagga,[9] the Pare and the people from Kamba in Kenya, and not least the people from Arusha. By 1978, the village council had informally to ignore the land-use restriction. All in all, physical surveys and household interviews carried out in the village in 1994, suggest that the zoning restriction imposed by the village council influenced the distribution of cowsheds in the village.

Examining broad land-use distribution in Chekereni after 1978, it is clear that the village council's zoning plan produced a spatial pattern in which, with the exception of the northern part of the village where land rights are held under customary tenure system, farms were separated from homes. While this separation allowed land use to be managed separately, it is also made it possible to implement specific land-use regulations for specific purposes. However, such separation reduced proximity, control and monitoring possibilities because of the distance between the homes and the farms. It is, however, debatable which pattern is efficient and in which context. In addition to achievements made in regulating the broad land-use pattern, the Chekereni village council should also be praised for identifying and managing areas for community facilities, including the school, village market and office, cemetery, cattle dip and the road and footpath system, which makes circulation in the whole residential area possible even by car.

In addition to regulating land use the Ujamaa Village Council was also famous for the way it managed the village communal farm. But unlike the success achieved in respect of the land-use restrictions, there was chronically poor attendance at village works. Records of village council meetings show poor attendance at village communal projects right from 1971. This has remained an issue in village meetings until today.

Villagers not only associate this poor attendance with the four days a week one had to work on the farm, but also, and probably most importantly, they felt that they could not discuss or contribute anything as to how the proceeds were distributed and shared. The issue of sharing proceeds may not be important from a land-use planning point of view, but considering that between 10 to 15 per cent of the village land was converted into public land and that the participation of villagers in the farm limited their time for their private farms, it should be discussed. In addition, the village communal farm is at the heart of the Ujamaa philosophy.

In this section, we present two stories illustrating how the communal farm proceeds were used; and secondly, that it was not only difficult but also punishable to question leaders' decisions.

Nasib Msuya is the head of a young family in Chekereni. He joined the village in 1979 well after Ujamaa had stabilized. He blames the low payment from the village farm for his poor living conditions. He argues that if he had worked as a casual labourer elsewhere, he would have been able to erect a better house within his compound. He felt really embarrassed by the quality of his house. According to him, the option of working as a casual labourer on private farms elsewhere did not exist because he had to work for four days a week on the village farm. The three days left in a week were not sufficient both to attend to his private farm and also to work for money elsewhere. To elaborate his point, he said:

> I attended work on the communal farm for all four days. But I doubt if all my workdays were properly recorded. I think most of my days were recorded for the relatives of village leaders. Although I participated every day, I never received more than Tshs. 400/= as my annual payment in any single year. I received Tshs. 120/= in 1980, which increased to Tshs. 270/= in 1981. And you could hardly do anything with that amount of money. When I received the Tshs. 400/= in 1982, I became very angry. I bought one kg. of sugar, a small amount of cooking oil, one Coca Cola and that was all. One year's work was finished. [10]

Nasib's story was disputed in one feedback session but admitted to be correct in another. Mzee Makishingo, a former village chairman who attended the feedback session, disapproved of the story as being unrepresentative and said that Nasib was not telling the truth. He added that Nasib's attendance at communal activities had not been very good and that he was paid accordingly. He also insisted that no one leader was able to favour his or her relatives in the allocation of workdays.[11] In the other session, which was attended mainly by the current cluster leaders, the story was accepted. Mzee Leonard Joseph, formerly the record-keeper of work-days on the communal farm, declared openly that:

> Leaders were not very strict. We had our corrupt practices-*tulikuwa na magendo yetu*-where few people attended work but many were listed for sharing the harvest. It was common for leaders to add the names of their relatives and friends to the list of working parties. Because of this, some villagers worked very hard but were paid very little, as they had to share with those who did no work.[12]

It was not only Msuya who found the handling of the proceeds from the communal farm irritating. Other villagers were also not happy with that practice. But it needed a strong person to criticize the Ujamaa village council openly.

Mzee Joseph Makoko, who joined the village in 1974, was daring enough to try and caution the village council about the low payments and to say that, people were not happy with the way the harvest from the communal farm was being distributed. Mzee Makoko was concerned with equity and fairness in the distribution. He raised the issue at the village annual meeting held in Chekereni on 28th February 1976. He argued that the distribution was unfair, since it favoured the leaders and their relatives.

Obviously the leaders were not happy with this accusation being made publicly. The leaders withdrew Mzee Makoko's membership, took back his two private farms, and ordered him to leave the village.

Mzee Makoko managed to use the authorities of the district, region and even the Prime Minister's office in Dar es Salaam to be allowed to stay in Chekereni. But he has not been able to recover his farms since. Stories similar to this, where villagers try to question leaders' decisions but are ignored or even punished, are many, and we shall hear more of them as we proceed.

In addition to regulating land use and managing the communal farm, the village council also received praise for its good management in respect of water use and maintenance of the village canal. The council adopted the *Wameeku wa Mfongo* traditional irrigation institution (see Chapter Two). With the villagers' involvement, three old men were elected to supervise the water-use schedule in accordance with an agreed programme. The village council would assist in cases of conflict or when it was necessary to clean the canal or carry out other maintenance tasks. Most of the villagers who were asked about the management of the canal said it was fine. Problems were solved locally. They all participated in the frequent calls to clean up the canal.

By that time, those using irrigation were few. Each would have access to water for irrigation once a week for about six hours. Water was being used continuously, on a 24-hour basis. Farmers did not care whether their turn came during the day or at night. They seem to have co-operated very well, since few conflicts were reported.

Most of the people interviewed claimed that there were no water shortages so serious that crops dried out. There was plenty of water available, and farmers had not been able to clear all the area earmarked for irrigation. The size an individual farmer could cultivate was limited not only by the length of water use, but also by the amount of family labour available and the capital required to run the tomato and vegetable gardens. This was a blessing in disguise, since it meant that irrigators were only able to manage small farms, and therefore it was possible for many smallholders to benefit from the canal.

It is important to emphasize the fact that the mixed farms which were established later with bananas, tree crops, fruits and maize, etc. did not require a similar amount of water every day. Less water was required as crops stabilized. It was therefore possible, at least at the beginning, to extend the area under irrigation continuously using the same amount of water. However, as more people joined the village and extended the farming area, competition for water intensified. The water situation became even complicated after the introduction of modern irrigation practices, through the Lower Moshi irrigation Project.

At this stage in the Chekereni narrative, we shall end the discussion on water management. It will certainly come up again, more actively in chapter seven and thereafter, and then we shall have an opportunity to compare the modern and traditional institution and the traditional system under Ujamaa.

In this chapter, we have seen how the Ujamaa system facilitated and controlled access to land through the village council as the main actor. The village council, regulated land and water use, and to some extent resolved or suppressed conflicts. The village constitution and Ujamaa ideology were key points of reference for the various decisions relating to land use. Neither Ujamaa nor the constitution could be questioned, and thus most of the leaders' actions were final. It was like a 'take it or leave it' situation. Villagers like Nasib did not try to question the leaders but kept their disagreements until they found an opportunity like the one offered to Nasib by this investigation. Some daring villagers like Makoko tried but suffered the consequences. The experience of these two and other villagers provides us with a link to the next chapter, where we shall examine in more detail the Ujamaa way of dealing with land conflicts.

Chapter Six
Land Disputes Handling Machinery at Work

Introduction

This chapter discusses land-related conflicts resulting from the decision to convert private land rights into village or communal ownership. In one of the stories, we shall show a case in which landowners who could not defend their lands instead despaired and moved to other villages. The second case is that of a villager who sued the village council. The second case, which is rather long and difficult to assess, will take us back to the peak days of Ujamaa in Chekereni and in Tanzania. It is interesting to follow this case up to the liberal stage of development in Tanzania and to show how it has influenced the land use intensification initiatives in the village.

When Citizens are Terrorized, Leaders Enjoy Absolute Powers

Following the 1973 Presidential visit, and especially after irrigation became possible in Chekereni, the number of registered people increased from 60 in 1973 to 96 in 1974. This was a dramatic change compared to 46 registered villagers in 1972.

Since the village council relied on communal projects, especially the communal farm, an increase in members meant an increase in labour and thus a corresponding increase in the area of the communal farm. The village council thus decided to expand the village communal farm. In June 1974, about 50 acres of private land were added to the farm. In June 1976 another 71 acres were annexed to the communal farm. In total the farm measured 183 acres. Those most hit by the decision were Mzee Wetundwa, most of the migrants who joined Chekereni because of the 1968 floods and Mzee Mbindyo who lost all his land.

The reader will remember Mzee Mbindyo's resistance and how he protected his land rights against the decision made by the District Commissioner (see chapter three). However, on this occasion he did not resist but simply moved out of Chekereni into the nearby village of Oria, where he acquired three acres of land and established a new home. If we refer to the date of his arrival in Chekereni, i.e. 1944, we see that the decision meant abandoning a home established, developed and used for thirty-two years. This must have been a difficult decision to make. When he was asked as to why he did not resist or appeal as he did in the 1960s, he replied:

> No, I didn't want to do that. This business of land is very dangerous. I have seen people die because of land. I do not want to die because of land.[1]

The change in Mzee Mbindyo's attitude to his land rights is interesting and should be understood. He saw how Ujamaa was introduced in Chekereni. He became a member but could not cope with the communal work. He saw the President and the Regional Commissioner visit Chekereni and praise the village leadership. The District Commissioner was also in full support and made frequent visits to the village. If he were to appeal, he would have to start with the District Commissioner. That would not make sense: he would not receive much support. He simply had to give up. Political scientists, for instance Nyong'o,[2] describe Mzee Mbindyo as an example of 'the terrorised native', who yielded to authoritarian rule and allowed the leaders to enjoy absolute power over the natives.

For their part, the villagers who were interviewed associate the change in Mzee Mbindyo's behavior with his poor health. Because of asthma, he could not cope with what the appeal might have involved. Whatever the reason, Mzee Mbindyo decided to leave the village as his way of coping with the conflict. During the interview eighteen years later, he still remembered how bad he felt when he had to leave his home and land to start life afresh in his late fifties. It is a case of a suppressed conflict kept in the mind, like that of Nasib in chapter five. It is not out in the open, but it is there.

In the next case, we shall follow Mzee Wetundwa, whom we also remember as one of the flood victim migrants. In his case, the matter was more touchy, as most of the land which had been allocated to the flood victims he had led into Chekereni was converted into village communal land. It can be argued that Mzee Wetundwa, as their former leader, felt he should try and fight for his people. He opened a case which we shall follow as an illustration of the Ujamaa conflict-processing mechanism at work in order to establish the strengths and weaknesses of that system. At the end of the story, we may be in a position to reconsider our present understanding of Mzee Mbindyo's decision to remain a 'terrorized citizen'.

Judgement by not Making a Ruling

> " I lost hope and kept on just watching what was happening in the village."[3]

The case started in June 1976, when Mzee Wetundwa appealed to the Moshi District Commissioner against the decision to incorporate fifty acres of land owned and used by the flood victim migrants, into the village communal farm. He therefore wanted to have the decision reversed. As a response, the Commissioner organized a public meeting at Kahe, a market center located south of Chekereni village. According to Mzee Wetundwa, the Commissioner addressed the meeting in very general terms. She warned village leaders that *'in implementing Ujamaa, they should respect private land rights; Ujamaa does not mean confiscating land'*. After a brief talk, the meeting ended. The Commissioner did not address the Chekereni village leaders openly, nor did she deal with the case directly on that day.

A few days after the meeting, Mzee Wetundwa made a second visit to the Commissioner, who then promised to look into the case. In his view, the Commissioner was very sympathetic and appeared keen to resolve the conflict. But after Wetundwa's second visit, it did not take long before Mama Halima was transferred and a new District Commissioner appointed. Everything concerning the case stopped.

Mzee Wetundwa believes that the new Commissioner was not as keen as Mama Halima in tackling conflicts relating to the implementation of Ujamaa and instead strongly supported decisions made by Ujamaa village leaders. The following section shows how Mzee Wetundwa pursued the case after the Commissioner was transferred.

> Everything stopped. People lost hope of getting their land rights back. The village council became very strong, and the leaders went ahead in acquiring private lands. No one could fight the village government. I remember that I had given part of my farmland to my sister, but that land was also taken away. My sister moved to Mabogini village. I do not know how she got land there. After Mama Halima was transferred I had nowhere to go. I lost hope and kept on just watching what was happening in the village. And I tell you, had it not been for God, and the government, there could have been a war. I kept on asking myself, where will my son John live, where will my son Daniel live, where will my grandchildren farm? No answers. I continued with frustrations and pains until 1988, [when he started the case afresh]. [4]

In 1976, Mzee Wetundwa did not achieve much except may be the meeting at small town of Kahe. But that did not give him his land back, and neither there was an opportunity to question the leaders. He therefore remained frustrated, as he said, and probably also as 'terrorised' as Mzee Mbindyo.

In Tanzania, the period from 1975 to 1985 was a hard decade for most people. Ujamaa and especially central government powers and control over land became very strong. Village councils like Chekereni were also very strong, their decisions were final, always right and unchallenged, so long as they could be associated with the development of Ujamaa. To most people who experienced government administration in that period, it was a tough decade that will not be easily forgotten.[5]

After 1985, the government relaxed its muscle over socialism and villagization and adopted more liberal policies. No new legislation was passed. But through speeches, villagers were allowed to de-villagize, that is, to move back to their pre-villagization lands. The speeches gave powers and hopes to landowners like Mzee Wetundwa. Cases of land rights taken to the courts or the President increased substantially at national level as well as in Chekereni.[6]

Wetundwa is among those landowners who decided to start all over again.

> I cannot remember the exact date, but what I can be sure of is that I started the case in early 1988. I decided to go to the District Commissioner's office and reported my case once again. I met the District Administrative Officer [the second in command in matters related to administration]. I made several visits to the District Administrative Officer. On 12th October 1988, he wrote a letter to the ward executive secretary, directing him to visit the disputed land and settle the conflict. I brought the letter to the ward executive secretary. He read the letter and promised to visit Chekereni to inspect the disputed land. After the directive from the District Administrative Officer, it was not long before the ward executive secretary visited the village. When he arrived, he first had secret talks with the village secretary, and then I was allowed to join them to inspect the disputed site. I showed them all the land I was claiming - 48 acres [located in the present village communal farm]. Before the ward executive secretary left, he told me to visit his office for a letter to take to the village secretary. After a few days, I went to the ward office to collect the letter. I did not get any letter.

> I went back to the District Administrative Officer, who wrote a second letter to the ward executive secretary. The letter, dated 9th November 1988, did not produce any positive action. So there was no solution to my problem that year.[7]

Within a year, all local government institutions, the district, ward and village council became involved and three letters were written, but the case was not resolved. By then, paddy cultivation under the Japanese financed Lower Moshi Irrigation Project had started in Chekereni, and as will be shown later, production was also very high in the communal farm, making Mzee Wetundwa more forceful with regard to the case. Since the ward executive secretary did not respond to the letter from the District Commissioner, he decided to report back to the Commissioner.

On 1st March 1989, I returned to the District Commissioner's office and reported to the Administrative Officer, who wrote a letter to the Divisional Secretary,[8] directing him to meet the ward secretary and find out why he had ignored my case. On the same day, I brought the letter to the Divisional Secretary. She took the letter and said, 'You can now go home. I will come to Chekereni in another day.' I then asked her to send me a private letter to my address when she decided to visit Chekereni, because if she wrote through the village secretary, he may not give the letter to me. She said 'Yes'. But she neither wrote nor visited the village. If she did visit the ward office I was not informed, so I don't know if she came. I think she did not. On 20th March 1989, I wrote a long letter to the District Commissioner seeking his permission to sue the village secretary, village chairman and ward executive officer in that order for confiscating my land. I did not get any response.

Six months later, I went back to the District Administrative Officer to inform him that the Divisional Secretary promised to visit the disputed land, but she did not come to Chekereni. On the same day, 11th September 1989, the District Administrative Officer wrote a second letter to the Divisional Secretary directing that: "You should solve Stephen Wetundwa's case. Why are you not dealing with it?" As usual I brought the letter to the Divisional Secretary's office and left. Again nothing happened. On 25th September 1989, I went to the District Administrative Officer, who gave me a copy of the previous letter. I took the letter to the Divisional Secretary. There were two other people from the District Administrative Officer, also going to see the Divisional Secretary on land issues. We went together. When we got there we sat outside the office, waiting to be allowed in. While we were waiting, the Divisional Secretary came out of the office. She saw me with the two people. She did not greet me, although she knew me.[9] When I had brought the first letter she received me very well, but not this time. I was surprised. She called in the two people, and I was left outside the office to wait for my turn. But I was not allowed in.

I went back to the District Administrative Officer. I told him, 'What I want now is a letter which I will take to the court to sue the Divisional Secretary. She has insulted me heavily.' I was so furious that the officer had to calm me down first. After some time I relaxed. The District Administrative Officer said, 'I will write letters [to the ward executive officer and the Divisional Secretary] and require them to visit my office to meet a delegation which is visiting us so that they can see the importance of attending the meeting. I will not write that they are being called in to discuss Wetundwa's case, because then they may decide not to come.'[10]

The case had now been running for two years since it was reactivated. Within this period, six letters were written, sent and ignored. We also saw that Mzee Wetundwa was 'ping-ponged' between district administrative institutions. And from the last sentence in the above passage, and also from the fact that the letters were ignored, we can say that the district had no authority over the lower levels.

Although Mzee Wetundwa did not declare it in the interview, I came to learn later that in fact he was also pursuing the case on behalf of the flood victim migrants. The migrants held secret meetings in Chekereni to advice Mzee Wetundwa as to how to proceed. During these meetings, contributions were made to finance his trips to the different offices. This may have been the reason why the divisional secretary accused Mzee Wetundwa of 'inciting people in the village'. Related to this is the additional finding that there were people in Chekereni who wanted to pursue their land rights but did not want to be known to the authorities. They therefore hid behind Mzee Wetundwa.

After the District Administrators the Land Tribunal Joins In

As Wetundwa continued visiting the district administrative officer at least once a week, the officer became tired. On 5th October 1989, she wrote another letter and ordered that Wetundwa's case should be dealt with and concluded before 9th October 1990, that is, within a year. A meeting was called in a separate note. The district administrative officer's trick worked. The meeting took place on 1st November 1989. Since Mzee Wetundwa knew the importance of the meeting, he came with Mzee Hosenieli Hassani, formerly the TANU[11] chairman for Kahe, which covers Chekereni village, and Mzee Joel Maya, formerly Mangi of Kahe area that included party of the Chekereni, who gave evidence that he was the rightful owner of the disputed land.[12]

It was decided in the meeting that since the witnesses had attested that Mzee Wetundwa's ownership rights had their origin in customary rights, the proper court to preside over the case was the Customary Lands Tribunal, not the district court.

Mzee Wetundwa was therefore given another letter, which he brought to the clerk in the Regional Customary Land Tribunal Office on 24th January 1990. He then opened a case, which was registered as case number 14 of 1990 concerning '48 acres of land acquired through allocation by

TANU in 1968, but confiscated by Chekereni village council under the villagization programme in 1976'. By that year, 1990, Mzee Wetundwa had been struggling for three years, in addition to waiting for twelve years, only to remain where he was in 1976, that is, starting to report a case.

We continue the story based on an interview with Mzee Wetundwa, a talk with the tribunal clerk and a review of the case file.

Two days later after the case was registered, the tribunal clerk wrote to the ward executive officer to request information about the case and also to order the officer to inform the defendants.[13] On 2nd February 1990, the defendants made a written statement about the case as required by legal procedures. The statements were received and filed. The ward executive officer made a visit to Chekereni on February 15, 1990 to obtain information about the case.[14] The ward executive officer inspected the area of conflict and made a sketch, which shows that the disputed land is right inside the village communal farm and within reach of the village canal. Thus judgement in favour of Mzee Wetundwa meant ruling against Ujamaa, which would amount to the privatization of communal lands. That would certainly have undermined the status of Chekereni as a model Ujamaa village.

On 16th February, the ward executive officer wrote a report in which he advised the tribunal as follows:

1) to investigate the case carefully, as there might be some underground plan to undermine the village council and its successful communal activities;

2) the tribunal committee should meet the village council and hear its views;

3) the land, which is being claimed by Mzee Wetundwa, has been used by the village council for almost twenty years without claims; it was thus surprising for Mzee Wetundwa to have kept quiet for such a long time, only to make a claim after fourteen years![15]

The case was dormant until 15th August 1990, when the tribunal clerk told the defendants and Mzee Wetundwa to prepare witnesses for a case hearing on 29th August 1990. The case was heard as scheduled. It was agreed that the next hearing should be planned after the tribunal committee had inspected the disputed land as and when Mzee Wetundwa (the plaintiff) provided them with transport. Thus a third site visit was being planned at Mzee Wetundwa's expense.

In early September 1990, Mzee Wetundwa informed the tribunal clerk that he was ready to finance the trip. On 7th September 1990, the tribunal clerk informed the defendants and the plaintiff of their intention to visit the area on 11th September and that they should be there to receive the tribunal committee members, show them the disputed land, and answer any questions. The tribunal committee visited Chekereni as scheduled, and requested for a copy of the minutes of the meeting in which it had been decided to extend the village communal farm.

Two days later, the village secretary sent a typed one-page letter headed 'Minutes of the Village Assembly Meeting held on 15th July 1970'. The letter raises a point of interest, which we should bring out here.

First of all its structure is notable. The letter dated 13th September 1990, stamped and signed by the village chairman and village secretary, does not contain minutes of any meeting. It is different from a normal report of a meeting in that it does not contain a list of attendants or agenda for the meeting, or details of any deliberations or resolutions. If anything, the document is a letter and not minutes of a meeting. In fact the document is a report from the village chairman on the development of Chekereni village from July 1970 to early 1984. The letter contains nothing about the extension of the village communal farm but only shows that the communal farm was 108.5 acres in area.

From a procedural point of view, the minutes requested by the officer are relevant to check if the decision was made in accordance with the requirement that the village council holds one meeting in which the decision is first discussed, and then holds a second meeting in which the proposal by the village council is presented, evaluated and approved or not approved by all members of the village who are 18 years old and above, in a village assembly meeting.

This procedure, if followed, encourages participation, the possibility to question decisions and maybe transparency. The question before us is whether any of that happened.

Since the village council was elected in February 1971, it was not possible for the council to hold a meeting in July 1970 as suggested. Documents from the village archives suggest that, the meeting to decide on the extension of the communal farm was never held, and there is no evidence, which shows that the village council or the assembly ever considered the decision. We can therefore say that the village council did not follow the right procedure in making that decision.

After the site visit by the tribunal committee and the receipt of the letter from the village, the case fell silent again, this time for three months. On 17th December 1990, Mzee Wetundwa reported to the Regional

Commissioner, who instructed the Land Tribunal Committee to deal with the case and to serve a stop order on whoever was using the disputed land. Mzee Wetundwa brought the letter to the land tribunal clerk. Again nothing happened until 4th February, when the tribunal announced a case hearing on 13th February 1991.

The case hearing could not take place because only two members of the tribunal committee were present, the quorum being five. The case was postponed until 25th February 1991, on which day only Mzee Wetundwa came with his witnesses, not the defendants. The case was scheduled for the next day, but once more the defendants were not present. Mzee Wetundwa attended with his three witnesses. The case was postponed until 3rd March 1991 and a warning written to the defendants. Again the defendants did not attend but claimed later that they had had to attend a seminar at the Regional Commissioner's office.

After the five postponements within two months, Mzee Wetundwa reported his case to the office of the Member of Parliament for Moshi District. On 21st March 1991, the personal assistant to the MP wrote to the tribunal clerk to speed up the case. He also repeated the directive to issue a stop order to whoever was using the land and told the clerk to keep the MP's office informed. The letter cautioned that

> Mzee Wetundwa was an old man, like your parent- *kama mzazi wako*- and that the practice of delaying decisions made citizens hate the government for not providing them with their rights.[16]

Again nothing happened despite the serious warning. On 10th May 1991, Mzee Wetundwa went back to the Regional Commissioner's office, where he had been a year before. He was directed to meet the secretary to the Regional Commissioner, who wrote another letter to the tribunal clerk directing him to 'see to it that the case is finalized and the Regional Commissioner is informed'.

The tribunal clerk received the letter and scheduled the case for hearing on 8th September1992, seventeen months ahead. Mzee Wetundwa was patient enough to wait. But again the hearing did not take place. This time it was also Mzee Wetundwa's fault because he came late and with only two witnesses. Otherwise, only one of the defendants was present; the other defendant, the former village secretary, was said to be attending another meeting. The hearing was thus postponed. The tribunal committee decided to deal with other cases.

The case was mentioned again on 1st October 1992 and scheduled for the 7th of that month, on which the hearing could not proceed, since there was only one tribunal councilor. None of the defendants attended and they did not give any reason or excuse. Mzee Wetundwa was present with one witness. The two tribunal committee members, showing sympathy and wishing to minimize expenses on Mzee Wetundwa's side, promised to give a ruling on the case within two weeks of that date. Up until March 1996, no judgement has been made, and the case is still pending. Mzee Wetundwa remains patient and hopes that one day he will get his land back.

On 9th November 1992, while the case was still running, the official government gazette announced that a bill seeking to extinguish customary titles in villages established during villagization would be presented to a parliamentary sitting on 1st December. The bill was interpreted as a government strategy to deal with cases similar to Mzee Wetundwa's.

The Presidential Commission of Inquiry into Land Matters submitted its report on 12th November 1992 arguing that cases such as Mzee Wetundwa's should be decided in favour of the landowners. On 13th December, the bill was tabled in the Parliament in Dodoma by the Minister for Lands, Housing and Urban Development and was endorsed and subsequently assented to by the President.[17]

However, the High Court and the Court of Appeal later declared the bill unconstitutional. The contradiction between customary claims and those based on villagization and Ujamaa allocation, both in Chekereni and in Tanzania generally, has yet to be officially and openly clarified. In his speech to people with land disputes in the courts of law, the Minister for Lands, Housing and Urban Development appealed to them;

> To be patient and to wait until a proper formula in compensation procedures is available.... People should understand that the villagization operation affected both parties, those who moved from one village to another and those who were residing in the new village...the original fault was the government's.[18]

It was expected that, the 1995 land policy and the subsequent land law might make cases like Wetundwa's workable. To a certain extent that has been the case because the Village Land Act, number 5 of 1999 confirms validity of land allocations made under the villagization programme.

Focusing on the land disputes handling mechanism it is clear that it has not performed well. Mzee Wetundwa's case has run for thirty years without a ruling. It has involved the administrative and legal as well as political structures of the region. None of the actors was or is ready to make a ruling. In the early stages of the case, we learned that the district officials did not have sufficient administrative authority over the division, ward or even village council. Orders from the district were ignored. We concluded that this was a weakness in the administrative system, one that may also undermine effectiveness in enforcing planning decisions.

As we proceeded with the case, actors who are supposed to have greater powers and authority were brought in. But we were surprised to see that even the regional Customary Lands Tribunal, which is directly answerable to the Minister for Lands Housing and Urban Development, could not give orders to the village leaders. Warnings from the tribunal did not change the defendants' behaviour. We also saw the tribunal committee receiving false evidence but not taking legal action. From another perspective, the tribunal did not honour orders from either the Regional Commissioner or the MP's office.

On the basis of the case, it appears that the formal hierarchy of administration and political powers became confused. In that situation, which was common when Ujamaa was at its height in rural Tanzania, laws were consciously overlooked, thus leaving room for corruption and undermining the goals of fairness, equity and openness in decision-making.

On the other hand, the actors in the case appear to show, at least in their communications with others, that they are very sympathetic and would like the case to be decided. One may be inclined to think that they were teasing Mzee Wetundwa, writing letters in such a way as to make him feel that the case was to be decided the next day in his favor. The interview with him shows that he still had that feeling and although that may have been a false hope, we may attribute his and the flood victim migrant's patience to it.

Land disputes not withstanding, the government was still keen to intensify the land use in Chekereni and in the surrounding villages. Thus in the late 1970s the regional government approved the introduction of modern irrigation farming in Chekereni. We pursue the planning and implementation of that project in the next chapters.

Chapter Seven

Planning for Modern Irrigation in Chekereni

It is sometimes of paramount importance not so much what is said, but who speaks. [1]

The Land Use Situation in Chekereni before the Introduction of Modern Irrigation

In order to understand the land use changes introduced through the modern irrigation farming system, it is important that we briefly outline the land use and economic situation in Chekereni before the Lower Moshi Irrigation Project was introduced. With traditional irrigation in place in Chekereni in the1980s, villagers intensified land use through traditional mixed farming which most of the Ujamaa migrants were used to.

There were therefore two farming systems in operation, dry and irrigated. Both had conservation potential, especially in maintaining soil fertility to a given level. Permanent cultivation through irrigation, where perennial crops such as trees, bananas and fruits are grown, has an added advantage not only in terms of protecting the soil from direct sunlight, but also in minimizing water loss from evaporation. The trees planted on the irrigated farms also reduce the strength of wind erosion. Traditional irrigated farming provided smallholdings with a wide range of crops, including maize, finger millet, cotton, cassava, bananas, vegetables and fruits and to a limited extent paddy. According to most villagers, the food situation was fair, and farms, which on average were between three to four acres, were reliable as sources of family food.

Despite the emphasis on crop cultivation, livestock did not receive any less attention than crops but was also a part of the farming system. Village leaders' estimates show that the village had 762 livestock units in 1980, with 450 cows, 800 goats and 450 sheep, which depended on grazing resources in and mostly outside the village.

According to findings from a structured survey carried out by the author in the village in 1994, household income-generating activities were many.

Crop farming and keeping livestock were the main ones, followed by casual labor, salaried employment and trading activities. It was common for a household to have several sources of income.

In the following chapters, we shall show how integrated development planning and its implementation were introduced in Chekereni. Through that type of planning, it was decided to transform 3320 ha.of land in the plains from dry cultivation to modern irrigated paddy cultivation under the Lower Moshi Irrigation Project. Out of the proposed area, 850 ha. were earmarked in Chekereni village.

The importance of the irrigation project to the Chekereni narrative is not only its influence on the land use intensification process in Chekereni, but also the opportunity it offers to experience the decision-making process in the irrigation project, from planning through to execution and how the system of land and water management worked.

Approving the Integrated Development Plan for Kilimanjaro Region

On 1st February 1979 the regional development committee approved the first Integrated Development Plan for Kilimanjaro region. Within the planning and administrative structure of Tanzania at that time, the Regional Development Committee (RDC) was the highest decision-making authority for planning, budgeting and development implementation in the region. Like other committees in other regions, the Kilimanjaro Regional Development Committee was comprised of the Regional Commissioner as chairman, the Regional Development Director as secretary, six members of parliament from the electoral districts, five district commissioners, twelve councilors, two from each district, and the six district executive directors. With the 1996 shift to decentralized planning and development to the district level, this structure has changed.[2]

The Plan, which was approved, included development projects in industry, infrastructure, agriculture and the environment. Eight sub-projects were listed under agriculture, among them the Lower Moshi irrigation project covering Chekereni and other eighteen villages in the plains south of Moshi town.

In the following sections, we examine the plan and the planning process in order to show how the Lower Moshi area including Chekereni was identified as suitable for the project. We start with some background to the integrated plan.

The decision to draw up the Integrated Development Plan for Kilimanjaro region was made in 1972 by the central government as part of its 1972 decentralization policy. It was actually drawn up by the regional authorities as a contribution towards national development planning as required by the decentralization programme. Under that perspective, the plan therefore identified development projects to be incorporated into the third National Five-Year Development Plan (1976-1981).

Another context, which may have triggered the plan, is that, during the 1970s Tanzania suffered from a serious food shortage.[3] In that situation, projects like the integrated plan, which were intended to improve agricultural production, were accorded a high priority.

On the global level, the 1970s were the peak period for the idea of 'integrated development planning'. Donor communities, for instance the USA, German and Britain, advocated this concept as a planning approach suitable for third-world conditions.[4] Tanzania accepted the concept and a nationwide directive was issued for each region to prepare its integrated plan, mostly with donor support. Kilimanjaro was assisted by the Government of Japan through the Japan International Co-operation Agency or JICA, which was already involved in development activities in the region.

Preparation of the Kilimanjaro Integrated Development Plan started in 1972. The planning team, comprising both Japanese and local experts, surveyed the whole region of Kilimanjaro. Among the areas identified as having development potential in agriculture was the land south of Moshi town or Lower Moshi. As usual, a technical suitability evaluation was carried out.

The suitability study included soil surveys leading to soil fertility rating, a water availability assessment, and an assessment of the social and economic capacity of smallholders in coping with a cash-crop economy under modern irrigation practices.

On the basis of this analysis, the planning team was convinced that the land in lower Moshi area, which was mostly used for grazing, seasonal cultivation, and traditional irrigation in small patches was fertile, and that with proper irrigation, improved technology and high-yielding rice varieties it would be possible to increase the yield from 1.8 to 6 tons per ha.

The planning team therefore concluded:

> It has been noted that in the whole region (covering 13,309 sq. kms) there is less than 3,000 sq. kms of land suitable for agriculture. This does not take into consideration, however, *technological know-how*, which can make even presently *unsuitable areas very productive*. It is, however, of interest to note that the lowlands [the Lower Moshi] are a logical place for future socio-economic

development based on the diversification of economic activities. [5] (Author's emphasis)

Several sites including the Lower Moshi area were identified for intensive agricultural development. Since we are interested in the Chekereni village land, we shall focus on the Lower Moshi irrigation project and on how that site was assessed and justified. Since it proved difficult and was not possible to interview members of the planning team, we shall examine the reasons outlined in the plan.

Location and size

Among the first reasons is that the proposed area was large and well located. It covered 4200 ha. of land skirting the southeastern side of Kilimanjaro mountain, at an altitude of 700-800 metres above sea level, which was suitable for irrigated paddy cultivation. Accessibility is very good, as the area is located between 5 and 25 kilometres southeast of Moshi Town and is bordered in the north by the Moshi to Dar es Salaam road.

Land reform proposed

Land rights became an issue because the project was to be implemented within smallholdings. With respect to land parcels, the plan noted that fragmentation had reached an alarming level. It therefore recommended a land reform in which paddy plots would be leveled and standardized in size in order to facilitate easy management in the administration of inputs such as water and fertilizer.

Low population density

The plan argued that the Lower Moshi area, where the main land use was seasonal cultivation and grazing, had a very low population density, estimated at 92 people per sq. km. Compared with the 500 people per sq. km. in the highlands, that was very low. In a region where the demand for productive land was very high, agricultural intensification might be a strategy for accommodating the region's population increase.

We should probably remember that the low density and perceived openness of land use in the plains has also been used as a reason for government intervention since the 1960s.

Soil fertility also rated high

The report described the soils of the area as follows:

Soils in the area were very fertile...there is no doubt about the fertility of the lowlands in the Kilimanjaro region. The few peasants who have moved to the lowlands and are cultivating there prove this. Areas such as Arusha Chini are very fertile. [6]

As well as referring to the few peasants cultivating in the area as evidence of the high fertility rate, the planning team's fertility rating map, which is based on their surveys, showed that most of the central part of the proposed project area fell into the 'medium fertile soils' category. A small tip towards the north was shown as having 'high to medium fertile soils', while a considerable part towards the southern boundary was rated as having 'low fertile soils'.

Socio-economic Capacity of Smallholders Assessed

Since the project was to be managed by individual farmers, the following aspects were taken into account.

1) The introduction of paddy cultivation as a cash crop would be facilitated by the fact that farmers had been accustomed to growing cash crops since the 1930s - coffee in the highlands and cotton in the drier lowlands. The smallholders in the area were therefore expected to be able to apply their experience in managing the inputs supply and marketing aspects of cash-crop production in paddy;

2) The farmers were used to irrigated agriculture. By then, the ratio of smallholders as well as large-scale irrigated farms in Kilimanjaro region was 17.5 per cent, four times higher than the national average of 4 percent. Given the high ratio of irrigation, by 1972 agriculture was consuming 94.3 per cent of the total volume of water used in the Kilimanjaro region.

Of the four districts, Moshi had 98.2 per cent, which was the highest in utilization of groundwater sources, and 94.9 per cent, the second highest in surface-water utilization. That finding did not affect the decision to invest in the Irrigation Project in Lower Moshi.

Water Availability

We saw in the previous chapters that water is a central issue for crop farming in the plains. It would become even more important with the project's implementation, because paddy needs more water than the crops, which had previously been introduced in the area. For this reason, we should deal with the issue of water in more detail.

The plan noted that rainfall in the area did not exceed 590 mm. per annum. The possibilities for irrigation were then examined. Eighteen river systems in the plains were analysed, and the following conclusions made:

> The major sources of surface water are the Rau, Mue, and Weruweru rivers, but downstream they have virtually **no drop of water to offer for irrigation purposes.** The only river that has some spare capacity to serve as a new water source for irrigation is Himo river.... The shortage of surface water is a very keenly felt problem...as can be seen from the monthly volume of river flow at 20 percent probability discharge. There is some surplus water during the rainy season of April and May, but this surplus water is utilized by the Nyumba ya Mungu dam downstream, **thus making it very difficult to develop a new source of surface water in this district in the future.** Due to the lack of surface water, an increasingly larger volume of subterranean water is now used in the middle and lower areas.[7] (Author's emphasis)

From these conclusions, it is clear that there were difficulties in introducing irrigation in the plains if the project were to rely on surface water. The only possibility was to draw on the spare capacity of the Himo river. Otherwise the other main rivers in the plains, Kikafu, Weruweru, Rau and Mue, were noted as being the most intensively used. In addition, the plan noted that the basins of these rivers are densely populated, making the existing demand for water, irrigation and domestic, very high.

The fact that Moshi Town was also located within these basins and therefore competing for its share of water for urban activities from the same sources was not discussed.

However, in order to ensure that the irrigation project would not suffer from water shortages, the plan made the following recommendations:

> The directions in which the water utilization schemes...should be pursued in the future would be to attain better and more efficient water utilization in the upper zone by way of a re-arrangement of the traditional furrows and lining of the irrigation canals, and to construct a number of small-sized dams. What is necessary in the middle and lower zones would be to use subterranean water...to be pumped by electricity.... It has become clear that, as the results of recent survey show, there are many groundwater resources all over the district. [8]

There are at least four points to emphasize here:

1) ways of enhancing water utilization efficiency throughout the catchment area, especially upstream, should be considered;

2) in order to catch and store surplus water during the April and May rains, small dams should be constructed;

3) in the plains, where the project is to be established, groundwater, which is plentiful at a depth of 50 to 100 metres, should be exploited through electric pumps and efficient use made of that water with the aid of a reservoir.

4) investment in an electricity supply and the construction of reservoir dams were necessary.

In short - a point which was to become controversial later - despite the plan ruling out the use of surface water sources for the project at implementation, such warnings were ignored. As we shall see later, that resulted in the implementation of an irrigation project in which water shortage has remained a big problem for the farmers and the project management.

Following the technical analysis, the plan showed that agricultural intensification through irrigation was possible in the plains, and twelve projects were put forward. One of these projects was the Chekereni area covering 320 ha out of the total planned area of 3320ha. Proposed water sources for the Chekereni area included six bore holes and the Rau river. In total 29 boreholes were proposed and with supplement from rivers the 118 cusecs of the water required would be available for the whole project. Chekereni alone was expected to consume about 11 cusecs.

Thus, as regards our interest in land-use change in Chekereni, the Kilimanjaro Integrated Plan, which was finally approved, proposed to incorporate 4200 ha. of land in Moshi District into an agricultural development project, of which a total of 3320 ha. were to be transformed into a modern irrigation scheme using mainly groundwater. In the following section we focus on how the plan proposals were to be realized.

Implementing the Approved Plan: Experts versus the Planning Team

The plan was approved, but the region did not have the financial ability to execute the proposed development projects. Execution had to wait for about fifteen months, when the Government of Japan agreed to finance some of the projects, including the one in Lower Moshi. At that point, the details of the Lower Moshi Irrigation Project were presented to the Kilimanjaro Regional Development Committee, which not only approved it but also recommended a revision of the implementation schedule so that actual construction could start earlier than planned.

However, the minutes of the regional development committee meeting which agreed to shorten the period do not give reasons for this decision, and attempts to interview the then members of the committee have not been successful. Probable reasons are many.

Tanzania experienced the first oil-price shock in 1975-1978. Agriculture's share of GDP averaged 38 per cent in 1974-78. The collapse of the East Africa Community[9] in 1977 increased the burden on public spending. The war with Uganda in 1978, the second oil-price shock in 1979 and the general decline in the world prices of agricultural commodities also eroded the value of export earnings. According to Morrissey, in 1977 Tanzania was facing a severe food crisis and about 230 million Tshs of the national budget were being spent on importing maize, rice and wheat.[10]

The fact that the Lower Moshi irrigation project was intended to increase food production was sufficient reason to speed up its implementation, as this would lead to a recovery of grain production, which was a national priority. By revising the schedule, the regional development committee was also facilitating the execution of the third Five-Year National Development Plan (1976-1981), whose main objective was to increase food production. In short, the Japanese experts who presented the plan were given a clear go-ahead, which they rapidly put into effect.

Thus after April 1979, the Integrated Plan acquired the status of a guide for the realization of the Lower Moshi irrigation project. The first step was therefore to carry out a more detailed study of the area in order to confirm its economic feasibility, as well as make detailed designs for the construction works.

In this section, we continue pursuing the planning of the irrigation project. We shall focus on both the feasibility report for the Lower Moshi Irrigation Project.

It was not possible to study the terms of reference for the feasibility study, but by referring to the contents of the report, we may conclude that its main purpose was to 'find out' if the proposed project was economically feasible and for how long irrigation could be carried out in the Lower Moshi area without detriment to the water supply and other inputs. Since the project's implementation schedule was to be speeded up, a private company was commissioned to carry out the studies.

In November 1979 a Japanese private company, Nippon Koei, was invited to undertake the feasibility study for the Lower Moshi irrigation project. A contract was concluded, and surveys commenced a month later. The main activities during the feasibility period included aerial photography to establish the levels for designing the water flow system, detailed soil investigations to establish soil and water suitability, and a detailed socio-economic survey. A draft report was ready in March 1980.

The experts returned to Tokyo, where they finalized the report. By August 1980, this was ready. The experts found out that the Lower Moshi irrigation project would be feasible for fifty years. It was therefore possible to start implementing it. How was the issue of water treated?

It should be remembered that the Integrated Planning team recommended the use of groundwater through bore holes and electric pumps. Findings by the experts on the availability of groundwater came to the same conclusion. The only additional information was that the annual groundwater recharge was about 500 million cubic metres. Given this volume, the experts suggested that there was a development potential of 50 million cubic metres annually. However, they cautioned that the quality of the groundwater was such that there might be problems if crops with a low salt tolerance were cultivated.

At a more detailed level, the experts proposed that instead of the 29 boreholes proposed by the Integrated Planning Team, only twenty should be sunk. No reasons were given.

The experts estimated that 0.93 cubic metres of water would be the yield from the twenty boreholes, which would then irrigate a total of 1020 ha. of mainly upland crops, i.e. maize and beans. The reduction in the number of bore holes to twenty also meant a reduction in the contribution made to the project by groundwater. According to the experts, groundwater sources would contribute thirteen percent of the total project water requirement. The rest would be drawn from surface sources. In the Integrated Plan, the planners cautioned about relying on surface water. The planners analyzed data on discharge from the potential surface sources dating from 1952. They concluded that the Rau and Mue rivers which were the main potential sources "have no drop of water to offer for irrigation" They therefore proposed that surface water should not be relied upon but should only supplement groundwater. The experts on the other hand, believed that groundwater sources should supplement surface water. How did the experts justify their proposal?

First the experts started by rejecting the available data on discharge. They wrote:

> The discharge of the above three major rivers [Rau, Himo and Mue] and springs has been observed since 1952. However, most records are interrupted occasionally and hence available discharge for rivers is estimated by means of reservoir model simulation. Available spring discharge is estimated based on the observation records.[11]

Two different methods were therefore used to establish the discharge volume for the surface sources. The water available from Rau, Himo and Mue was established using assumptions derived from what the experts called a 'reservoir simulation model', while the available data were used for the springs.

The issue of data reliability was discussed during interviews conducted for this research. The water experts I talked with[12] were of the opinion that there might be gaps in the discharge data for most of the water sources in Tanzania at that time, making them difficult to use in extrapolating a reliable trend. The data situation has not improved since. For instance, at national level the hydrological data collection system broke down in 1977, since when no systematic data has been collected. Therefore in terms of quality the experts could be right in suspecting the data. That notwithstanding, relying on simulations to estimate potential capacity is subject to drawbacks for a number of reasons: The reservoir simulation model is supposed to use data generated from computerized rainfall records, which should be available on a continuous basis. But because data of that quality was not available, the experts made assumptions on the basis of which they generated rainfall data, which they then used in the model. The data summarized in Table 1 was produced using this approach.

Table 1: The Average Overall Annual Runoff for Selected Water Sources

Water source	Average annual runoff (million m³)
Njoro Springs	121.3
Rau River	69.8
Miwaleni Springs	50.3
Himo River	15.1
Total	**256.5**

On the basis of the estimated annual runoff, the experts concluded that;

The Project would use the Rau and Himo rivers and Miwaleni and Njoro springs as the water source for irrigation, while the other rivers as well as the Soko and Kileo springs are excluded from the project use because of little development potentiality. [13]

Following that conclusion, the project command area was extended from what the planned and approved area of 3320 ha. of land to 6320 ha., of which 2900 ha. were to be irrigated for paddy and the rest designated for upland crops. The total water requirement also doubled from 118 cusecs or 3.34m3/s to 224 cusecs or 6.68 m3/s. The experts reduced the number of projects from 12 to nine. For Chekereni the total area covered by the project as proposed by the experts amounted to 850; paddy area covers 700 ha and maize and beans 50 ha. The maximum water requirement for Chekereni was 1.11 m3/second.

Phasing for Implementation

The next stage in the planning process was to decide which of the three water-source schemes should be implemented first. Economic calculations, including the 'internal rate of return model', were applied to work out which scheme was most feasible from an economic point of view. The experts made the assumption that the project should run for fifty years starting from 1987, when construction would be completed. Although the fifty-year life span was not proposed in the report, calculations were made on the basis of that assumption. Conceptually, the 'internal rate of return' discounts the future cash flows associated with investment into equality with the initial capital investment. It is therefore expressed as a percentage of capital invested.

According to the feasibility report, the overall Lower Moshi Irrigation project was worth the investment at an 'internal rate of return' of 13.1 percent, while the Rau system in which Chekereni is located, was well above that figure, at 16.1 per cent, although the plan reported that these sources were already over utilized. The ground water schemes on their part were evaluated as having an 'internal rate of return' of 9.6 percent which was the lowest. The Rau system was therefore given priority in construction and justified thus:

> (T)he project is technically feasible and economically sound. Although the project is found feasible as a whole, the four schemes (Upper Mabogini, Mabogini, Rau ya Kati, and Chekereni and Oria villages) in the Rau river system have advantages over other schemes... in respect of construction cost per hectare and operational costs. Therefore it would be recommended to set out the Rau river system as the first stage development.... The direct benefits would come out in 1984 and increase year by year. It would attain its maximum level of 70.2 million Tshs in and after the twelfth year, after commencement of the project implementation. [14]

In brief, the above extract justifies the irrigation project and therefore it was ready to be implemented starting with the Rau system. The Rau system commanded a gross area of 2300 ha, where by 1100 ha was zoned for paddy, 1050 ha for upland crops managed by individual small holders and 150 ha managed partly communally and partly private.

According to the plan, there would be two harvests every calendar year. It was planned that in the rainy season, i.e. from January to June, the whole area would be cultivated. During the dry season, from approximately July to December, it was proposed to irrigate 800 out of 1100 ha. zoned for paddy. No maize cultivation was planned for during the dry season, because water was considered insufficient. In conformity with the plan, a total of 1900 ha. of paddy (1100 in the rainy season and 800 during the dry season) was to be cultivated in each year, with an expected annual harvest of 8550 tons at an assumed yield of 4.5 tons per ha.

One more concern was on the smallholder cultivators' ability to pay. That was also well argued by the experts. According to the feasibility report, farmers whose land would be included in the irrigation project were expected to pay for water charges and also to contribute in recovering the project costs. Payment was to start after a ten-year grace period.

Farmers' capacity to pay was worked out by comparing returns of farmers cultivating oilseeds with those producing paddy. A farmer cultivating paddy under irrigation was assumed to be able to generate a primary income of Tshs. 16,100/=, while one producing oil seeds was expected to generate an annual income of Tshs. 12,190/=. With an average expenditure of Tshs. 7,600/=, the paddy cultivator was obviously found to have a greater ability to pay. However, the experts realized that even if paddy producers had a higher ability, the amount of money to be repaid was just too high to be repaid by the farmers, possibly requiring a number of generations to raise that amount. To get around that problem, the experts proposed a subsidy from the government, on the argument that it would maintain sufficient incentives for paddy cultivators. In other words the experts recommended subsidies for farmers in producing paddy for their own income and food.

All in all, the team of experts completed its assignment. The team confirmed that the Lower Moshi irrigation project was feasible over a fifty-year period and that the project would reach its maximum level in 1999, that is, twelve years after 1987. Since the experts feasibility findings were considered technical in nature and that they were guided by the approved integrated plan, the Regional Development Committee did not consider it important to have the experts reports presented, examined and approved as it was the case with the plan. Among the consequences that assumptions concerning water availability and economic returns could not be re-examined or questioned. There was also no intention or time to involve the smallholders (or their representatives) whose lands were to be included in the project area.

On the basis of the experts' technical findings, the issues that received most attention were soil fertility, water availability, the socio-economic capacity of the farmers and a very limited consideration given to the environmental aspects. At that time it had not yet become a condition in Tanzania to carry out an environmental impact assessment (EIA) for such projects. However, as from the early 1990s in Tanzania, it is common for some public institutions, for instance the Ministry of Lands and the Tanzania Investment Center to demand an EIA report before approving request for land or an investment project. Once the Environmental Management Act 2004,[15] becomes law, large projects like the Lower Moshi one will in have to be approved by the ministry responsible for the Environment. An environmental impact assessment will be a prerequisite.

The Ministry of Agriculture Finances another Plan for Chekereni Village

While the experts and the regional development director's office were implementing the irrigation project in Chekereni, land use planners from the district agricultural office in Moshi, were busy producing a land-use plan for Chekereni village in 1986. The village land use plan could have been an important tool for interpreting the irrigation project and its implications for the overall land use in the village. But that was not the case. After examining the land use plan it is clear that the irrigation project and the land use plan are completely independent interventions. This is interesting especially given the fact that the village land use plan was financed by the Ministry of Agriculture, which was also responsible for coordinating the irrigation project in the Lower Moshi area. We were keen to find out the reason behind such a decision.

Let us start with the views of the district agricultural officer:

We had a land-use planning [i.e. preparation of plans] project for Moshi District, which was financed by the Ministry of Agriculture. Our land-use planners were supposed to show areas in each village plan for residential, grazing, crops production, forests etc. They were also required to provide a guide for the villagers on how they should use their land and solve or avoid conflicts, for instance, between crop farming and grazing. Village leaders are supposed to observe the plan proposals, so consequently, when the land use planners made the plan they involved them.[16]

The response by the district agricultural officer seems to point out that the land user planners were concerned with showing the villagers how to use their land and to assist in avoiding land use conflicts. Apparently the conflict between crops and grazing was already noted by the village leaders during the early days of Ujamaa in Chekereni and tried to address it but failed. Since the district land use planners did not consider the irrigation project in their plan they also did not seem to be aware on the potential conflicts among water users in the village.

However the argumentation by the officer is not sufficient to convince us as to why a plan for the village was being drawn up while another was already being implemented. The officer was again requested to elaborate on the issue, and responded thus:

> In each financial year, we are accustomed to preparing a list of villages, which we shall draw up plans for. That is the basis on which we are allocated funds from the District Council or the Ministry of Agriculture. Even if there were other projects in a listed village, our intention is to deal with one ward systematically, covering each village in that ward. In this case, Mabogini ward, which consists of Chekereni and other three villages, was our priority area. Each village had to be covered with a land-use plan. Before I came to this office, the land-use planning section used to prepare plans for villages located in different wards without a system! Then I directed that, we should avoid that practice and deal with one ward comprehensively. We have prepared land use plans for three villages located within the Lower Moshi Irrigation Project. We have not dealt with the fourth one because it is not only located in another ward but also in another administrative division.[17]

Whether the plans were comprehensive or not, that for Chekereni and the other villages within the irrigation project have remained of no use to the village leaders.

In reality, the Chekereni village leaders who were interviewed did not regard the drawing as a plan. Instead, it was glued to the wall in the village executive officer's office, evidently as a wall decoration. This is contradicted the district agricultural officer who believed that if there was a follow-up, the villagers could be made to observe the plan's proposals. In the following extract the officer describes the process through which the plan was produced and monitored by the office:

> I cannot say that we visit the villages. But our approach was to produce plans to cover all the villages in a ward first, and then during phase two we will start visiting the villages to do a follow-up on the performance of the plans. Unfortunately, funds were stopped before we could cover all the listed villages.

After 1986 we were told that the responsibility of formulating village land-use plans has been shifted from the Ministry of Agriculture to the Ministry of Lands Housing and Urban Development. However, even if the project had still been within the Ministry of Agriculture, it would still have been difficult to enforce the plan. We have no powers. Maybe the Land Use Planning Team established recently [in 1987 under the 1983 National Agricultural Policy.[18]] will have such powers.[19]

All in all, a number of observations can be made here. First, it is clear that there was no coordination, not only between the regional and district authorities in the same region, but also between the officers in the same ministry.

Secondly, the plan was made and public money was used to pay the land use planners, but with neither contributions to village land use planning objectives nor benefits to the land users. A third lesson is that, while village land use plans, as the one made for Chekereni may be valuable, the one originating from the district agricultural office could not be useful, not only because it excluded the villagers, but also because the issues it addressed were not the real practical concerns facing the villagers during that time. In addition to village plans made by the district agricultural officer, the regional land-use planning team, which, using funds from the National Land-Use Planning Commission[20] and the Ministry of Lands, Natural Resources and Tourism, drew up four village land-use plans for four villages within the Kilimanjaro region. This time Chekereni was not included in the list. The four plans were approved in 1993 but like those from the agricultural officer, not implemented.

The regional town-planning officer outlined three reasons for the lack of implementation of the approved village land use plans:

1) The problem is the traditional land tenure *(Land tenure ni kali sana)*. There is no land that is free and unclaimed; every piece of land is occupied already. We cannot acquire such land and make or implement the plan. And it is very difficult to acquire the land beforehand.

2) There are no funds to implement the plans. We cannot even demarcate the different land-use zones identified in them *(tunazungumza kinadharia tu);* we speak in theory only. The big problem is funds from the central government. We cannot rely on funds from private investors; we are not certain about such funds..

3) The Director for Urban Development directed that we should tell the District Executive Directors to set aside funds to implement village land-use plans. But we cannot do so for a number of reasons. First of all, the director will not understand us. The district has no money and is faced with more tangible commitments: schools, dispensaries etc. And even if we had funds for

demarcating different land uses, we would be creating conflicts over land rights.[21]

Judging from these remarks, the regional town-planning officer, like the district agricultural officer, is hinting that village land-use plans are prepared for their own sake, only in theory. He seemed convinced that it is difficult to have the plans implemented. He was however of the opinion that, if the plans were submitted to the district and to the villages, maybe it would help. The plans may influence some investment decisions in the district and the village.

Experience from elsewhere in Tanzania indicates that not much can be expected. Johannson[22] examines in considerable detail the process and methods with which a land-use plan for Dirma village in the Arusha region was produced and made the following conclusions:

1) Procedures for plan preparation as outlined in the Town and Country Planning Ordinance, 1956, were not closely observed. The plan thus produced is administratively not legal.

2) Villagers' problems are not considered. For example, the water issue, which is so pressing, was not adequately addressed.

3) Implementing the plan is not feasible. Without the use of force, some of the proposals, for instance, extinguishing customary land rights to warrant taking away village land for a proposed large-scale farm, will not be easily accepted by landowners in the village.

Apparently, the scenario observed from the village land use planning attempts in Kilimanjaro and Arusha is a typical one in Tanzania, which if not changed, the scarce public resources will continue being used but without making any significant contribution to addressing pertinent problems in land use and natural resources management. As a poor country we cannot afford such spending of public money.

In summary, neither the district agricultural officer's plan nor the regional town planning officer's plan made any impact on land use intensification practices in Chekereni. The irrigation project did. Because of that, we are thus interested in following up the irrigation project so as to show its role as a land-use intervention in the land-use intensification process in Chekereni village. The implementation of the project from the land and water use management perspective is therefore the focus of the following chapter.

Chapter Eight

How Farmers and Village Leaders Pursued their Interests at the Start of the Project

Compensation is a Bad Precedent

In order to facilitate smooth management of the project implementation the project staff needed to locate offices, staff housing, seed experimentation sites, trail farming areas and a demonstration farm in which the farmers could be trained in the project area. For the Rau system, Chekereni village was earmarked for the location of the facilities. In total, Chekereni village had to set aside about 81ha of land. The central attraction in Chekereni was the already established village communal farm, which could be developed into a pilot farm without getting involved in land ownership problems because the farm was under the control of the village council. The fact that the village communal farm was also strategically located in terms of ease of irrigation made it still more appropriate. The location of the pilot farm therefore attracted other project facilities for reasons of nearness. Ten hectares of private land close to the village centre were zoned for the project office, staff housing, tractor workshop and a large part as a trial farm. As we shall see later, although the Ujamaa village council was not involved in the decision to locate the facilities in their village, they were instrumental in implementing that decision, especially in facilitating the project in acquiring private lands.

Chekereni village leaders, especially the former village chairman, who was behind the decision, justified their decision to allocate land to the project by arguing that, the allocation was part of their strategy to take advantage of the potential benefits that were likely to accrue to the village from the project's activities if they were located in Chekereni. The village chairman, who was in power when the project started in Chekereni, defended the allocation of the ten hectares as follows:

> The land earmarked for the trial farm was a seasonal swamp. When it rained it used to act like a channel collecting and directing floodwaters to our houses in village residential area where I live. Since the project was concerned with water and since the Japanese are experts in controlling water, it was an opportunity to contain the floods in the area.[1]

Records suggest that the allocation of the private land was done in a village meeting. When the villagers were asked whether or not they could question the allocation decision, they formed the opinion that the intention of the meeting was to inform them about a government decision rather than to discuss the allocation. They added that since the plan had come from higher authorities, it was difficult for the village leaders and the villagers to stop it. One village councilor remarked:

> We were already used to receiving and accepting orders from above. Who will question orders from above? To us, the Region is like our father: we have to say 'Amen'. If the Chairman and Secretary agree, then it has to be accepted; *'Mwenyekiti na Katibu wakikubali basi lazima ipite'.* [2]

The villagers continued and said that when they agreed to have paddy plots established on the communal farm, thinking that the project would be confined only to that area and not to their private farms. But that was not the case. For, whatever the reasons given by the former village chairman, the important factor in the allocation was the structural relationship created through Ujamaa, in which decisions from above were easily honoured and put into effect by the lower levels. While the village council did not question decisions from the Ward or district, the villagers on their part had to accept decisions sanctioned by the village leaders. This helped greatly in facilitating the process of land acquisition in Chekereni.

However, the individual villagers who were to lose their lands reacted differently. As the land allocation decision took place in village council meetings, and since no efforts were made to inform landowners of the decision, the owners only became aware of the new status of their land, when construction started. First the five landowners, who claimed ownership of the ten hectares, approached the village chairman and requested him to stop the construction. Their request was turned down. As usual, the landowners reported their case to the District Commissioner, who wrote a letter directing the village chairman to find alternative land for the five farmers as compensation. From 1982, when the conflict was first reported to the Commissioner, to 1984 at least four letters were written and several visits made to the offices of the District Commissioner and the ward executive secretary by the farmers. But no land was allocated to them. The letter, which made the case a silent one, at least in the village files, was that from the village chairman to the ward executive secretary, which read:

> [The Lower Moshi Irrigation Project] has been brought from higher authorities

at national level *(ngazi za juu kitaifa)* and is of national significance.... If the government wishes to help the farmers, then let the District Commissioner's office declare it openly and show us the alternative land they are referring to. The office should also say how much land they should receive. If the District Commissioner has land, he should go ahead and allocate it to Kiriki and his friends.[3]

From the letter, at least two issues can be raised. First, there is a clear lack of respect for the Ward Officer and also for the District Commissioner's Office. We noticed this same type of relationship between officials when we were following Mzee Wetundwa's land case narrated in chapter six. Secondly, the way the decision was justified leaves a lot to be desired. To the village chairman, a project from above can override individual rights, and that should not be questioned. The agricultural extension officer in the meeting gave a similar type of justification where Mzee Mbindyo's case was discussed, back in the 1960s. This seems to be the easiest way for decision makers in Tanzania to justify their decisions, even if the reason is not accepted. The five farmers were not able to stop the project being implemented. To my knowledge, the land conflict has not been resolved. However, the clearing of the village communal farm was also not without resistance. One farmer refused to leave his farm, and instead of using the usual administrative system to pursue his claims, he decided to resort to force and scared the village leaders.

Mzee Elisadi was one of the villagers who had farms close to the pilot farm and had improved his farm quite well through irrigation from the village canal. Like other farmers in that location, he was required to give way to leveling works in establishing the pilot farm. But he refused. The episode started after Mzee Elisadi refused to let his farm be cleared and was ready to fight. At first, the project staff wanted to contribute money to compensate Elisadi for his well maintained farm alongside the village canal. The farm was planted with sugar cane, cassava, bananas, vegetables, trees, etc. Mzee Joseph Makoko remembers very well how difficult it was for the village council to convince Mzee Elisadi to allow his farm to be cleared. Eventually they had to use the police to force him off his land. The following story told by Mzee Makoko[4] illustrates the case:

When the village council ordered Mzee Elisadi to clear his farm so that the tractor may start the leveling, he completely refused. He was warned that the village council might have to sue him. He was not moved. The Japanese came and saw that all the land except that belonging to Mzee Elisadi had been cleared. They asked the village secretary for advice on what to do with the farm. The experts were told to proceed with the clearing and that Mzee Elisadi would be considered later for another farm in the village. The experts did not clear the farm as they were told. Instead, they tried to convince Mzee Elisadi to rescue some of his crops, after which they would clear the farm. They told him when he was allocated another farm by the village council, they would assist in clearing it for him (as a form of compensation). Mzee Elisadi accepted the offer on condition that he got the alternative land first so that he could directly transfer some of the plants to the new farm. [5]

According to Mzee Makoko, although the village secretary was not keen to have a dialogue, the experts were, and it produced a positive response acceptable both to them and to Elisadi:

The project experts then contacted the village secretary for the promised alternative land so that they could clear it for Mzee Elisadi to enable him to start harvesting and also to transplant his crops.

I do not know if the village secretary was jealous or not, but he did not show them any land. The experts insisted, but the village secretary argued that if the village council were to allocate land to Mzee Elisadi it would form a bad precedent, and if other farmers come forward and makes similar claims it will not be possible to honour them.[6]

Obviously, if compensation took the form of alternative land, there was not sufficient land to cater to all possible claims, which was probably the reason why the village secretary was not keen to entertain claims for compensation in terms of land. But in any case Mzee Elisadi and the five landowners had a right to be compensated. However, the Japanese experts were not happy with the village secretary's arguments. They reported the case to the regional development director, who supported the village secretary's position. Since the negotiations between Elisadi, the project and the village secretary were delaying the clearing and leveling of the pilot farm, the village secretary called in the police, who arrested Mzee Elisadi for two days while his farm was cleared.

Mzee Makoko's story was discussed during one of the feedback sessions. The feedback team agreed with the story but said it was a bit exaggerated. Some members agreed with the argument that if Mzee Elisadi had been compensated it would have formed a bad precedent others did not.

In the cases of the five farmers and of Mzee Elisadi, the central point of conflict was compensation. The village council was aware of the potential problems if a policy of compensation was adopted.

Certainly this would have complicated project implementation, as neither the regional authorities nor project management were prepared for it. On the other hand the law, by then the Land Ordinance (cap 113 of Tanzania Laws) enacted by the British Colonial Government in 1923, and as revised in 1961, provides for compensation, but only of the unexhausted improvements on the land. In that case it would have been the crops on the land in question. But typical of the system of decision making in Tanzania especially during the early 1980s, that law was ignored by the government authorities.

Land Reform to Modernize Traditional Farms

Unlike the traditional irrigation practice, modern paddy cultivation requires that farms be standardized, leveled and roads and canals constructed according to international standards. Land reform was therefore a prerequisite. Before the farms were leveled and the plots standardized, farmers were required to clear their farms and rescue some of their crops. Farmers were informed about that requirement in a public meeting, which was called in December, 1984. The first announcement was that the paddy cultivation that had already been established on the village farm would now be introduced on the villagers' farms. And because the project only covered part of the village farms, the project experts described the area to be covered by the irrigation project. Thus farmers with land in that area were required to clear their farms so that tractors could start the leveling. The meeting thus basically concerned those farmers who became part of the project.

Mama Kahumba is one of the farmers who attended the meeting. She told me the following story in an interview:

> We were told to harvest as much as possible from our farms because Japanese experts wanted to level them, *Mjapani anataka alime*. We were expected to rescue as much as we could. I could not harvest all my crops, especially the bananas, mainly because of storage problems. I asked for assistance from my neighbours. We harvested for two days. On the third day the tractor arrived into my farm and cleared everything. [7]

Most of the people interviewed report that they were given time to remove their crops from their farms. Some say it was a few days, others several months. But whatever the period, the important thing is that consideration was given to the existing crops on the farms. Mama Kahumba was mainly concerned about her limited ability to harvest and rescue her crops.

Other farmers had more serious worries. They feared that clearing the land could prove to be another government strategy to acquire their lands. Their experience with the implementation of Ujamaa shows that their fears were justified.

Mzee Kirumbuyo is one of those farmers who had established a well-maintained farm in Chekereni. It was to be leveled. He was among those who were worried that once the farm was cleared and standardized, it would become government property. During the public meeting, he raised a question about compensation. Here is a part of the response according to an interview with Mzee Kirumbuyo:

> The government officials who introduced the project admitted that [our private] farms were really well kept and valuable, but they advised us that we should benefit a lot from the paddy project and would also be able to have *two harvesting seasons a year*. And because of that we should allow tractors to level the land and create paddy plots. You should not ask for compensation for the area to be cleared, since the land is still yours. It is not possible for the government to pay you compensation and at the same time clear your land, make paddy plots for you and re-allocate the land to you. The official asked. 'Do you all agree?', and we all said, 'Yeees'! [8] (Author's emphasis)

It is important to note that, the public meeting in which the project was introduced became an interesting forum for dialogue, though rather short. It was an opportunity for farmers to raise their concerns, but to the project staff it was not a forum for decision-making. The farmers who agreed with the decision followed it. The others had to find other opportunities to pursue their interests. As shown below some farmers were able to realize their interests outside the short village meeting.

Although most farmers at the meeting agreed to clear their farms by saying 'Yes', some were not ready to accept the change in land use. Nothing said at the meeting could remove their fears. They tried to influence the scale of the project to keep it off their farms. Mzee Athman Bahari, one of the pre-Ujamaa migrants and a paddy cultivator in Chekereni, claimed that the village leaders were able to persuade the project staff to revise the size of the paddy farms in Chekereni with a view to maintaining their permanent mixed farms under irrigation and obtaining paddy fields elsewhere in the village:

> The village leaders were very clever. They did not want to have all their private farms converted into paddy plots. They were already able to irrigate them through the village canal, and they thought that under the project they would still be able to get water and irrigate their bananas, pawpaws, cassava, maize, vegetables and trees. They therefore decided to find reasons to keep the project away from their farms. They argued as follows: 'Since Chekereni is a famous Ujamaa village, it is important to maintain a particular area of block farms, so that future generations will be able to see the way private farms under Ujamaa were organized.' The village chairman together with other village leaders identified the area very close to the pilot farm as the most suitable area to be

conserved. That is the area where the village leaders have their private farms. The Japanese experts were persuaded and agreed not to clear that area. That decision meant that, the block of paddy farm proposed in that location was reduced to almost half its intended size. [9]

The minutes of the meeting at which the village council deliberated on this issue could not be found. It is also questionable if that was a sufficient justification for the project experts to review the plans. In one of the feedback sessions, members of the feedback team who had also become village leaders by then agreed with the story. One member reported that several meetings were held informally at which the idea was discussed and a strategy developed and agreed upon. They therefore requested the former chairman, who then approached the project experts. Most of the village councilors were involved in the meetings, but they could not all benefit from the decision because the area agreed upon was too small to include as many farms as the councilors would have wished.

This is a brief story, but it shows that as farmers, the village leaders were not ready to change over completely from the traditional mixed farming system to the modern irrigated paddy farming system: they wanted a bit of both. But it was the same village leaders who had publicly and openly supported the project as of national importance. However, as we shall see later, they could not continue with irrigated traditional mixed farming in that area because, contrary to their expectations, all the water was directed to the project area.

Mzee Bahari's story is not unique to Chekereni village but was a common phenomenon in the other three villages in the project. Farmers wanted to continue with mixed farming or if possible carry out paddy cultivation on one plot and mixed farming on the other. There are also stories that some farmers were so scared that they sold their farms in the initial stages of the project. In the neighbouring village of Rau ya Kati, some villagers were also able to stop tractors clearing their farms. Several old men are said to have 'bribed' the surveyors to avoid their farms when mapping the area for the project *(tusaide ramani ipite pembeni)*. They were successful and have retained their traditional mixed irrigation farms.

The action of village leaders and a few rich farmers in Chekereni and in the other villagers within the project, corresponds to actions by farmers in the well-documented case of the Ilocos Norte Irrigation Project in the Philippines, where it was reported that in 1981, three upstream Zanjeras [or communities] resisted an irrigation project [which was also being planned and carried out in a similar manner to that of Lower Moshi], to the extent that the original designs were changed. [10]

As it will be shown later, farmers who managed to use either political or economic powers, outside the formal decision making arena, to keep the project away from their land and continue with mixed farming, were able to use their land on a continuous basis. Those within the project were not.

While the pre-leveling harvesting was taking place on the farms whose owners were not able to keep the tractors away, the village land allocation committee was busy compiling a register of villagers with land in the area, which had been earmarked for paddy cultivation. The register would be important for the land re-allocation exercise once the leveling had been completed. Unlike in the three nearby villages within the project, where villagers acquired plots of land in different ways and thus of different size, the land that was zoned for paddy cultivation in Chekereni was acquired mainly through the village land allocation committee. Individual farms were thus assumed to be of more or less equal size, either an acre and a half or an acre and a quarter. It was therefore believed to be 'uncomplicated' for Mzee Martini Sabiniani and Mama Atanasia Juma, who were active members of the village land allocation committee, to prepare the land register without involving the actual owners.

As the committee members were also involved in land allocation during Ujamaa, they were expected to be conversant with existing land rights in the cleared area, to know who owned what land and of what size. Under that assumption, no other villager or project staff except the village agricultural extension officer was involved in preparing the register. It was completed smoothly, and no conflicts were reported before the re-allocation started. Pre-allocation conflicts were probably minimized because the list was neither displayed nor presented to the scrutiny of the landowners. It was only when it was used to determine the size of farm plots that each owner was to receive during the re-allocation that it became an important reference for decisions and thus a source of conflict.

The source of conflict was not only the size, but because of the prospects for modern irrigation, the land which had become part of the project increased in value and became more likely to be attractive to leaders and farmers as well.

Our present interest in land reform is not only due to its importance in the land-use intensification process in the Chekereni story. This process is also likely to become a common land-use planning strategy in rural Tanzania in reorganizing rural settlements for better efficiency in production. We may therefore learn from the land reform process in Chekereni as well. We therefore focus on more details of land reform in the next chapter.

Chapter Nine
Managing Land Reform

Introduction: Village Committee and Project Staff Collaborate

Once farmers had rescued some of their crops and the land had been leveled and converted into paddy plots (locally known as *maboda*) each measuring 100 by 35 meters, it was time for land re-allocation.

The re-allocation process was initiated in a letter dated 2nd December 1986 from the project land surveyor. He informed the village chairman that paddy plots in all ten blocks in Chekereni were ready for re-allocation. The letter included a re-allocation schedule indicating the amount of land to be allocated to each landowner and a brief description of the way the re-allocation schedule was reached. Since the amount of land allocated to each farmer was an issue, let us examine the surveyors' calculations.

First of all, the letter draws the village chairman's attention to the fact that according to the village register prepared by the two members of the village lands allocation committee, the gross area of cleared land amounted to 263.48 ha. However, the project survey team, which presumably took more accurate measurements of the farms, came up with a gross area of 294.0 ha. The difference is significant. Since the survey team used more advanced equipment, their figure is expected to be more reliable compared to that of the villagers. If that assumption holds, there were about 30.52 ha of land more. The experts did not correct the village committee's figures. Instead they ignored their own calculations and applied those produced by the two villagers in working out the re-allocation schedule. In arriving at a re-allocation factor, the 'net designed area' from the survey team's measurements is expressed as a percentage of the villagers' estimate.

Mathematically, the net area after subtracting land occupied by roads and canals is 91.72 per cent of the total area. This means that the land reform exercise took up only 8.28 per cent instead of the 25 per cent, which had been projected as the maximum land loss[1] expected from the infrastructure works. Taking into account possible discrepancies from errors or from landowners' names not being on the register, the surveyor reduced the net area to be allocated to 91 per cent.

The reduction increased the amount of land loss to 9 per cent, the ratio used to work out the schedule, which was submitted to the village chairman.

About seven weeks later, on 20th January 1987, the surveyor wrote another letter to the village chairman and told him that the earlier schedule should not be used, since it had typing errors, which had to be corrected.

The new schedule did not contain any new calculations but was scattered with corrections here and there in the respective entries. On the last pages of both the first and the revised schedules, the re-allocation does not appear as systematic as one would have expected. Substantial changes were, however, made on pages 11 to 14, specifically to the re-allocation schedule for one of the blocks (RS 4-1) which had became a point of contention in the land conflicts resulting from the land reform in Chekereni.

The village council accepted the second re-allocation schedule and organized a public meeting to announce the re-allocation procedures.

The late Mzee Musa Chami was one of the farmers whose land was converted into paddy plots and was therefore an interested party in the land re-allocation process. He recalled the procedure he followed during re-allocation:

> A meeting was held at the village office compound. We were told that we should all be present in the farms to receive our new plots. We were required to pay fifty shillings for each paddy plot re-allocated, because the team, which was assisting in the re-allocation, had worked extra hours and had to be paid some money for lunch. They worked from morning until 6.00 in the evening. The re-allocation was easy for the team, since the plots were already numbered and were guided by the schedule. Like every farmer, I paid Tshs 50/=, got a receipt, and went to receive my farm. You were shown your new plot and you were told that your plot number is so and so. It was a strange thing [to the farmers]. You could easily forget and get lost because all the farms looked alike. I was shown plot number 613 full, i.e. 100m by 35m, and part of (80m by 35m) plot number 614, all in block RS 4-4. My former *shamba* measured about an acre and a half and I received what I was entitled to. Although the location was not exactly where I used to farm before, that did not bother me.[2]

This account makes the re-allocation procedures appear very clear and without problems. However, it is important to emphasize a number of points. First of all, farmers were willing to pay, and they paid to facilitate a smooth and quick re-allocation. Thanks to the payment, the re-allocation team was motivated and worked harder, including after office hours. That was necessary for the farmers to know their plots and have time to prepare them for the new season. Like Mzee Chami, most villagers were aware of the calculations and the amount of land they should expect with respect to the surveyor's schedule. They could ask if they felt that they had not been treated well.

Nevertheless, stories from other villagers do not portray a process as smooth as the one described above. Out of the 213 households interviewed, 80 had their farms incorporated into the paddy area, 19 of the latter expressing dissatisfaction with the land reform, especially the re-allocation process, for various reasons. Some were simply not listed in the village register and thus did not appear on the re-allocation list. Others were not satisfied with the amount of land they had received. In most cases, they felt that the land allocated to them was too small in comparison with their original plots and the size they had expected from the re-allocation schedule.

Others complained that land was allocated to officials who had had no land in Chekereni village before the land reform. They pointed to the village agricultural extension officer as an example of officials who had acquired land in that way. One villager remarked in a group interview, 'There are a lot of dissatisfied farmers; they report to the village council, but receive no attention' There were also complaints from farmers who had received land in locations different from where they used to cultivate before and in two or more different places.

A point to note here is that conflicts are inevitable in any land reform exercise such as that carried out in Chekereni. The issue which is of our current interest is how prepared were irrigation project officials and the village council to deal with these conflicts and how did they actually manage them? To illustrate this point, we shall follow up two conflicts. One concerns farmers who had land before the project but whose names did not appear on the village register and therefore not on the re-allocation list either. The other involves farmers who were not satisfied with the amount of land they received after the re-allocation. The two conflicts were pursued in different ways, and success also varied. We start with the first type of conflict.

Landowners Join Forces

The area covered by the irrigation project in Chekereni included both lands held under customary rights and lands held after allocation by the Ujamaa village council. Among the farms leveled by the project some belonged to absentee landowners residing in Uru settlement north of Moshi town. Probably because they were not registered in the village, the village council had not allocated them land, they were therefore not known by the members of the village land allocation committee who prepared the village land register. Thus their lands were leveled and allocated to other farmers while the 17 landowners organized themselves in trying to reclaim them.

On 18th December 1986, the Chekereni village executive secretary received a letter signed by seventeen people from Uru village in the highlands. The letter accused the village council of illegally allocating their 32 acres of land to village and district officials and demanded that they get their land back.

The village executive secretary did not respond to the letter. A month later, i.e. on 20th January 1987, the landowners wrote another letter, this time addressed to the District Commissioner. Like the first , copies were sent to the Regional Commissioner, the ward executive officer, and the Chekereni village chairman. The letter claimed that their land had been illegally allocated to village officials (without names) including members, relatives and children of the Village Lands Allocation Committee, some of the irrigation project staff and some district council officials. As usual, there was no response. The ward executive officer, however, managed to call a meeting between the group of farmers and the village council. During the meeting, which took place on 24th March 1987, it was suggested that the farmers should be allocated paddy plots in the pilot farm that is from the former village communal land, on a temporary basis until their case was resolved. The group refused and insisted on a permanent allocation. Because of this disagreement, the meeting was not properly concluded.

After the meeting, the group wrote a stronger letter to the Regional Commissioner. Attached to it were the names of the officials who had been allocated land in that area. The letter was copied and taken by hand to various important offices in Dar es Salaam, including the President's Office. A copy of the letter was obtained from one of the group members. A close examination of the 56 names listed shows that most the beneficiaries were the children of members of the village council and the village lands allocation committee. It appears that the land reform was really an opportunity for the leaders to achieve their goal of acquiring land in Chekereni for them, their relatives and children.

The letter became an issue in the district and regional offices, mainly because of the names that were attached. Several strong letters were exchanged between the District Commissioner and the ward executive officer. While that was going on, the group of farmers decided to file a case in the district magistrate's court against those listed in their letter. Publicizing the names increased fear and pressure on the village council, for each person listed would be required to defend his tenure of the land in Chekereni. That would have been difficult in an open public court. Before the case came up, the village council decided to try and pacify the group of farmers by allocating them land in the pilot farm. On 6th December 1990, the village council allocated seven paddy plots amounting to 2.1 ha. from the pilot farm to eight people from the group. According to the allocation letter the eight farmers were given permanent rights over the paddy plots in the former village communal farm. We have not been able to find out what happened to the other nine landowners.

However by privatizing part of the pilot farm, it became possible to pacify the group of farmers and thus maintain the 'illegal' allocations. Some villagers described that as a clever exchange as it would have been too open for the village leaders and their relatives to have allocated themselves land from the village communal farm. It is also interesting to note that it was the same land on the pilot farm that was the subject of the long case being pursued earlier as already shown in Chapter Six.

Most villagers interviewed did not know that part of the village communal land had been privatized. Those who were aware considered the allocation temporary. They did not accept it as a permanent allocation because they believed that the land in the communal farm belong to the whole village; if it were privatized, therefore, it should be with the villagers' approval. The village leaders, for their part, claimed that the decision was based on an order from the District Commissioner.

The villagers were also not happy with a similar decision, when part of the Chekereni village primary school plot was privatized. The reason given for this was that families with homestead plots in the paddy fields were subject to frequent attacks of malaria and other water-borne diseases. Those families were therefore allocated plots within the 25-acre school plot, so that they could move from the paddy fields. The village leaders also justified this as 'an order from above'.

Privatization of public lands by village councils is a concern of some officers in Moshi District Council. For instance, in 1994, the district education officer, being concerned with encroachment on to primary school plots in villages in the district, wrote to all village councils saying that they should demarcate the school plots in their respective areas and have the land officially surveyed and beacons erected. But that has been difficult to implement. The district lands development officer is aware of the importance of that request but he does not know how to finance the survey.

Public Meeting Becomes a Decision-making Forum

Mama Tabu Ramadhani migrated to Chekereni in 1964 from Arusha town following the death of her husband. She came to the village with her ten children. In Chekereni she was remarried to Mzee Ramadhani Hassani. Together with her new husband she approached the local traditional leader for land. They were allocated twelve acres of land in the present paddy area. A few years later, they separated. Mzee Ramadhani allowed Mama Tabu to keep only four of the twelve acres as her property and kept the rest for himself.

She continued to cultivate maize and cassava on the four acres until 1984, when the land was cleared for paddy cultivation. During the re-allocation, in January 1987, she was surprised to realize that her land had been allocated to other people, including the project staff and village lands allocation committee members and their relatives. She narrates:

> When the time for re-allocation came, we were told to go to the village office and pay fifty shillings for each paddy plot. As I had a big farm (four acres), I thought I should pay at least Tshs 100/=. When I went to the village office to pay I produced Tshs. 100/=, but the village accountant refused to receive my money. I complained to one of the village lands allocation committee members, but she insisted I should pay fifty shillings only. Okay, I paid. Then we went into the paddy fields, to the area where I used to farm before. They started to take measurements with the chain, and when they were right on my plot I said, 'That's right, this is the right place for my farm'. Surprisingly they did not listen to me; instead they dropped the measuring chain and left. They did not show me any plot. I followed them and begged them very hard to go back to the fields, but they refused.

> I continued begging for several days but was not successful. When I realized that the re-allocation team had totally refused, I decided to report to the village chairman. I made several visits to the village office until I became tired. I then thought I should try with higher authorities. I started at the District Commissioner's office. By that time, Mr. Ruben Matango[3] was the Commissioner for Moshi district. On 7th April 1987, a few days after my visit to the District Commissioner's office, Mr Matango made a visit to Chekereni village and inspected the disputed land. We were called into a meeting, as

there were a lot of us. We were asked a few questions by the village leaders in front of the District Commissioner. After a long discussion and exchange of words between the Commissioner and the village chairman, the Commissioner directed the village council to allow me to cultivate in one of the paddy plots in the village communal farm.[4] He added that, once those who were cultivating on my farm had harvested their crops, I should be allocated my land back. The District Commissioner left. I was not allocated a plot on the pilot farm nor in any other area in the village.

Several months later, the District Commissioner was replaced. I went to see the new one concerning my land dispute. He also visited the village and directed the leaders to see to it that I was allocated my land. But nothing happened. There were several transfers in Moshi; I do not know why. It was as if whenever a District Commissioner began to be acquainted with my case, he or she was transferred. I went through the same procedure, but nothing happened. We decided to form a group, thinking that we should be able to help each other and perhaps be more effective. In all we were fifteen villagers dissatisfied with the re-allocation schedule in that particular area.[5]

In addition to the interview Mama Tabu was kind enough to allow me to read and make copies of letters she had written or received on the matter. Let us examine the documents briefly.

The first thing Mama Tabu's group did was to write a letter to the District Commissioner, in which they officially reported their land dispute. The letter from the group was also copied to the Water Users' Committee and to the district party secretary. A few days later, on 10th May 1988, the district administrative officer wrote to the Central Water-Users' Assembly Sub-Committee in Chekereni and the project officials.

The letter, written in Swahili, reads (author's translation):

We have received complaints from fifteen farmers in relation to land re-allocation within the irrigation project in Chekereni. They claim that they are not satisfied with the amount of land they received after their farms were converted into paddy plots. We are directing you to thoroughly investigate these complaints and submit a report to the District Commissioner well in time before 21st May 1988.[6]

Nothing happened after the letter was sent to the respective authorities. Mama Tabu's group did not despair. Eight months later, on 4th January 1989, three farmers representing the group reported their case to the regional party office. They made a number of visits and exchanged several letters, but their case was not resolved. They lost hope of any assistance from the political party leaders in the regional office.

Their hope was invigorated on 21st February 1991, two years later, when some of the group's members were called to a meeting with the District Commissioner in his office in Moshi Town. The letter inviting the farmers was written on 20th February 1991 and required them to be in the District Commissioner's office on 21st February, at 10.00 am. However, the letter did not reach them in Chekereni until the afternoon of the 21st. For example, Athumani Bahari, one the active members of the group, claimed to have received his letter at 1.41 pm. on the afternoon of 21st February 1991, too late for the appointment. So none of the farmers attended the meeting. Most of them considered the delayed invitation a trick to avoid them. They then decided to try with the higher authorities, beyond the regional level. On 4th June 1991, they wrote to the Minister for Home Affairs, who was also the Member of Parliament for Moshi rural district. They told him that their case dated back to 21st June 1986 and to date it had not been addressed. They added that, they had been to all the relevant officers at both district and regional levels and were asking for his assistance.

They listed their names in the letter, and copies were sent to the Prime Minister's office in Dar es Salaam and the Regional and District Commissioners in Moshi. Again there was no response, not even from their Member of Parliament. On 11th July 1991, they wrote another letter to the Minister, including their names and signatures to give further weight to it, but still they received no response.

For almost a year and half the group's representatives kept visiting the district offices without much success. On 13th May 1993, they decided to try the village council once again. They wrote to the village chairman to ask for his assistance, but received no reply. The villagers despaired as a group. Each started to pursue the case individually, and the group disintegrated.

On 5th June 1993, a public meeting was held in Chekereni. The guest of honour was the MP, who was also there in his capacity as the Minister for Home Affairs. Mama Tabu Ramadhani attended the meeting and had an opportunity of presenting her case to the Minister. She showed him copies of the letters relating to the case that had been exchanged since it started six years ago, a large bundle of which had accumulated. Mama Tabu narrates on what happened during the meeting:

> The Minister was very sympathetic. He directed the ward executive officer to make sure that I was allocated one paddy plot and that I would be able to participate in the next cultivating season. The ward executive officer was also

directed to ensure that I should eventually be allocated the rest of my land. The Minister insisted that I should receive the paddy plot immediately and that the officer should inform the Minister about the result of his directive within seven days. Otherwise, the ward executive officer would be fired.[7]

On 7th June, the ward executive officer wrote to the Chekereni village chairman to call a village council meeting to witness the re-allocation of land to Mama Tabu. The re-allocation took place on 10th June 1993. It is worth emphasizing here that unlike the many directives issued by the Party and the Regional Commissioners, the Minister's order had a penalty for non-compliance, which is probably what made the difference. Action followed the order of the Minister. However the land re-allocated to Mama Tabu was already re-allocated and used by two village land allocation members. Certainly they would not sit back and watch, they would try to re-possess their land.

The two-committee members[8] who had been cultivating on the re-allocated land were not satisfied with the decision and tried to stop Mama Tabu from cultivating the land. Since at the beginning of each season irrigators had to pay service charges to the project, the committee members thought that if they could stop Mama Tabu from paying, she would not be able to cultivate her plot and would eventually have to surrender it to the original users.

The committee members conspired with the village leaders and the clerk to the water-users' assembly in the Chekereni village office.

On 14th July 1993, when Mama Tabu went to pay, the clerk refused to accept her money. She reported to the ward executive officer that the village chairman had said she could not pay because the farmers who used to cultivate the farms were not satisfied with the re-allocation and she was informed that they had appealed. On the same day, the ward executive officer wrote to the village executive officer and the village chairman, informing them that:

> Mama Tabu is the rightful owner and user of the plot. If there is any appeal, it should be processed and approved by the District Commissioner after which a copy shall be sent to the ward office. The ward executive officer will in turn inform the village chairman officially when it can be implemented. Since there was no known appeal, Mama Tabu should be allowed to pay and participate in the season.[9]

After that directive from the ward level, the water users' assembly clerk[10] accepted payment from Mama Tabu. Thus, it took five years for Mama Tabu to have her land back. In other words she lost at least ten harvests amounting to several bags of paddy, from her land.

However, the village council was not happy with the Minister's order. They decided to challenge it. The leaders resolved to create an argument based on their interpretation of the tenure status of the land in question.

On August 26th 1993, the village executive officer, representing the views of the village council, wrote a letter to the District Commissioner, claiming that, the land under dispute belonged to the village government, as it was within the village boundaries. Since the letter raised issues of importance in understanding the land tenure complexities in rural Tanzania, let us examine it in more details. The logic of the argument in the letter is simple: The basic argument by the village executive officer is that, all land within Chekereni village was acquired by the village council under the villagization programme of 1975 and was re-allocated afresh. The assumption here is that once a village is registered under the Villages and the Ujamaa Villages Designation, Registration and Administration Act, 1975, then individual customary land rights cease to operate and that the village council assumes powers over land allocation within the jurisdictional area of the village. So, since Mama Tabu and the other farmer's claims were based on allocation by the traditional chief, the village council was not ready to entertain them. It was then the responsibility of the village council to re-allocate the land, which they did. It was also pointed out by the village executive officer that:

> During villagization, Mama Tabu like other villagers was allocated village land. She was allocated a homestead plot, a maize farm measuring one and half acres, and another farm, which has been included in the project. Also, her four children were all allocated land: a homestead plot and a farm. One of the children, Husein, was only allocated a homestead plot. All that land was not their traditional land (*maeneo hayo hayakuwa yao ya asili*) but was owned by other people who surrendered the land to the village council.[11]

With this clarification of the village council's position, the village executive officer requested the District Commissioner to reverse the Minister's order so that the allocation carried out by the village council still held. But the Commissioner did not respond. Mama Tabu, the rest of the group and the village council are still struggling with the land dispute in that area.

The position held by the village council may be interpreted as an example of what Fortmann found in his study of a struggle over property rights in rural Zimbabwe.[12] He argues that in defending property claims, different versions of the same event are told by different claimants. It is not only the poor and the dispossessed that tell stories to claim rights, but also the powerful, in order to preempt the discourse of the powerless.

The situation of unclear land rights is partly contributed to by the lack of clear governmental position on rural land rights. For instance, the ministerial order may also be an illustration of the confusion of politics and the law, because procedures require that such cases are determined through the Customary Lands Tribunal. On the other hand we also learn that Mama Tabu was successful partly because she knew how to exploit the opportunity provided by a public meeting, where her case was decided

In fact the Chekereni village council spent a significant amount of time and funds to pursue a process in which they acquired a certificate of title to the village land in October 1992. The powers of the village council over this land may also have increased after the village received its land title in October 1992.[13] However, the village shall have to surrender that title and apply for "certificate of village land" in accordance to Village Land Act, No. 5 of 1999. With the village title, the assumption among members of the village council was that, all customary claims over the village lands were by implication extinguished. The reasoning applied in the village executive officer's letter dated 26th August 1993 is therefore justified by the village title. The village executive officer tried to use equity, in the sense that Mama Tabu had been allocated land elsewhere in the village and therefore ought to surrender her rights to the disputed land, equity here being used to formalize and justify re-allocation of the land.

After the enactment of the Village Land Act, No. 5 of 1999, the government position with respect to rural land rights has become clearer than before. The Act did among other things, provide for the following:

a) Legalize land rights acquired through village allocation during Ujamaa;

b) Recognize customary claims over village lands; and

c) Give powers to village councils to manage village lands including land use planning, land allocation and issuing of certificate of customary land rights. *"Hakimiliki ya kimila"* to respective landowners in the village.

Although some authorities may interpret the new law as also providing land rights to the village councils, in my interpretation it does not. Following the new law, villages holding "certificates of title" similar to Chekereni may have to surrender them and apply for a "Certificate of village land" or *"Cheti cha Ardhi ya Kijiji"* in accordance to Section 7 of the new law, on the basis of which such a village council can acquire the above mentioned powers over the village land.

Despite all these attempts land rights claim in Chekereni and most rural areas in Tanzania are largely unresolved. It is expected that, the enactment of the new land law, will improve the situation. However that depends on how prudent will the operation of the law is.

The disputes caused by the land reforms notwithstanding, the project was implemented. In addition to reforming the land rights, the irrigation project also introduced a new system of managing irrigation water. We therefore follow up the water management issues in the next chapter.

Chapter Ten
Paddy Cultivation Starts: Plan versus Reality

... If the Project is to be operated following the [initial] design, there will be almost no harvest of paddy. [1]

The Actual Water Situation in Chekereni

In this chapter we shall deal with the reality of the water situation in the project and in Chekereni, the aim being to demonstrate its effects on land use. The main focus regarding the water issue is first to establish the volume of water available and the actual project consumption by using real-life situations, and secondly to describe the different ways in which the project management has been coping with the water shortage. Basically there were three ways.

In September 1986, the Lower Moshi Irrigation Project was almost fully operational, with paddy cultivation being in its third year in two villages, and clearing and leveling close to being completed in the other two villages including Chekereni. Since a large part of the area brought into the project had been under irrigation in the traditional system, the furrows had to be realigned, reconstructed and combined into the project canal system under the management of the project experts.

In addition to the physical changes, the traditional irrigation institution, locally known as *Wameeku wa Mfongo*, was replaced by a new institution called the Water-Users' Assembly. In each of the four villages within the project, a sub-committee of the Water-Users' Assembly was established. A Central Water Users' Committee, with members from the different sub-committees, was created for the whole project area. An important observation here is that the local traditional management system was replaced by the project's centralized water-use management system, in which the engineers had a say regarding water use and distribution.

When cultivation started, the Central Water Users' Committee and the sub-committees worked together with the project experts in preparing and enforcing water-use schedules, cultivation plans and overall project management.

By 1987, the institution was already facing a big challenge through water shortages. According to the project design standard, it was calculated that at least 1,310 cubic metres of water would be required to irrigate 800

97

ha. during the dry season (see chapter seven). However, the actual amount of water consumed by the 473 ha. irrigated in the dry season in 1987 was 1,326 cubic metres. In the event, therefore, an approximately equivalent amount of water was needed to irrigate half of the proposed area. This big difference in water use per hectare between the design and the actual amount used was said to be caused by the 'high rate of percolation, which was not anticipated by the plan'.[2]

Findings from this study suggest that, there were more reasons than percolation. Climatic conditions in Moshi District, particularly in the Lower Moshi area, were not favourable in the 1985/86 cultivating season. There was a serious drought to the extent that the regional development committee at their 1986 and 1987 meetings discussed it. Because of the severity of the drought, the committee advised farmers to plant crops that did not require much water. The committee also proposed to restore traditional irrigation furrows in the district, in order to reduce potential stress from food shortages.

Rainfall data collected by the Lower Moshi project office in Chekereni show that from 1982 to 1990, average annual rainfall varied from 401 to 932 mm (see Table 2). The lowest rainfall occurred in 1987, when the project was in its first cultivating season at a fully operational level. Thus as from September 1987, the irrigation project started to experience serious water shortages.

Table 2: Annual Rainfall at Chekereni Station, 1982-1992

Year (19...)	82	83	84	85	86	87	88	89	90	91	92
Rain (mm)	792	417	506	568	597	401	546	657	932	569	662

Mathematically, additional 0.914 cubic metres would be required if the project was to cope with the proposed cultivation of 800 ha. of paddy as the minimum area for the dry season. The volume of water available to the project could only irrigate 500 ha. in a season. Water is extremely vital in irrigated paddy cultivation.

To ensure good yields, sufficient water had to be supplied to each plot every fourth day so as to keep pace with the growth pattern, especially during the pollination stage. If water was not supplied for more than ten days during critical stages of plant growth, the grain yield risked being zero. In order to avoid a tragedy, project management had to fight for more water by any means possible.

Project management adopted three strategies. First, they decided to make an application for water rights, on the understanding that a legal right would ensure the project the amount it required and also give it powers to control other water users within the area. Secondly, they decided to reschedule the cultivation plan so that the irrigation area corresponded to the amount of water available. Thirdly, they intensified their attempts to control land use and thus irrigation activities upstream, so that as much water as possible was released downstream, at the end of the river, for the project's use. The process to acquire water rights started in early 1986, after implementation of the project had started but before it was fully in operation. Because the process of acquiring water rights took four years, we shall first describe the other three, shorter-term strategies. Then we shall return to the water-rights application process and describe it in detail in the next chapter.

Revising the Cultivation Schedule

A meeting between the Central Water-Users' Committee and the project experts was held on 19th March 1988. The main agenda was to review the cultivation schedule. At the meeting, the reasons for the water shortages were outlined by the project staff, as follows:

1)   increased water use outside the project, especially upstream;

2)   climatic: drought and low rainfall in 1987; and

3)   the fact that the project had just started *(upya wa mradi)*, meaning that percolation was rather high, which increased water consumption from the design standard of 1.31 to 2.9 litres/s per ha.[3]

Because of percolation, the project experts argued, even if the amount of water flowing were increased, time would be needed for the soils to stabilize in order to reduce water loss. With such arguments, and given the reality of the water shortages, the meeting had no option but to agree to the proposal, hoping that with time the situation would improve. The cultivation schedule was thus revised from two harvesting seasons per farmer per year to one.

We should remember that, this represented the second rescheduling, as the first reduction of the area under the project was effected in 1986, through which the proposed cultivation area of 1050 ha. for upland crops was abandoned, although the area had been partly cleared. The decision to abandon upland crop cultivation meant a reduction in the planned project command area from 2300 to 1250 ha. by 1986. In Chekereni village, the 1986 decision withdrew about 143 ha. of private farms which had already been cleared and the irrigation infrastructure (roads and canals) already been built.

In reality that decision meant a reduced potential harvest, which would affect not only the internal rate of return of the project but also the expected harvest to individual farmers.

The 1988 cultivation schedule was such that the project as a whole would have three cultivation seasons in a calendar year but each plot only one harvest. Thus the promise made at the public meeting in Chekereni in December 1984, that farmers will harvest twice a year, became invalid. In general the individual farmer's expected returns were therefore reduced by a half.

The new plan was implemented during the first season of 1988. In Chekereni 140 plots out of the 768 plots were cultivated during the January to June session. For the May to October season, 483 plots were cultivated, while the September to February session 280 plots were irrigated. Thus a total of 903 plots were irrigated in 1988, suggesting that only 135 plots or about 17 per cent, had two harvests during that year. For the plots with two harvests, 63 were located in the village communal farm.

Within the 1988 schedule, paddy cultivators in, for instance, Chekereni were assured of at least a harvest each year, and in the 1987/88 seasons farms were idle for only two months. The gap between one season and another was quite short. As a result, farmers could not complain much with respect to the two seasons that had been promised when the project was introduced.

According to Mzee Chami, one of the main paddy cultivators in Chekereni:

> The gap between seasons was quite short, only two months, even before weeds could grow. Some farmers had not even finished selling their previous harvests before they were told to start farm preparations. It was like that from 1988 to 1990.[4]

Most of the farmers interviewed refer to the first four years as the best period, when they earned a lot of money from their farms. They also said that during that period water came as scheduled. Fertilizer, seeds, advice and tractor services were available on time. Some farmers associated this with the presence of the Japanese experts, most of whom left in 1991. From 1988 to 1990, there was a tremendous increase in area cultivated per year. The number of plots cultivated in Chekereni increased from 0 in 1986 to 202 in 1987, and again rose to 903 in 1988 and to 1131 plots in 1990.

The idea of rescheduling the cultivation plan was very productive and was later praised:

> The amount of annual paddy production in the project is almost the same as the

amount expected in the design: it is 8550 tons in the design [4.5 ton/ha, 1900 ha/year] and about 9000 tons in actual [6 ton/ha, 1500 ha/year]. Actual production was achieved after discarding the initial paddy cropping system in the design. The differences are mainly in the water requirements of the paddy plots, varieties of rice (growth period) and planting seasons. If the project were to be run according to the design, there would be almost no harvest of paddy.[5]

We should point out that these achievements are based on the increase in yield per ha. from the planned 4.5 to 6 tons per ha. The maximum area that was ever irrigated, i.e.1497 ha. in 1990, was no more than 78.8 percent of the scheduled area of 1900 ha. per year, or 65 percent of the 2300 ha. planned total project command area. However, as will be shown later, the year 1990 was a turning point for irrigation in the project. Floods occurred which, like those of 1968 in Mkonga, were followed by a drought, from which the project still has not recovered.

Attempts to Control Upstream Land Use Fails

As the shortage of water intensified, the project manager thought that by using the legal powers of the regional water engineer, he could influence land use and irrigation activities upstream so that more water would be made available to the project. The desire to limit irrigated paddy cultivation outside the project area was officially announced by the project manager on 16th July 1987 in a letter to the regional water engineer, in which he complained about five furrows extracting water from Njoro springs without formal permission.

Since the furrows had no water rights, the manager asked the regional water engineer to close them down.

The regional water engineer responded promptly to the manager's letter on July 18th 1987:

At the time of writing your letter (i.e. in July), the five furrows mentioned, which are located in Moshi urban area, were dry and therefore cannot be blamed for affecting water flow to the project. You should, however, consult the Town Director concerning the role of the furrows and consider if they can be closed to avoid problems later. I, together with the Lower Moshi Project agronomist, had inspected irrigated paddy cultivation in Mandaka Mnono and saw about 200 ha. of land under irrigation. You should consult the Regional Agricultural Officer for a solution. Irrigated paddy cultivation in that area was practiced before the Lower Moshi Project started and was not a new land use or water user, so I do not see how it can be blamed for influencing the water available to the project, which came later.[6]

These communications between the project manager and the engineer

101

point to a conflict between formal and the traditional water rights. It is also interesting to note that the manager criticized the farmers upstream for not having a formal permit, even though by then the project was also operating without one. The letter from the regional water engineer also shows that Moshi Town, which was never mentioned in either the integrated plan or the feasibility report as a water user in the Rau catchment area, now finds itself being brought in very actively by reality.

There is no evidence to suggest that the manager consulted the agricultural officer or the town director as suggested. However, on 7th August 1987, the project manager replied to the regional water engineer. He argued that the 200 ha. of irrigated paddy in Mandaka Mnono were consuming 300 liters per second, which was affecting the project, and that the regional water engineer should investigate the issue and take the necessary, preferably legal, steps. We could neither establish if there was response from the regional water engineer nor if legal measures were taken. Indeed, it was not possible to take legal measures, as there was no relevant law.

On 11th September 1987, the project manager wrote to the regional development director, the administrative boss of the regional water engineer, to complain about the latter's lack of attention to the matter. He added that he expected the regional water engineer to:

> ...Apply legal measures to the irrigators above Njoro intake weir, because they are drawing water from Njoro spring without a granted water right. But the engineer argues that it is not possible to apply legal measures because the farmers had already been using the furrows before the project. [On this point, the project manager added that] the traditional cultivators had only been used to one cultivating season before the project, but of late they have introduced a second harvest during the dry season, which is the main cause of the water shortage in the Lower Moshi Project. ...we want to make this clear, in case there is a water shortage in the Lower Moshi Project. ... one of the main reasons is water use by farms outside the project.[7]

From the letter, it is clear that the project manager wished farmers upstream to be restricted by law and that they should only be allowed to cultivate for a single season, especially during the rainy season, when there was enough water to share with the project. In other words, the district council would be required to institute a land-use regulation with respect to irrigation in Mandaka Mnono and in other upstream areas, which would only allow irrigation in specific periods of the year.

The project manager's letter, which is partly quoted above, was copied to the Moshi District executive director, who was the first to reply. On 24th September 1987, he wrote to the regional development director, cautioning that:

As time goes on, problems within the Lower Moshi project are increasing. The different actors should meet and resolve some of the issues which can be resolved and deliberate on those which need more time to deal with. A meeting should therefore be called as soon as possible.[8]

As a response, on 2nd October 1987, the Regional Project Implementation Committee held a meeting to deliberate on the issue. The committee comprised of officials, experts and politicians, adding up to 31 members, agreed to form a sub-committee of four experts[9] to investigate the water use situation around the project. For almost the whole of October, the team carried out investigations on land and water use in the whole area of Lower Moshi and in the settlements located upstream. While carrying out the investigations, the technical team had an opportunity to attend a meeting of the Central Water-Users' Committee, held in Chekereni village on 16th October 1987.

The team then presented their tentative recommendations, which included the following:

1) that water should be shared according to availability and not according to earlier plans

2) that a neutral local institution similar to the Central Water User's Committee but covering the whole area should be established and become responsible for allocating water, in other words, management at catchment area level.

3) suitable sites should be identified for groundwater drilling within the project area.[10]

As for the recommendations on sharing water among different users, the team informed the Committee that:

The idea of sharing water between upstream users and the project was totally rejected by upstream users. They argued that water is their gift from God-*maji ni zawadi toka kwa Mungu*-and that it should not be controlled by the project.[11]

According to the report of the technical team, some members of the Central Water-Users' Committee were not happy with the attitude of the farmers outside the project. They therefore suggested to the technical team that:

...the water-use conflict should be reported to higher authorities, and that an immediate solution, such as the use of force, should be considered in order to rescue the Project.[12]

Thus no concrete agreement was arrived at in the meeting between the team and the Committee. However, a report was made and presented to the Regional Project Implementation Committee.

On 14th November 1987, another meeting, attended by the Central Water-Users' Committee, representatives from the four villages involved with the project, three top officials from the project office and the district executive director, was held in the project office in Chekereni. Among the issues raised was irrigation outside the project, especially in Mandaka Mnono. One of the members cautioned that:

> Farmers upstream have customary rights to the use of water from Njoro and Rau rivers. It is important to investigate the volume of water to which the farmers are entitled through such rights and allocate it to them. Once that is done, then we can issue regulations on water use, cultivation schedules and so on.[13]

Members of the meeting agreed to the idea, and it was resolved that the issue of cultivation outside the project should be dealt with more actively by Lower Moshi Project Operation and Maintenance and by the district executive director. But after the meeting there was no follow-up to these agreements. It seems that none of the water users were ready to compromise his or her share. This is probably why, in a period of about a month, two different groups deliberated on the conflict between the project and the upstream irrigators and made recommendations, without suggesting a clear mechanism as regards how to affect them.

On 18th April 1988, the regional project implementation committee held another meeting to find a way of controlling irrigation cultivation upstream, especially in Mandaka Mnono, so as to release more water to the project. In opening the meeting, the committee chairman, who was also the regional development director, said:

> Water shortages have made the project unable to achieve even half the target in terms of area cultivated in each season. And without addressing the water issue, the Lower Moshi Project, which during its planning stage was projected to produce substantial economic benefits will be considered a loss-*Wakati wa mandalizi ulionekana ni wa manufaa makubwa kiuchumi, sasa utaonekanan ni hasara tu.*[14]

The regional development director requested the members of the meeting to deliberate seriously on the issue of the water shortage, as it was their responsibility to make sure that the project was managed successfully. The introduction came to an end, and the meeting started to discuss the report of the technical committee, which had been set up by a similar meeting in October 1987. The suggestion that available water be shared among different users was among the issues discussed. Members of the meeting, at which the key water users were neither present nor represented, came to the following agreements:

1) water should be shared between the project and users upstream. Priority

should be given to the project. Two-thirds or 0.367 cubic metres of available water should be allocated to the project. Farmers upstream should receive one-third;

2) the proposed rationing should be presented to Moshi District Council and later to the Regional Water Board[15] for implementation;

3) to make the farmers outside the project honour the new allocation system, it was recommended that the ruling political party office (CCM) at the regional and district levels should inform and educate the farmers *(ziwaelimishe)* on the new ratio and on how best to utilize the amount of water allocated to them;

4) in order to control the allocation of water, it was also recommended that control gates on intakes of the main traditional furrows should be installed. It was thus agreed to make a costing for erecting the gates and that, that amount be included in the 1988/89 regional annual budget;[16]

5) to look into the possibility of implementing the Miwaleni springs irrigation scheme, as recommended in the 1980 feasibility study, which was also a second priority in terms of the 'internal rate of return' after the Lower Moshi Project.[17]

Of the five recommendations, the one on public meetings was closely followed. The district executive director, together with the divisional secretary and two experts from the project, visited Mandaka Mnono on 29th February 1988 for a public meeting to inform and *educate* the farmers. The farmers were told about the proposed rationing of water between them and the project. At the meeting, the farmers argued that it would be difficult to implement the recommendation immediately, because during February paddy was still in the fields and required water. Because sharing water at that period would have affected its growth, it was agreed that the rationing be applied after the paddy was harvested. The request would be discussed further at that time and a plan made. No other suggestion was discussed.

Since there was no follow-up on the part of the project or the district, after harvesting the paddy, farmers continued with their irrigation practices as usual. There was therefore no effective action in terms of controlling upstream irrigation, as irrigated paddy cultivation continued and even expanded in area.

At this stage of the Chekereni story, i.e. after 1987, water shortages within the project were a big problem. The area under irrigation had been reduced and cultivation re-scheduled, but the available water was still not enough and the amount was decreasing with each season, mainly because of natural causes like changes in rainfall, but also because of poor water-use management. How to manage the water shortage situation is a complicated issue for the project, especially considering that huge investments had already been made and expectations rose, but available water was not sufficient.

The events leading to that situation provides a number of lessons to managers of irrigation systems. Several meetings were held which could have been a potential starting point for continuous dialogue among water users in the whole area. However, the meetings were not fully exploited by the actors. The recommendation of the team set up by the regional project implementation committee was to establish an institution, which can facilitate discussions on how to share the water, in principle a basic structure for managing irrigation systems, but that was neither taken up by the project nor the government authorities in the Kilimanjaro region.

We can also conclude that the project manager's desire to apply legal measures and therefore force the irrigators upstream may have undermined and probably did undermine the possibility of negotiation and did not improve the situation.

As a reaction to the conflict, several committees were established but they had no political or administrative status on which to base their decisions. As a result, they made recommendations in their reports with no follow up.

The fact that no regulation was enforced over water use, especially in the upstream area, has been associated with laxity among the leaders of the district and the region who are said to have wanted as much water and as many cultivating seasons as possible for their own private farms.

In an article entitled 'Leaders are Killing the Lower Moshi Irrigation Project' in the people's forum, the writer accuses leaders with farms outside the project in Mandaka Mnono, Mwangaria and Njoro of directing all the water to these farms. The article concludes by requesting the President to intervene 'so that the country is saved from the shame of killing such a healthy and useful project'. [18]

It seems neither the leaders nor the upstream irrigators wanted to control water use. Nevertheless the project located at the end of the river required a more reliable water supply and needed upstream irrigation to be controlled. Based on the belief that formal water rights would give the project more power to control water use in the area the project management therefore initiated a process to secure such rights. This is examined in the following chapter.

Chapter Eleven

Interests of Foreign Donors Are More Important than National Regulations

> We believe an already existing irrigation project cannot be closed down so that a new domestic demand can be met.... We believe this might jeopardize the interest of foreign donors in similar projects....[1]

Applying for Water Rights for the Lower Moshi Project

In this chapter we shall follow the process through which the project acquired their water rights, showing factors taken into account and roles played by different stakeholders and institutions in the struggle for water in Kilimanjaro. We join the process on 10th April. 1986 when the regional irrigation engineer in the irrigation section of the Ministry of Agriculture wrote a letter to the regional water engineer, under the Ministry of Water,[2] in which he applied for two water rights in accordance with the Water Utilization Act of 1974, amended 1981.[3] The application was submitted to the regional water engineer in his capacity as the regional water officer responsible for the Kilimanjaro region and initiated a process to obtain legal access to use water from the Rau River and Njoro springs for the Lower Moshi irrigation project. In other words, the water, which the project had been using for about four years since 1982, was being acquired informally. The project therefore wished to formalize that access.

Before getting involved in the details of the process, it is worth having some idea of the technical and political factors, which are taken into account in allocating water rights. With that knowledge we shall be in a better position to not only understand the decisions but also evaluate the outcomes. Since the application forms indicate the factors that are supposed to be taken into consideration when granting or refusing a water rights application, I shall examine them in some detail.

Amount of Water and Area to Be Irrigated

The two application forms indicate that water amounting to 1.802 cubic metres was taken from the Rau River to irrigate a total of 1525 ha, of which 1100 ha. were for paddy, 245 ha. for maize and 180 ha for fruit. Similarly, the 1280 cubic metres from the Njoro spring would irrigate a total area of 1075 ha., of which 655 ha. were for paddy, 300 ha. for maize and 120 ha. for fruit. The two applications were meant to provide irrigation for 2600 ha.

Compared with the planned project command area as recommended by the feasibility report, an additional 300 ha. had been created. Whether intended for upland crop irrigation or other crops, that is a large overstatement. The exaggeration in the area to be irrigated appears again in the letter, which accompanied the application forms.

One of the sentences in that letter from the regional irrigation engineer, which was intended to demonstrate the importance of the project, reads:

> The Lower Moshi irrigation project is a contract project between the Government of the United Republic of Tanzania and the Government of Japan. When fully completed, the project will have a net area of 2300 ha. under irrigation.[4]

The letter presumably gives weight to the application in terms of showing that the project is a national scheme covering a large area and that it should be given priority over other local water demands. The irrigation engineer's letter is in accordance with the feasibility report but contradicts the information on the application form.

Water Users to Be Affected

The application forms indicate the regional development director, regional water engineer and regional irrigation engineer as representing the *only* institutions, which may be affected if the water right is granted, as they had other water-use projects within the catchment area in question. None of the other water users with traditional or statutory water rights within the area including Moshi town and further upstream were listed. It seems as if only the official users within government projects were worthy of consideration. Not mentioning, and thus not taking into consideration, the Kahe Railway Station located further downstream from Chekereni, for example, which would create a problem later, as the station would not be able to operate without water. In reality, users downstream were already being drastically affected by the project, because in 1985 all the water in the Rau river was being diverted to the project farms.

Possible Pollution

The section on possible pollution from the irrigation project and the proposed measures to deal with it reads 'nil'. That again cannot be true because in principle any irrigation activity has a potential for pollution and it should have been prudent to identify the extent of pollution so that mitigating factors could have been considered before it was too late.

We shall now set aside the application forms for a while, and follow up the application procedures.

Although the office of the regional water and the irrigation engineer are both located in Moshi Town, the application forms were not received by the water engineer's office until five days later, on 15th April 1986. The forms were sent to the hydrology section, where they were examined and posted to the Principal Water Law Officer in the Ministry of Water in Dar es Salaam for further processing. He received them on 17th April 1986 for registration and processing before presenting them to the Central Water Board for approval. On 20th May 1986, the Principal Water Law Officer wrote back to Kilimanjaro, directing the regional water engineer to prepare hydrological reports for the two applications within forty days of sending the application, as stipulated by the 1974 Water Utilization Act. The regional water engineer received the letter on 28th May 1986. The forty days elapsed without a report from the regional water engineer, and consequently the application lying in Dar es Salaam could not proceed further.

While the Principal Water Law Officer was waiting for the hydrological report, the Lower Moshi irrigation project manager learned about the Moshi Town Council's plans to draw 0.122 cubic metres of water for urban domestic use from Njoro springs (the same source). The manager therefore became keen to have his applications approved first.

On 8th August 1986, four months after the application was initiated, the project manager wrote directly to the principal secretary at the Ministry of Lands, Water, Housing and Urban Development, who was also responsible for urban development and indirectly for the water supply to Moshi Town. The letter from the manager read:

> It has come to our notice that your Ministry has already allocated funds to start (extraction of) water from (Njoro Springs) for domestic use. We also note that you have instructed that we should presently be allowed to extract 1.28 cubic metres, which will be reduced in future depending on domestic demand. Lastly, you also directed that we should not be allowed to extract water from Rau River below half the minimum flow.[5]

It is important to note, however, that the regional water engineer had already written to the same principal secretary on another occasion to clarify the water flow in Njoro spring. He informed the principal secretary that the total flow in the Njoro River was 1.616 cubic metres, while the Lower Moshi irrigation project's application requested 1.280 cubic metres from the same river. If the 'half minimum flow' condition were to be respected, only 0.808 cubic metres could be extracted. The project manager was also aware of the implications of observing the 'half minimum flow' rule for his applications and argued around that condition too:

> This amount, i.e. the flow of 1.616 cubic metres in Njoro, was observed in the month of January 1980, whereas the critical month-minimum flow-is in June, which has a flow of 1.24 cubic metres, and that is when the Lower Moshi Project is using 1.2 cubic metres. There is therefore no surplus water.[6]

In the project manager's argument, it is clear that if the 'half minimum flow' rule were applied, the project would only qualify for 0.62 cubic metres per second, which was half the amount used by the project. In this case, the 592 ha. already under irrigation would have to be reduced further to 296ha. Reading between the lines, the manager's reasoning was that the flow from the Njoro spring was so low that the 'half minimum flow' rule should not apply. In other words, the project needed and had already been using all the water from the Njoro River and should therefore be allowed to continue using that amount even if it was against the water use regulations.

Another issue of concern for the manager was the priority given to the domestic water supply for the residents of Moshi Town. On this point, the project manager argued:

> We believe that an already existing irrigation project cannot be closed down so that a new domestic demand can be met. If the Water Office goes on with the project...to draw water amounting to 0.122m cubic metres from Njoro spring, it will mean a reduction of irrigable area in the project by 10 per cent, and this will imply that approximately Tshs. 10 million in investment costs (1982 prices)...has been wasted; roughly 60 per cent of that amount is in foreign currency.... *We believe this might jeopardise the interest of foreign donors in similar projects*.... We would therefore kindly request you to look for another source to meet your requirement as discussed and agreed on 7th April 1986 in the Regional Development Director's Office between your staff in the region and ours. *We again regret that the water rights for the Lower Moshi Irrigation Project were not applied before the commencement of the project...due to oversight by the Officers concerned.*[7] (Emphasis by the author)

At this point, we should recollect the important points in the letter. Arguments in favour of approving the application were given by the project manager. They included the fact that the project had already been drawing all the water from Njoro spring and therefore could not be stopped, because this was a project of national importance between two governments. Also, if the application were not approved it would mean the loss of Tshs. 10 million, whereas approving the application would assure good relations with donors who might agree to finance other projects.

This way of reasoning seems political. It may be argued that the project manager decided to use political arguments, because they could not justify the application through technical grounds. It is obvious that it would be very difficult to explain why such a big project that involved many "experts and planning" did not consider water rights application important. While this reflects the power of international donors, it also reflects the laxity among Tanzanian policy makers and experts towards observing their own regulations. As we shall see later in this book, ignoring regulations, which is not only common in Kilimanjaro but also in other parts of Tanzania, is one of the sources of conflicts in the use and management of natural resources in Tanzania.

Attempts to Consider Water Users other than the Project

We shall probably remember that, upon receiving the applications, the central water law officer requested the regional water engineer to provide hydrological reports containing technical data in respect to the two applications. Although regulations require that such reports be made available forty days after sending the application, it took the regional water engineer about six months to reply. The request made in May 1986 was not responded to until November 1986. The regional water engineer reports to the principal water officer included a list of the existing water rights, which would be affected if the applications were granted. Since the hydrological reports provided an opportunity to consider water users other than the irrigation project, it is important that we examine them in more detail.

According to the reports, the application to draw water from the Rau River was to affect two water rights together with several traditional users below the point of abstraction. The one for Njoro spring would also affect users with traditional rights downstream and at least four water rights already in use for several years. Specific to the traditional water users, the engineer cautioned that:

> In all cases, farmers with traditional user rights below the abstraction point, especially Kahe railway station and Kahe Town, have objected to the applications.[8]

111

As regards the application to draw 1.80 cubic metres from the Rau River, the regional water engineer made the following recommendations:

> The applicant should be granted at least an amount that will not affect downstream users. Also, the applicant should consider the question of drilling boreholes around the area to be irrigated.[9]

As regards the Njoro spring application, the recommendation was:

> The applicant may be granted at least half the amount applied for. Downstream users of this river should be considered, especially those in the Kahe area. The applicant should consider the question of drilling boreholes around the area to be irrigated.[10]

Probably because of the data that the regional water engineer had on the water situation in Njoro spring, he was specific and suggested to the Central Water Board an allocation figure of 0.8 cubic metres. Lack of data on the Rau river may have led him not to make any specific suggestion to the Water Board as downstream users do not seem to have received much attention. He does not suggest how they should be considered. It has not been possible for the author to find out why the information on the water rights that would be affected by the application was not included with the application forms when they were submitted. This is probably the same question that made the Acting Principal Water Officer write the letter below.

Five days after sending the hydrological reports together with the additional information and recommendations, the regional water engineer received a letter dated 31st October 1986 from the Acting Principal Water Officer.

Apparently the letter was written after a visit to the area. The Acting Principal Water Officer made an official visit in Kilimanjaro from 7th to 11th October 1986 to inspect the water-use situation in the region, including the Lower Moshi area and Kahe, where he received complaints that the project had diverted all the water and that Rau river was dry in the Kahe section.

The letter, which we shall examine in detail, had two main purposes. First, it reminded the regional water engineer about the letter sent to him on 20th May 1986, which called for the hydrological reports. Secondly, it informed the regional water engineer of the results of a four-day official visit by the Acting Principal Water Officer to the Kilimanjaro region. The letter observed;

> During the visit, I received complaints from the stationmaster at Kahe concerning the 40,000 gallons of water that they were allowed to draw from

Rau River through water right number 656, issued to the Railway Authority on 3rd May 1951. Since the stretch of Rau River after the project and in Kahe is dry, that water is no longer available. In addition, the Railway Authority had already written to the Regional Development Director, with a copy of the same letter being sent to you. You should therefore be well aware of the issue. I am surprised that you did not mention the complaint when the application forms were submitted to the Ministry of Water in April 1986.[11]

The Acting Principal Water Officer included a list of the water rights, which were affected and should have been included in the application form, namely four water rights for Njoro, amounting to 6 cusecs and 2800 gallons per day, and 19 water rights for Rau River, amounting to 28.75 cusecs, and 77,000 gallons per day, both located below the project. He then directed the regional water engineer as follows:

> Carry out a detailed investigation concerning the water-use situation in Rau River to facilitate a good decision-*Uamuzi ulio bora*-by the Central Water Board in the allocation of water-use rights in Rau River.[12]

The directive also required the regional water engineer to evaluate the application for Moshi Town in terms of the existing water rights that would be affected. This suggests that the application for Moshi Town had already been received by the Acting Principal Water Officer and was thus being processed together with that of the project. Another point in the letter was an order to investigate four traditional furrows within the Rau river system, to establish if they were still operating and how much water they were drawing above the confluence between Njoro and Rau rivers. Within four days, that is on 12th November 1986, the regional water engineer replied to the letter as follows:

> Some water rights, for instance number 189 issued to Usagara Farms Ltd to irrigate (70 h.) acres of land for cultivating sugar cane and maize in Lower Moshi area, was incorporated into application number 4807 for Njoro, which also ensures that water is made available to the private farm.[13]

> Most of the furrows operating under traditional rights were converted into application number 4708 for Rau, since *the project was implemented in the same area that was irrigated by such furrows.*

> For the Kahe area especially, Kahe Railway Station was already affected because the Lower Moshi Project was drawing all the available water in Rau River.... As a recommendation, drilling underground water was necessary and the application for drawing water from Rau River should only be *approved on condition* that the amount drawn should not affect water users in Kahe area.[14] (Emphasis by the author)

There is a minor but rather interesting point to be made here. As a private company, Usagara Farms was issued its own water right. Incorporating private water rights to the right issued to the regional development director may be interpreted as combining private and public rights, or the revocation of the right, which would then be vested in the regional development director. Later, the incorporation of the water right into the Project produced a conflict that was resolved after several meetings.

After the regional water engineer's two consecutive letters to the Ministry, there was a silence, which lasted for seven months. However, the central recommendation in the regional water engineer's letter was the proposal made by the Kilimanjaro integrated plan in 1977 concerning the drilling of groundwater, which we have observed was ignored by the feasibility report for the Lower Moshi Project. The engineer also suggested that conditions should be imposed on the project to ensure that other water users would not suffer because of the project.

The Tragedy of Rau River

The three application forms, presumably including the project manager's long letter, the regional water engineer's recommendations and the field report by the Acting Principal Water Officer, were discussed by the Central Water Board in May 1987, fourteen months after the application was logged.

On 25th June 1987, the Acting Principal Water Officer wrote to the applicant, the regional development director, to inform him that at its meeting of 27th May, the Central Water Board evaluated the three applications and made the following remarks:

> The Board was impressed by your wise decision to give priority to water for domestic use in Moshi Town. However, the Board failed to make a final decision because you did not indicate the share of water, which should be allocated under the application for domestic use from the two applications for agricultural use. In addition, the issue of other users-those residing downstream with water rights and users with traditional rights drawing water from the river with buckets (*ndoo, debes*, etc.) -has not been dealt with thoroughly in your application. With respect to the limited water flow in the two rivers, the Board directs you to provide information on the amount of water you recommend for each application, also ensuring that existing water rights and people downstream will not suffer if water is allocated under the two applications for irrigation.[15]

After receiving the letter, the regional development director decided to obtain advice from the regional water engineer and the Lower Moshi project manager. On 6th July, he wrote to the two officers directing them to work together in co-operation and advise him how he should respond to the questions raised in the letter from the Ministry. To the project manger, the letter from the regional development director was an opportunity to revise his application on the basis of the knowledge that the application for domestic use by Moshi town was also being processed. Ten days later, the project manager responded by writing to the regional water engineer:

1) During the dry season, the only crop to be cultivated is paddy. Water requirement during the dry season is 2 litres per second per ha. Also, the area that is recommended for cultivation is 650 ha., which includes 300 ha. in Mabogini and 350 ha. in Rau, Oria and Chekereni villages. With these changes, the water requirement becomes 1.300 cubic metres per ha., which is slightly below the design standard of 1.310 cubic metres.

2) There are two water rights that have to be considered, Usagara Farms Ltd, with the right to extract 54 litres per second from Njoro River, and Chekereni village canal, with the right to draw 135 litres per second from Rau River. The two water rights were incorporated into the application made by the Lower Moshi project.[16]

In his letter, the manager justified the application by using data that he claimed to have been acquired from the regional water engineer. He argued that the dry season flow in the Njoro River was 1.616 cubic metres and in the Rau river 0.380 cubic metres, adding up to 1.996 cubic metres as the total volume of water available and thus to be shared by the irrigation project, Moshi urban and existing private water rights, and users below the project intakes.

He then proposed sharing the available water (1.996 cubic metres) as follows:

1) Irrigation project; 1.489 cubic metres;
2) Moshi town, 0.120 cubic metres;
3) Water right number 574 for Kahe Sisal Estate, 0.101 cubic metres;
4) Water right number 656 for Kahe railway station, 0.002 cubic metres;
5) Individual users, 0.284 cubic metres.[17]

The 'minimum flow' rule was ignored in the project manager's suggestion as his allocation proposal exhausted the whole amount. All the water had been shared out. Whether there would be water flowing in the river would depend on the individual users.

Even if the proposed 1.489 cubic metres, or 75 per cent of the available water were to be made available to the project, this would still have been far below its water requirements, as it will only be sufficient to irrigate 500 ha., not the planned 800 ha.

Judging from the regional engineer's response, which arrived on 18th July 1987, the manager's proposals were not accepted and neither the manager nor the engineer made attempts to consult each other and work together as directed by the regional development director. Each worked independently, making it more difficult to reach an agreement. The engineer's letter to the regional development director made two important points:

1) the Lower Moshi Project has diverted all the water from Rau and Njoro rivers, and water users downstream have no water at all;

2) a recent investigation revealed that the following canals with registered water rights have no water at all: number 656 for Kahe Railway Station, number 574 for Kahe and Soko Estates, and number 2163 for the Chief of Kahe [presumably for the Kahe community], and the rest of the traditional furrows downstream.[18]

The main point emphasized in the regional water engineer's letter is that the project had drawn all the water from the two sources, but unlike the manager, the engineer did not come up with any suggestions as to how to share the available water in Rau river, which is what the regional development director expected. He received the letter from the regional water engineer but did not write back to the Acting Principal Water Officer. On 9th August 1988, the regional water engineer responded to the latter's letter on behalf of the regional development director, making the following suggestions:

The water right application to draw 0.122 cubic metres of water from Njoro springs for Moshi township should be approved as requested. The Lower Moshi project should be *advised to drill ground* water so that some water is added back to Rau River to provide at least some amount for the users downstream to supplement the existing water supply in Kahe.[19] (Author's emphasis)

Even though the engineer's suggestions were based on a professional investigation, it was not possible for the irrigation project to accept them, as they implied a further reduction in the area being irrigated and the additional expense of drilling groundwater. On the other hand, the regional water engineer was consistent with his advice. But the central question raised in the Acting Principal Water Officer's letter to the regional development director was not answered, namely how to share the water in Rau and Njoro springs among the current users.

The Acting Principal Water Officer had to write back to Kilimanjaro to request an answer to this question. He insisted that:

The regional development director, who is the applicant for the three conflicting water requests, is supposed to know the volume of water available and advise the Central Water Board on how best to share the little water available among the three applications.... The regional water engineer should properly inform the regional development director on the water situation in the two rivers so that the regional development director is brought to a better-informed position.[20]

It is very clear that the Principal Water Officer wanted a more satisfying answer, especially as regards suggestions on how to share the water in the Rau River. After this rather strong letter, the exchange of letters between the regional engineer and the Principal Water Officer ended, which marked a big change in the whole application process.

Two months later, on 28th October 1988, the project manager made a new application on behalf of the regional development director. In the covering letter accompanying the application forms, he wrote as follows:

We wish to re-apply for water rights.... Rau River and Njoro springs are the sole water sources for irrigation in the Lower Moshi Project. About 1135 and 804 litres per second respectively is being abstracted to irrigate 2335 ha of maize and paddy. [21]

The two application forms were addressed to the regional water engineer, with copies to the Principal Water Officer and for the first time to the Zonal Irrigation Officer[22] in Moshi. In the second application, the total volume of water applied for was 1.939 cubic metres, which was less than the amount in the first application, but exceeded that which the manager had earlier suggested, i.e. 1.489 cubic metres. The author was not able to establish the basis of the second application or the reason for changing the amount of water applied for. Documentation of the second leg of the process was also not available.

Nevertheless, on 12th May 1990, four years after the first application was made, the project was issued with two water rights: number 4807, to abstract 0.804 cubic metres from Njoro spring, and number 4808, for 1.135 cubic metres from the Rau river. By May 1990, the application for domestic water for Moshi Town was still pending.

Thus after May 1990, the irrigation project was entitled to draw 1.939 cubic metres from the Rau and Njoro rivers for irrigation purposes. Restrictions with respect to 'minimum flow' and consideration for downstream users, as well as the question of drilling for ground sources, which were raised and discussed in the first application, were ignored.

The Kahe community, one of the downstream users most seriously hit by the project, decided to draw water from Miwaleni springs through a furrow which takes water from Miwaleni Springs to the dry the Rau river valley. According to Mangi Joas, who co-ordinates the Kahe Water supply project, water was to be made available to the community in Kahe a few weeks after June 1994, when the author interviewed him. The water was to follow the old course of the Rau River to the Kahe settlement, where it would be used for irrigation, livestock and domestic purposes.

During a feedback discussion[23] the author was informed that with a close follow-up from the then Member of Parliament for Moshi Rural District, a Provisional Water Right no. 4848 had been issued on 2nd September 1988 to four villages in Kahe to draw 1.0 cubic metres from Miwaleni spring. The implications of that decision for other water users dependant on Miwaleni springs, for instance Estates, settlements and the Nyumba ya Mungu Hydro-Power Dam, have not been worked out, and negative consequences cannot be ruled out.

On the basis of the actual water consumed in 1987, that is, 2.9 litres per second per ha, the 1.939 cubic metres granted to the project by the water rights is sufficient to irrigate about 668 ha. If the volume of water indicated in the water rights is available to the paddy cultivators in the project - and given the new plan to cultivate 500 ha. per season - there should have been no water shortage. In reality, this has not been the case, because the amount specified in the right has never been available for the project. Judging from the area cultivated each season; the amount of water available to the project did not exceed 0.9 cubic metres. Thus, granting of the two water rights did not solve the water shortage problem, but gave more powers to the irrigation project to fight for their water rights in the area.

According to the Acting Principal Water Officer, it is common in Tanzania for people to receive less water than they are entitled to. Actually, water sources are drying up and thus reducing the yield capacity of the sources. It was the responsibility of the water officers - in the case of the Project, The Pangani Basin Water Authority (PBWA)[24] - to review the water rights according to the available water and suggests allocations proportionately.[25] Apparently that was not done. However a number of lessons relevant for policy makers and planners can be raised from the water rights application process. It is clear that the amount of water, which a rights holder receives, is not necessarily determined by the water right in place. While the project was granted a right to 1.939, in reality, only about 30 per cent of what has been allocated by the central water office was available.

We also saw that in this struggle for water, information was provided on a selective and careful basis. In the initial application, the many water rights existing in the area were not listed. Had it not been for the visit to Kilimanjaro by the Principal Water Officer, the conflict with downstream users probably would not have surfaced during the application process. Although the application was granted, at least the Kahe community was heard and could obtain the support of their Member of Parliament.

We have also observed that instead of having a meeting where the main actors could declare their interest more openly, the process was conducted through the exchange of letters between the project, the region and the Ministry. Again, by confining the process to the bureaucracy of letters, none of the traditional water users were able to penetrate the negotiations.

At this stage in the discussion, we have so far looked at three strategies adopted by the Lower Moshi irrigation project in trying to cope with water shortages. We started with the revision of the cultivation schedule, then with the attempt to control water-users upstream. We have now examined the process through which the project obtained an *idealistic* water right. By and large, the water problem remained unresolved at the project level with serious implications to the land use intensification process at village level, especially at the end of the river in Chekereni village. In the following chapter, we shall start in 1987, with the first cultivation season in Chekereni, to see how the smallholders coped with modern irrigation paddy cultivation.

Chapter Twelve
Water-Users' Assembly at Work

Introduction

In this chapter, we shall experience farmers' reactions to the modern farming system and the capacity of the local institutions in managing water and the new land use. In principle, the project experts employed by the project through the Ministry of Agriculture managed paddy cultivation within the project area. The experts worked together with the Water-Users' Assembly from 1986 to 1993, when the Assembly was transformed into a registered paddy producers' co-operative union known as CHAWAMPU. The discussion in this chapter will only cover the period before the Water-Users' Assembly was 'empowered', when both the experts and the Assembly were active in the operation and maintenance of the project.

In each of the four villages involved in the modern irrigation project, the Water-Users' Assembly was structured as follows: It included individual smallholders at paddy-plot level, the watermen, sub-block leaders, block leaders and the chief block leader as the foreman in paddy cultivation at village level. At project level, members from the four villages elected a Central Water-Users' Committee with a chairman, secretary and councilors. In total, for the local management of the project there were four chief block leaders, 17 block leaders, 70 sub-block leaders and 34 gatekeepers or watermen.

In order to understand how the different actors in the assembly worked, we shall select stories from individual farmers who had experienced some of the leaders either directly or indirectly.

Block Leaders and Project Experts Work Together

Mzee Chami, who, it will be remembered, joined Chekereni village in 1976, had his farms within the paddy project. He was among the most prominent paddy cultivators in the village. He was also lucky enough to be employed as a block leader. He narrates his experience as an illustration of the work of block leader:

> I was elected a block leader to supervise water allocation in block (RS 4-4), where my paddy plots were located. My main duty was to make sure that water distribution was in accordance with the schedule (drawn up by the project). I was at work full time. I used to wake up at midnight to inspect the irrigation works on the farm. That was my work.

As a block leader, I also organized and supervised self-help activities in maintaining the canals and also ensured that individual paddy plots were cleared and ready in terms of the planting schedule. Without keeping closely to the schedule, water allocation would turn into chaos. Farms have to get through a particular cultivation stage at the same time. If a farmer is late and cannot cope with the activity schedule, he or she has to employ additional labour. If he or she fails and does not turn up, I am allowed to engage labourers and recover the costs from the respective farmer before or after the harvest. In that situation I normally get a loan from the Water Users' Assembly Clerk in the village. The farmer later repays the loan, or else the Clerk confiscates the harvest and recovers the money with a fine. It is necessary to make sure that each plot is cultivated; otherwise we cannot keep away vermin and weeds, which may affect productivity in other plots.

I am paid a salary for my work. I started with Tshs. 6000/= a month, in 1987. Currently (October 1994) I am paid Tshs. 7200/=. This is about Tshs. 240/= a day, and I work every day, no weekends or nights. It is work throughout. Although the payment is not enough, I accept it because I also attend to my plots.

My authority over water distribution starts from the point at which the water enters my block, at the turnout. Distribution within the block is my responsibility. Beyond the block it is the responsibility of the chief block leader *(Mkuu wa Shamba)*, who is mainly responsible for the overall paddy production within the village. [1]

According to this account, block leaders are very vital, not only in supervising water allocation but also in land-use management, because irrigated paddy cultivation is an intensive agricultural practice which requires a lot of co-ordination. And the fact that irrigated water use is centralized puts greater demands on co-ordination, because each piece of land has to follow the agreed cultivation schedule with very strict timing. Consequently, one of the duties of block leaders is to ensure that farmers operate within the time schedule laid down by the project. Farm management is therefore supported by the project staff and the Water-Users' Assembly.

In an interview with Mama Kahumba, another active farmer in Chekereni, the 'block leader system' was evaluated with respect to water-use management.

When cultivation started, there was no water shortage. Water for irrigation was not a problem, and there was no issue, as water has been closed down or diverted to other plots contrary to the schedule. Once water was directed to Chekereni, then it was available for the whole month. Therefore the watermen could not give the excuse that, 'I didn't irrigate your plot because there was no water'. The block leaders used to assign the watermen a number of paddy plots to irrigate, and they had to do so. There was no excuse. If one of them did not irrigate all the plots within the schedule, the block leader had to report him to the Water Users' Assembly office in the village. The waterman then was required to explain himself to the chief block leader. [2]

Judging from Mama Kahumba's story and also from other farmers interviewed by the author, one can conclude that as long as there was water in the canals, the system of watermen and block leaders worked well. Most of the villagers commended the watermen and block leaders and the hard-working project staff, especially the Japanese, who ensured that each plot was put into production at least once a calendar year. It was also the responsibility of the project staff, in co-operation with the Water-Users' Assembly, to relate the cultivation plan to the amount of water expected to flow to the project area. According to most of the villagers interviewed, the water supply was fairly reliable and the planning and management task much easier in the period from 1987 to 1990 compared with the years that followed.

Within a period of four years, income from a 0.3-ha. paddy plot increased from about Tshs. 29,000/= to Tshs. 54,000/=, which is about 44 per cent. Rent from a similar paddy plot had also gone up from Tshs. 3,000/= to Tshs. 20,000/= per three months season.[3] In short, the substantial investments made by the project contributed to the increase in land productivity and thus land values within the paddy area.

As shown on Table 3 below, the highest area cultivated in the history of the project was attained in 1990, when 1497 ha. were irrigated, representing a significant increase from 1431.41 ha. in 1989.

A turning point for the project in terms of water and land use management came after 1990. In April of that year, the village received 932.3 mm. of rainfall, which, because of the flat, low-lying nature of the terrain and poor drainage, several houses within the residential area were flooded.

Table 3: Annual Rainfall (mm) and Area Irrigated (ha.) in the Project

Year	1987	1988	1989	**1990**	1991	1992	1993	1994
Rainfall	401.1	545.5	656.9	**932.3**	568.7	661.7	n.a	n.a
Area	887.29	1286.84	1431.41	**1497.0**	1298	891	1015.7	664.4

The 1990 floods were followed by a severe drought over the whole of Moshi in 1991. Water flow in the Rau and Njoro rivers, the main water sources for the project, was very low, affecting the whole project area.

The effects were worst for Chekereni farmers at the end of the river resulting in one cultivation season being cancelled, as it coincided with canal maintenance. In Chekereni in that year, only 1025 plots or 300.5 ha. were cultivated compared to 1131 plots the year before. Thus after 1991, farmers' expectations of having at least one harvest per calendar year were not met. Nor did the situation improve.

For instance, the first season of 1992 was cancelled because there was no water, and in Chekereni only 170.21 ha. were irrigated. Slightly more than half the area cultivated in 1991 was irrigated. How, then, did farmers and their local institutions react?

Again we have an account from Mzee Musa Chami, the block leader, who claims to have lost more than half of his paddy harvest, mainly because of plant disease, which he could not handle because of the water shortage. During the first season of 1991, a disease unknown to him attacked young paddy plants in his plot. Here is his story of how he tried to rescue the paddy:

In 1991 a disease occurred in the paddy farms that (farmers) could not diagnose. We had not seen this type of disease before. It was much more pronounced in Block RS 4-4 than in any other block. The Water Users' Assembly Officer advised me, to report the matter to the project agronomist. I described the case to the project agronomist, who decided to accompany me to the paddy fields, to my plot. He uprooted one plant and said, 'Too late, this infection could easily have been cured by a particular chemical which we have just received from Japan, but it is too late now. You should have reported this earlier. Maybe the crops can be rescued by increasing the amount of water into the farms. So add more water to the whole block.' And then he left.

Yes, it was a good and cheap advice, but there was no water to add to the farms. That was a loss. I harvested fifteen bags instead of the forty I used to harvest before. Since then, water has continued to become scarce. Anybody could easily see that from the water level in the canal. Instead of 25 litres, there was only 7 to 8 litres flowing in it. When I noticed this low water level, I went for an explanation to the project's irrigation section. I wanted to know the cause of there being such a low flow of water in the canal. The experts answered: 'There is a big water shortage upstream, the water sources i.e. Njoro and Rau rivers, are almost dry because of the insufficient rainfall.'

But I was not convinced. In my understanding, we are practicing irrigated farming, which is supposed to be independent of the amount of rainfall. I said to him, 'We should not rely on rainfall as we used to before the project was implemented.'

We have continued with that situation, in which harvests are no longer uniform; some farmers get reasonable harvests, while others get nothing. There are occasions when farmers have had to leave their harvest in the fields because the amount of paddy involved was not sufficient to cover the expense of harvesting it. In my case, in the case of the specific plot in Block RS 4-4, which I have been cultivating since 1987, I used to harvest around forty bags (3200 kg.) up to the 1990 season. In 1991, I got fifteen bags. In 1992 I ended up with four bags and there was no season for us in Block RS 4-4 in 1993. It is like we are burying the little money we have into these soils.[4]

The story reveals a number of issues. First the support the project was providing to the farmers. With the support of the project experts in such areas as technical services and crop disease, the Water-Users' Assembly received praise. Farmers were assured of quick and reliable extension advice in case of problems. They were also assured of tractors, spares and pesticides from Japan. The project experts were developing seeds at the trial farm in Chekereni village. Although the district council employed an agricultural extension officer, who was stationed at Chekereni, he was not mentioned by any farmer I interviewed as having assisted them in giving advice on paddy cultivation. Farmers relied fully on the project.

We may agree with Mzee Chami that since the project depended so much on rainfall, its plan should have been flexible enough to cope with changes in the amount of water available.

For instance, farmers could have been allowed to cultivate other crops while they were waiting. In this way, Mzee Chami could have grown maize and beans in 1993, when he did not have a paddy cultivation season. With the water shortage, allocation became problematic, and favouritism and corruption set in. We have just heard Mama Kahumba praising the Water-Users' Assembly when the water shortage was not so severe. Since 1991, Mama Kahumba has been of a different opinion:

Watermen allocate water to those farmers who can talk to them as their age mates. If you are an old lady like me (she is in late 60s) you can't get water. You go home crying. That is why it is wrong to elect young people as Watermen, they do not have the experience of children crying for food. They also favour leaders, because they appoint them. And if the watermen knows how to sit with the leaders in the evenings *(kula na Wazee)* it becomes difficult for us farmers to get such a waterman or block leader out of work. Thus for a farmer really to be able to use his or her land effectively, friendship with the watermen has to be kept up.

The *Wameeku Wa Mfongo* were better than the watermen. They were better because the farmers in a particular block came together and elected a canal

125

leader from among them, a person they knew and trusted, who would not allow the water allocated to his group to be misused. If there were problems, we could easily elect another person. But in the project it is the Watermen who are given the powers; the water is in their pockets, and nobody asks them how the water is distributed. If the block leaders or the chief block leader does not bother to ask the watermen about water allocation, then what can a poor farmer like me do? [5]

Mama Kahumba's last sentence supports another story where one farmer, a sub-leader, tried to be responsible. The sub-leader was keen to ensure that water allocation was carried out in accordance with the project schedule. Thus he wanted one farmer who had violated the schedule to be fined. But the farmer apparently had connections with the chief block leader, who decided to transfer the sub-leader instead of fining the violator. Since Mzee Edmund's story refers to the problems of favoritism and corruption in obtaining access to water, let us discuss it in more detail.

> When the project started in Chekereni in 1987, I was appointed a sub-leader, an assistant to the block leader. My main duty was to assist in supervising the watermen when the block leader was not around. In that situation I would tell the Watermen, which plots to irrigate, and which pattern to follow. Unlike block leaders and watermen, sub-leaders are not paid a salary. The watermen have to be paid, because they work day and night. As a sub-leader, I only visit the farms occasionally and therefore could not claim payment. [6]

Mzee Edmund worked as a sub-leader for a number of seasons. He later resigned because he could not tolerate the malpractice and corruption involved in water allocation that followed the water shortage. Here is Mzee Edmund's account of how he tried to curb corruption in water allocation.

> One day, while on duty as sub-block leader, I told the waterman to start irrigating paddy plots from that end of the block where the plots were larger and took more time to irrigate than the standard plots. He agreed, and actually started. But even before the first plot was well irrigated, suddenly there was no water in the canal. I sent the waterman to find out what was wrong. He followed the canal and within a few minutes came back running and said, 'Oh! Mzee, there is one farmer who has decided to divert all the water on to his plot.' I was astonished. I took my bicycle and followed the canal. It was true. The farmer had diverted water from two tributaries into one and directed all the water to his plot. He was sitting there guarding the water flowing to his plot with a machete *(panga)*. That was at around 6.00 pm. in the evening. Water had just arrived, and we were supposed to irrigate our block overnight. In the morning, the water would be used for the next block. I approached the farmer and asked him, 'What is going on?' *(imekuwaje bwana?)*. The farmer

answered, 'I have decided and I am ready to die. Nobody should tamper with the water flowing into my plot. You should not even come any closer. Stay where you are, until I am through irrigating my plot'. I realized that I was facing a tough job. I sent the waterman to inform the chief block leader. Surprisingly he did not do anything immediately, not even coming to witness the episode. I think that was because the farmer was his relative. After waiting for the leader for some hours, still with the farmer irrigating by force, I decided to go home to sleep.

Very early in the morning, I went to the farms. I found a very bad scene. The farmer had finished irrigating his plot and had decided to let the so precious water flow loose out of control. The block was thus watered unsystematically, and a lot of water was wasted. I wanted to sue the farmer for what he had done, since I had enough evidence. I went to the chief block leader and I told him that, I was going to sue the farmer who had violated the irrigation schedule by keeping the water to himself throughout the night, and that he had prevented me and the Waterman from carrying out our official duties. I had sufficient evidence. But the chief leader said to me, 'I will take care of that myself' *(nitafuatilia)*, and that the waterman and myself should leave the case to him and continue with our other duties. A few days later, the issue reached the Water Users' Assembly Clerk in the village office, and I thought, OK, maybe the farmer will be called in and fined. I came to learn later that the farmer had conspired with the chief block leader to transfer me from that block. It seems the chief block leader agreed, even when he knew very well that my paddy plots were in that block and that was why I was working there. It will be difficult getting me transferred.

As I was waiting for the farmer to be sued, I was called into the village office, where I met the chief block leader. He told me that because the block I was responsible for was too large, it would be better if two young people were employed and took over from me and that I would be transferred to another block. I was surprised to hear this, as I was expecting to have a meeting where we would have considered the case of the farmer. I asked the chief leader, 'Do you think an incident in which a man threatens you with a machete is a minor issue? Anything could have happened,' The leader responded, 'I will talk about that later'. As I was not convinced, I told him, 'I have no plots in those other blocks you plan to transfer me to, and I work in this block because I was elected by the farmers in this block, as I have a farm there. The people who elected me are my neighbours. You should know that I am not an employee of the Water Users' Assembly. No one pays me any salary. And I work on *our* farms. Now if I am transferred, does it then mean that I am employed?' The chief leader insisted on me moving. Eventually I told him that I was not going to move and that I am no longer a sub-leader, because if we continue like this I may end up being killed and the Water Users' Assembly will keep quiet. That farmer is supposed to be sued, but instead I am the culprit and I have to be transferred! I resigned, and since then I have been just a farmer in a situation in which watermen and block leaders are becoming rich while farmers are losing.[7]

Most farmers in the project could not continue with this system of obtaining access to water. They increased their complaints to the Water-Users' Assembly leaders, the village council and project management, until it was agreed to change the water management institution over to the traditional system, where farmers were given more powers in electing and dismissing watermen. Elections were held and the system changed in such a way that each canal leader would be allocated water for, say, two or three days, and it was up to the canal leaders to make a plan of how to distribute the water among the members of his group.

The traditional system worked for two seasons, after which complaints started again. The watermen system was re-introduced and has continued since. As the amount of water was never sufficient, corruption in accessing water came back and it seems as if it is there to stay. It is clear that corruption cannot be curbed simply by alternating the systems of water management, but rather by having an effective enforcement mechanism. Whether the institution is traditional or modern, if regulations are not enforced, corruption will always take over.

This chapter brings us to 1992, five years after the irrigation project started in Chekereni village and water shortage has become a chronic problem. During the same period, the idea to decentralize project management to the Water-Users' Assembly was being discussed and it was decided that, the Water-Users' Assembly should take over the management of the project in 1993.

The basis for the decentralization policy was the 1980s economic crisis in Tanzania, which compelled the government to withdraw from implementing development projects at local level and adopt economic liberalization policies. From the late 1980s, the government adopted policies which were meant to give more planning, administrative and executive powers to local-level institutions, whether or not the institutions were ready and able. In 1982, for instance, the government enacted the Local Government (District Authorities) Act 1982, which led to the re-introduction of the pre-decentralization local councils. Other policy initiatives in the direction of liberalization included the introduction of multi-party politics in 1990 and elections in 1995. Trade liberalization and the recognition of private property rights in land were other aspects of the state withdrawing from direct involvement of local-level development activities. In this context, the decision by the government to withdraw from the Lower Moshi irrigation project in 1993 could be considered comparatively overdue.

Plans by the government of Japan and Tanzania to withdraw subsidies and manpower support in the operation and maintenance of the project were already announced in 1990. In the same year, the Tanzanian government sold the paddy-processing complex in Chekereni, which was constructed and managed by the project, to the Kilimanjaro Native Co-operative Union for Tshs. 137 million. In the same spirit of decentralization, in December 1991, the regional development committee directed Moshi District Council to establish a committee to manage the Lower Moshi irrigation project from June 1993, when the two governments decided to minimize their subsidies for the project.

In the following chapter we shall enter a different stage in the land use intensification process in Chekereni, in which local institutions, including the Water-Users' Assembly, the village council and individual farmers, reached a point at which they had to take over and supervise the irrigated paddy cultivation. The localization of the project's operations and maintenance is of interest to the Chekereni narrative for a number of reasons. In the first place, land and water resources within the project area are now managed by the smallholders themselves through the Water-Users' Assembly. The traditional top-down planning and decision-making approach was slowly replaced with local-level planning and management. Experiences of how the smallholders handle this new role may shed some light on the future of rural land-use planning in Tanzania. By following up decision-making processes, we shall experience the capacity of local institutions to operate with limited central government support, a considerably sudden adjustment for which they were not prepared. Let us see how they fared.

Chapter Thirteen

Irrigators' Association and the Village Council Take Over the Management of the Project

The First Challenge: Farmers Advised to Form a Cooperative Society

On 13th March 1993, the Government of Japan's contract in the Lower Moshi irrigation project officially ended and handed over to the Government of Tanzania, which implicitly meant that the smallholder themselves would take over its management.

Before the farmers could fully take over, the regional administration had to manage the transition period, by which point, most of the Japanese experts had left. It was thus the regional officials who made the decisions regarding the status of the project equipment, which they regarded as national property and therefore some of the tractors were transferred to other farming areas in the region. This meant withdrawing a number of the working tractors from the project which only added to the already critical water problem, as the Water-User's Assembly had to deal with a shortage of tractors as well. They could not cope with and as a result, farmers' complaints reached the President's office and the Member of Parliament, who was also the Minister for Home Affairs. In May 1993 he visited the project and had a meeting with the project staff and senior officers from the regional office.

At the meeting, the Minister ordered that the project tractors should be brought back to the project farms immediately. He also encouraged and assisted the farmers in the project to form a co-operative society as a legal entity to manage the project. Thus on 3rd June 1993, the Water-Users' Assembly was transformed into a registered farmers' co-operative known as the Paddy Producers Association (it's Swahili acronym of CHAWAMPU), which took over the duties of the Water-Users' Assembly at village level and those of the Central Water-Users' Committee at project level. A fifteen-member committee was then formed representing farmers within and outside the project area. On 17th June 1993, CHAWAMPU was fully registered, since when it has been quite active in running the project. We shall now hear accounts of how the association has been coping with running of the project focusing on land and water use.

131

Land Use Planning Attempts to Share Water Resources

After 1993, the regional authority was less involved in the project and the district council became more active in supporting CHAWAMPU. Complaints and conflicts relating to the water shortage were therefore directed to the attention of the District Commissioner.

In February 1994, the District Commissioner called a meeting to which he invited representatives from the four villages within the project. During the meeting, the Commissioner introduced a proposal to form a technical committee to advise on how to deal with conflicts over water, which were increasing. The representatives agreed to the idea, and a special committee under the leadership of the Zonal Irrigation Officer was set up.[1]

The committee, which included the CHAWAMPU Chairman, was required to investigate the water dispute in the Lower Moshi area and advise the District Commissioner accordingly. It was supposed to investigate irrigation and cultivation activities in four main settlements surrounding the Lower Moshi project area as shown on Map 2. The team formed a well-balanced local-level planning institution providing an opportunity for leaders and representatives of the different water-use groups to come together for the first time. It was also an opportunity to have an overview of the water-use situation in the whole project area. In this event, there was also an attempt to co-ordinate irrigation activities within the area. The committee visited each settlement and made specific suggestions. In some settlements the conflicts were resolved.

Drawing on information gathered from field surveys and by reading the committee's report, we shall outline the issues discussed by the committee for each area they visited, starting with Kisangesangeni village.

Suggestions for Kisangesangeni Irrigators, further Downstream

Since the implementation of the Lower Moshi project, farmers in Kisangesangeni have only been able to depend on the normal April rains, as their part of the Rau River had dried up. Traditional furrows and rivers in the area were found to be dry for a long period, and the settlement was threatened with drought. When the committee visited the area, the village chairman informed them that in the 1994 season, farmers had cultivated about 1500 ha. of maize which needed to be irrigated. In order to rescue the crops, the committee managed to convince farmers in Mandaka Mnono to release water from Mwananguruwe springs located in the eastern part of Njoro Forest Reserve.

The spring is also very important for the life of the Lower Moshi irrigation project, as it contributes water to the Rau River above the main project intake. It is in fact the first and only confluence with the Rau River after the Msaranga canal, which draws water from the Rau River for irrigation and domestic use in Msaranga village. The conflict between the project and the upstream cultivators in Mandaka Mnono basically concerns the amount of water allowed to flow into the Rau River from Mwananguruwe springs.

According to the technical committee, water flowed in Mwananguruwe spring throughout the year. In February 1994, the amount flowing from the main intake was 350 litres per second, most of it directed to paddy fields in Mandaka Mnono through traditional furrows. The committee also convinced the project management to allow water from the Rau intake back into the river to increase the water pressure from Mwananguruwe springs. Pursuant to that arrangement, about 100 ha. of maize in Kisangesangeni were irrigated. According to the committee's report, Mandaka Mnono village leaders promised to co-operate with farmers in Kisangesangeni not only during the dry season but also in other seasons. But they did not do so: no water was allowed to flow to Kisangesangeni after the January 1994 season.

Suggestions for Mandaka Mnono Located Upstream to the Project

Irrigation farming, especially of paddy, is an old tradition in Mandaka Mnono. The traditional water management system or *Wameeku wa Mfongo* is said to have been operating in the area since the 1930s. The institution has also advanced to the extent that a routine of weekly meetings to discuss water-allocation and furrow maintenance has developed. According to Mzee Minja, one of the farmers in Chekereni:

> The system in Mandaka Mnono should be admired and could provide the experience needed in the project farms. Farmers in Mandaka do not depend on tractors, they have not lost any of their land for wide farm roads and they do not have watermen. Conflicts never get out of hand for the police, as is in the case in the project. Payments from canal leaders come from fines, and if they are not paid, one is quickly cut off from the water supply. The system works without donors, maybe because there aren't any.[2]

However, the committee noted that the water available from Mwananguruwe spring was not sufficient to properly irrigate the 800 ha. which were under cultivation. There was also a notable degree of water loss because of inefficient irrigation structures and encroachment by

Map 2: Potential Conflict Points along Rau River

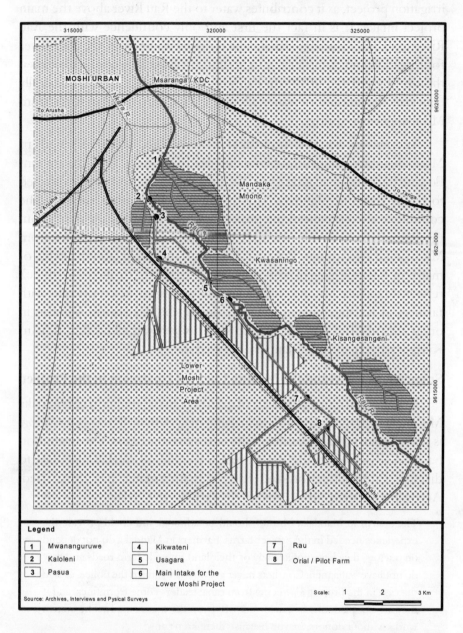

Legend

1	Mwananguruwe	4	Kikwateni	7	Rau
2	Kaloleni	5	Usagara	8	Orial / Pilot Farm
3	Pasua	6	Main Intake for the Lower Moshi Project		

Source: Archives, Interviews and Pysical Surveys

Scale: 1   2   3 Km

farming and grazing activities, which were too close to the intake. The committee recommended that village leaders should be responsible in protecting the spring and in discouraging farmers from extending the irrigated area, especially during the dry season, because the available water was not enough. It is also important to note that it would not be realistic to expect the Mandaka Mnono farmers to be able to let more water flow to the project or to their friends in Kisangesangeni if they continued to expand the area under irrigation as they were doing, a practice that, if allowed to continue, could result in that the conflict among cultivators in Mandaka escaping local control.

Suggestions for Kwasaningo Irrigators

Kwasaningo is another settlement that is active in irrigated paddy cultivation. Located to the south of Mandaka Mnono, its cultivation depends on water draining off Mandaka Mnono fields or filtering through the inefficient traditional furrows. Here, the committee reported that irrigation in Kwasaningo does not run smoothly because water is only available when farmers in Mandaka Mnono are satisfied and are willing to allow water to flow into Kwasaningo.

Thus most of the water flowing into Kwasaningo had already been used, making the threat of increased salinity levels very high. Already there were areas noted by the committee as having signs of high salinity and suggestions were made to the farmers to reduce the area under cultivation and change to less water-demanding crops such as millet, maize and beans. In addition to depending on infiltration from Mandaka Mnono fields, the farmers in Kwasaningo had constructed two furrows, which reduced the water flowing to the project. One furrow was located above the point where the tributary from Mwananguruwe joins the Rau River, while the second was below the confluence between the spring and the Rau River, very close to the project's main intake for the Rau system. Fights frequently occurred here between farmers outside the project and those within it, mainly over releasing the shutter/gate. In short, if the water gate at this intake were properly controlled, which it had not been, cultivation in Kwasaningo would be drastically affected.

Suggestions for the Project Area

The committee made two important findings. First, the lack of water had severely affected paddy cultivation in Chekereni village, especially on the pilot farm. Secondly, some farmers were violating the project's cultivation schedule. To increase the volume of water for the project, the committee conducted negotiations with Mandaka Mnono and Kwa Goa village leaders. They agreed to allow water to flow from the springs to the Njoro River a few days a week. Although the agreement was short-lived, at least it was a step towards a solution to the conflict between upstream paddy producers and the project.

General Suggestions

In addition to the suggestions made for specific sites, the technical committee made the following general recommendations on land and water use management for the whole area they visited:

1) exploitation of groundwater to supplement the available surface water;
2) application of by-laws to control cultivation within the project in accordance with the cultivation schedule;
3) water users should pay, and those who use more water should pay more;
4) a re-evaluation of existing water rights and if possible implementation of a water rationing project during the dry season;
5) the Water and Irrigation Departments should work together in order to assist village governments and the project in regulating the area they irrigate with available water.[3]

As usual, the recommendations went no further than in the meeting at which they were presented.

Managing Water Allocation through Guarding Parties

The first water-and land-use related management decision by CHAWAMPU was to revise the water allocation schedule. This started on 15th July 1994, when the CHAWAMPU chairman, secretary general and all block leaders toured the whole project area to assess the consequences of water shortage. The project's chief irrigation engineer also accompanied the team. After the investigations, it was decided to reschedule the water allocation system within the project area. The new schedule stipulated that water should be allocated to Chekereni and Oria villages for four days, and to Rau ya Kati village for two days. The new schedule replaced the old system, in which a given volume was made available to each village throughout the season.

Implementation of the new schedule started on 16th July 1994, and the waterman opened the gate at the Rau intake for water to flow to Chekereni and Oria at 8.30 in the morning and was meant to continue for four days. At 10.00 a.m the same day, cultivators from Rau ya Kati village closed the gate and diverted the water to their farms.

The CHAWAMPU team was furious and summoned an emergency meeting of the Oria and Chekereni farmers. At the meeting, paddy cultivators were asked to guard their respective intakes not only during the night, as they used to do, but also during the day.

It was proposed and accepted by those attending the meeting that for the six intakes and conflict points (see Map 2), Oria and Chekereni villagers should each contribute four strong men for the guard party during the day and six during the night. This meant that farmers whose paddy plots were in season had to contribute ten people each day. Since this was fully accepted, six people from Chekereni joined the Oria farmers and formed a guard party for the night of 17th July 1994.

According to one of the guard party, at around 8.30 in the evening, a group of young men from Rau ya Kati arrived at the intake prepared for a fight and released the gate and allowed water to flow to farms in their village. The members of the guard party were terrified and went to report the incident to the Rau village chairman, who suggested that the water should be left to continue flowing to the farms until the morning, when a meeting would be held and a resolution adopted.

On 18th July 1994, a meeting of all paddy cultivators in the project was held in Rau ya Kati village. The main issue was the violation of the new water schedule. The allocation schedule made on 15th July 1994 was reviewed. Chekereni and Oria villages were given three instead of four days, and Rau was allocated water for two days. The 'one-day buffer' was increased to two without explanation. After the meeting, water was directed to Chekereni and Oria as planned, and the flow was not disturbed for the first three days.

At 8.30 am on 21st July, the water was diverted to Rau village as agreed at the 18th July meeting.

The agreed schedule was respected, and there was peace at least for a few days. But towards the end of July, farmers got used to a situation in which water was always available according to schedule, and they started to neglect their participation in the guarding parties. This laxity was not accepted by CHAWAMPU.

On 2nd August 1994, Oria and Chekereni paddy cultivators were summoned to a meeting by the CHAWAMPU chairman, who announced that it was compulsory to take part in guarding parties and that any farmer who did not attend when his turn came would have to pay a fine of Tshs. 1000/=. This was accepted, and participation in guarding parties rose again.

The water flow continued as scheduled, and peacefully until a fight broke out. Mzee Kamuu, who attended a guard party that night, narrates this episode:

> On 19th August 1994, there was a fight at the intake from which water is
> distributed to either Rau or Chekereni farms. In the incident three people
> from Rau were arrested by the guard party from Chekereni and Oria and

brought to the police station in Moshi Town. After a day they were released. The police argued that there was insufficient evidence to prosecute them. Besides, there were no approved bylaws[4], which could be used in suing them. In the process of arresting the three, one person was injured and required medical treatment. The cost of this amounted to Tshs 6000/= and was paid by CHAWAMPU, because the guards who caused the injuries were working under the auspices of the Association.[5]

The guard parties continued with occasional conflicts, which CHAWAMPU had to settle, and sometimes with assistance from respective villages. Because the water shortage was more severe in Chekereni, the village council was very strict over the question of guarding water intake. Even sick farmers have to participate, as was described by Mzee Justin Ngowi:

As I was sick, I paid Tshs. 1000/= for someone to join the other farmers at the intake to guard water on my behalf. But when the water came it was not directed to my farm. I asked why, and was told to wait my turn. While I was waiting, the canal dried up. That means I lost my money.[6]

Thus even those who participated in guarding the intake were not assured water for their plot. According to Mama Kahumba, only those farmers who physically participated in guarding activities and were then able to follow the water to the respective paddy plots could be assured of water. Mama Kahumba, like other paddy cultivators interviewed, admitted that the situation was very difficult to cope with, and judging from an interview with, her the future does not look good either:

Mama Kahumba: The present condition is that only those who guard the intake during the night get water. If it had been like this before, things would have been better.

Interviewer: If you attend the night guarding party, how do you make sure you get water, because by the time you are at the intake water may be used on the farms?

Mama Kahumba: That is a problem. Those who are in the fields during the night control the water allocation. When the people from the intakes arrive in the morning, they quarrel with those who were on the farms during the night. It is difficult for anybody to stop them taking the water, as they have spent all the night in the intakes. Those who were in the intakes get priority in water allocation...those who go to guard during the night take all the water, and even if their plots are already irrigated the night before they irrigate them again. It's like they own the water.

Interviewer: Would you agree with the statement that, in this situation block leaders and watermen are paid without doing any work?

Mama Kahumba: That is true *(wanakula bure)*. They are paid without doing any work. If farmers harvest, then I may see a point to their salaries. Otherwise they are paid for nothing. There is no work that they are doing. Farmers have to visit their farms every day. It was officially announced that this is a dry season, water is a problem, and all farmers should work together with block leaders and watermen. But some farmers argue that if you employ someone and pay him yet you do his work, it does not make sense.

Interviewer: If you do not go to the farms, what will happen?

Mama Kahumba: That's how it was supposed to be. But if you are not there, when water comes, it won't reach your farm. But if you are around they will at least feel ashamed and you can also shout for your rights... In future it will be for those who are able to fight for water; those who are old and tired like me will remain poor. We shall die and that will be a loss.... [7]

Other farmers in Chekereni still have some hope and participate in guarding parties, where fights occur occasionally. Others, like Mzee Joseph Makoko, who was once the chairman of the Central Water-Users' Committee, are convinced that if there were more effective management it would be possible to achieve a better harvest. He argued that it is because of poor water-use management that they decided to guard the intakes:

> There are water disputes both between farmers within the project and between the project and those cultivating outside the project area, especially in Mandaka Mnono and Pasua. The Watermen cause conflicts among paddy cultivators in Chekereni. They don't follow the water distribution schedule anymore. If you give Tshs 1000/= to a Waterman, he readily diverts the water to your plot and thus disregards the irrigation schedule completely. The conflict between the project and farmers upstream is very serious. Farmers from Mandaka Mnono and Mkonga used to break the gates at the main intake and steal water. Similarly, farmers in Rau ya Kati village take more water than their planned share. For us in Chekereni and Oria, [with farms **at the end of the river**], we have to guard the intakes. And if the guarding is not done with care it may lead to war among paddy cultivators. In one incident people were beaten up and a project car was vandalized - that is not a good sign.[8]

Difficult to Enforce Decisions without Approved By-laws

Despite guarding the intakes and the occasional fights and arrests, water shortages became increasingly severe because the amount flowing from the source was decreasing. CHAWAMPU had to make additional efforts. On 27th August 1994, it organized another meeting in Chekereni village. As usual, the main point on the agenda was water allocation. The District Commissioner, the regional co-operatives officer and paddy cultivators from the four villages in the project attended. At the meeting, the Lower Moshi irrigation engineer reported that on that day, the amount of water flowing from the Rau river system to paddy farms in Rau, Oria and Chekereni villages was only 0.600 cubic metres. That is 53 per cent of the 1.135 cubic metres allocated to the project by Water Right number 4808.

The water allocation had to be re-scheduled again. Instead of allocating the water in terms of days, it was proposed to do so according to the old schedule based on volume, as follows: 200 litres for farms in Rau ya Kati village, 180 litres for Oria and the pilot farm in Chekereni, and 220 litres for the private farms in Chekereni. To control the flow of water in accordance with the scheduled volume it was proposed to control the gates with new padlocks at each turning point. The decisions made at the meeting were implemented swiftly since the plots had already been cultivated and because of the amount of water they would require. As a result, the 200 litres allocated to the farms in Rau ya Kati was not sufficient to irrigate the paddy that had already been planted. The farmers in Rau ya Kati were therefore not satisfied with the decision.

On the night of 3rd September1994, some unknown farmers vandalized the gates, destroyed the padlocks and diverted the water to their farms in Rau ya Kati. That same night, the chief block leader from Chekereni, accompanied by the project irrigation engineer, visited the water intakes to inspect guarding parties at different points. They arrived at the Rau farms' turning point at around 9.30 pm. The people from Rau who had destroyed the padlocks saw the project car and noticed that it had a policeman in it. They stoned the vehicle and broke its windscreen. The driver had to drive away very fast to avoid further injuries. As the people in the car could identify the Rau people who stoned them, the suspects were arrested the next morning. Later they were released, after village leaders in Rau ya Kati promised to raise money from the farmers to pay for a new windscreen. By March 1996, no payment had been made. Although CHAWAMPU bought a new windscreen a few days after the incident, there has been no court case.

However, the Rau village leaders who promised to pay did not commit themselves in writing. The only evidence of their promise to pay is the minutes of the meeting.

Following these two dangerous incidents, CHAWAMPU summoned a public meeting of all farmers on 4th September 1994. Five farmers were elected as representatives and were mandated to visit the District Commissioner's office to invite him to Chekereni to assist in dealing with the water allocation dispute, especially as regards those farmers who were not respecting the agreed water allocation schedule.

On 6th September 1994, the District Commissioner visited the project and inspected the farms in Chekereni village. He threatened that any farmer cultivating outside the schedule would be arrested and imprisoned. Following this announcement, on 7th September seven farmers were arrested in Mabogini and brought to the central police station in Moshi Town. They were later released without charge.

CHAWAMPU thought the farmers could be prosecuted in accordance with the project bylaws, but the police said that the bylaws could not be used because they had not yet been finalized, that is, not approved by the Minister for Local Government or the Prime Minister, and ratification by CHAWAMPU members was also still pending. The bylaws were finally approved in early 1995. However that did not lead to significant changes to the land and water use situation in Chekereni, as by then, the irrigation project was dealing with only 30 per cent of the overall area of operation. Thus the irrigation infrastructure, intake facilities, distribution canals, drainage ditches, tractors, paddy-processing factory, project experts and manpower were under-utilized at that level or below. The central reason is the decreased volume of water available.

Modern Irrigation becomes a Burden to Irrigators

The amount of water flowing in the Chekereni main canal in 1995 was so low that the period between supplies of water to any given plot had increased from the critical four to seven days, and in drier periods to ten days. In most cases water is supplied randomly according to who pays Tshs. 1000/= to the watermen first. Thus the one hour and forty-five minutes which is allowed to farmers are not sufficient, since the normal period required to irrigate one plot has increased to up to two hours and fifteen minutes. This is because soils dry up, so that it takes longer for the water to infiltrate and reach the paddy plants.

Since 1990, it has been common for farmers in Chekereni to wait for a period ranging from twelve to eighteen months from one season to another. The income from paddy has to be stretched over a longer period than before, when the waiting period was twelve months or less. The consequences for farmers of skipping cultivation seasons were increasing and were contributing to food shortages in the village. For instance, in February 1991 Chekereni village was listed among those villages in Moshi District requiring food assistance.[9] With the increase in the length of the period that farmers had to wait, and also the increasing risk of low yields, which is also due to the unreliable water supply, farmers now see the project as a constraint to using their land.

Mzee Musa Chami, who is among the villagers who praised the project when it started, is one of those farmers who were regretting it in 1994:

Now I am growing old, and farming is becoming problematic. When the government implemented the Japanese Project (*Mradi wa Wajapani*) in Chekereni, it created a lot of disturbance. (The paddy) project has really disturbed my plans. Before the project I used to travel a lot, trading in commodities from one town to another. I was able to stay away for three months by sending a small amount of money to my family, who relied on our farm, which supplied them continuously with bananas, fruits, vegetables and, in season, maize and cassava. There was no need for the family to spend money every day.

These days, when we only rely on paddy cultivation, the family needs not less than Tshs, 3000/= to meet daily family expenditure. You have to have that amount, and you do not have an income *(lazima uwe nazo, na mapato hakuna)*. I have lost hope; I cannot migrate to another village, I have no money. I cannot afford school fees for my children. If I have about 0.88 ha of paddy field and am so poor, what about other villagers who have no land? I have two and half acres of maize farm, but still I cannot see where we are heading to.... I have a lot of land, I cannot use it, I cannot benefit from it.[10]

In Chekereni, farmers with stories similar to this one are many. But Mzee Minja, a leader in CHAWAMPU and a paddy cultivator in Chekereni, thought that, the story exaggerated the water situation. He added that, maybe the reason Mzee Chami and other villagers had such stories was because they were not careful enough in managing their income from the paddy. Mzee Minja also associated such views with selfishness:

Due to selfishness *(ubinafsi)*, farmers like Mzee Chami are not ready to sacrifice and wait their turn. They do not co-operate in the water allocation plan. It is the farmers' selfishness in pursuing individual private interests, which contributes to corruption, favouritism and fighting over water allocation, which eats back on the farmers.[11]

Mzee Minja made an interesting point, which should be, elaborated further - that of the careful management of family income. Most villagers, like Mzee Chami, were not yet used to running a family on daily cash expenditure.

They used to rely on the continuous harvest they obtained from the traditional mixed cultivation, supplemented with occasional purchases, but certainly not on a daily basis. And probably, given the need to have cash and to make purchases daily- as Mzee Chami puts it, 'You have to have that amount - it is difficult to sacrifice and wait for the cultivating season'. While Mzee Minja is right as regards income, the real cultivation situation in Chekereni supports Mzee Chami's argument that farmers were unable to use their land for paddy cultivation and were keen to cultivate other crops.

On 8th October 1994, at a meeting of the Regional Project Implementation Committee, the issue of how best to utilize the paddy plots when they are idle was raised. The committee members suggested that farmers should be allowed to cultivate crops other than paddy, for instance beans. The suggestion was not accepted. The project manager, who was also attending the meeting, argued that, 'Allowing the cultivation of other crops in the paddy plots will amount to changing project plans' *(kutengua mipango ya mradi)*. However, the farmers did not despair but continued to bring up their request in meetings.

An interview with Mama Kahumba gives more reasons why, in villagers' views, the project management was reluctant to allow the cultivation of other crops:

> Requests that those blocks which do not get water for a long period should cultivate maize have been made many times. But the project experts claim that if paddy is cultivated together with maize, it becomes difficult to control vermin. Other experts argue that since the nutrients required by paddy are the same for maize, soil fertility is quickly depleted fast. But we challenged them on that: why is it that maize cultivation is allowed in other paddy projects, like the one in Same district (also in Kilimanjaro region)? And in traditional irrigated paddy cultivation, we used to plant maize in June and July, and after harvesting in December we would plant paddy in the same field. And there were no problems.[12]

There were conflicting views between experts and farmers on the issue of other crops, and farmers had living examples, which the experts could not really deny. Reasons like 'changing project plans' could not be accepted by farmers. Project management has also changed such plans since implementation started.

Another paddy cultivator in Chekereni, employed by the Irrigation Project as a driver, explains the reason behind the conflicting views:

> The project experts insist on paddy cultivation because, you see, when the project started, a good number of farmers were unable to cope with the costs involved. They then rented out their paddy plots for about Tshs. 3000/= per season. [Some land owners sold their blocks at only Tshs. 20,000/=]. Most of the project staff became tenant farmers while working on the project. In my view farmers who are unable to cope with paddy cultivation will certainly be

able to cope with maize cultivation. I therefore consider the experts' attitude towards maize cultivation to be a strategy designed to ensure that those farmers continue renting out their paddy plots.... There is also an argument that if maize cultivation is allowed the paddy plot level will be destroyed, which will make it difficult for irrigation water to reach all corners of the plot. But there are ways in which farmers can be careful and maintain the level. And if the project experts conduct closer supervision, there will be no problem..., I am sure at present that the farmers are adamant and are likely to push very hard with this request. And it appears that whether it is accepted or not, in the next season, that is January 1995, farmers with paddy plots that won't be cultivated will have to be allowed to cultivate maize. We haven't had a meeting on this recently, but if there is one I'm sure the experts will have to change their views.[13]

I interviewed the project manager over the issue of maize cultivation. His response obviously supported the views of the project experts, but he elaborated further.

It is true that farmers in the paddy project in Ndungu in Same District were allowed to cultivate maize within the paddy plots, but that was only for two seasons, after which it stopped for the following reasons:

1) maize cannot tolerate standing water and therefore the yield will be affected.

2) maize cultivation will require a tractor with a disc, which will destroy the level and cause problems in irrigation.

3) farmers argue that they will rely on rainfall, but that is not true. If the rains fail, farmers are likely to steal water, and that is going to cause more conflicts.

4) we have allowed cultivation of beans, but again, although beans require water, they do not like standing water. There are a few farmers who have tried to cultivate beans but they did not harvest much. But still, if we encourage this I am sure they will steal water. On the other hand, there are very few farmers who are really keen to cultivate beans, as it does not pay as much as paddy.[14]

Despite the reasons given by the experts against other crops being grown in the paddy fields, the respondent who predicted that the experts would not be able to prevent farmers from growing maize in the January 1995 season was proved right.

Mixed Crops Farming System Comes Back to Chekereni

In April 1995, CHAWAMPU announced officially that farmers would be allowed to cultivate other crops, though only rotors, not disc ploughs, should be used. Crops considered to be fast maturing and to require less water were listed, including millet, *serena,* soya beans and finger millet. The announcement also stressed that farmers who decided to plant such crops should plan in such a way that they harvest in July, in order to leave room for paddy cultivation. There were also a few farmers who decided to grow maize and tomatoes in their paddy plots, crops that CHAWAMPU had not listed.

Although the April permission to grow other crops was only limited to three out of the ten blocks in Chekereni, it marked a significant change in land use, nine years after farmers were encouraged to clear their traditional crops. In 1995, farmers were told to cultivate the same crops, though faster maturing varieties.

On 13th February 1996, CHAWAMPU announced another concession for the cultivation of other crops during the rainy season in five blocks. According to CHAWAMPU leaders, only farmers in Chekereni, at the end of the project, responded fully. This is understandable, since they were those most hit by the water shortage. Farmers in Mabogini and Rau ya Kati villages, who were better off as regards access to water, were not really interested in crops other than paddy, their first priority. Farmers in Chekereni who tried tomatoes and finger millet are said to have had a very good harvest. For instance, the cost of producing finger millet in the standard plot of 0.3 ha. is barely Tshs 40, 000/=. Unlike paddy, the amount of fertilizer required does not exceed 25 kgs. The harvest from millet ranges from five to eight bags, which can fetch up to Tshs. 200,000/=, a modest investment with modest returns.

If the trend towards other crops continues, paddy cultivation may slowly become marginalized. But the fact remains that if water is available, paddy is still the most rewarding crop. Farmers were therefore keen to ensure that an alternative source of water is established so that they can continue to grow paddy.

Groundwater Drilling in Chekereni: Farmers versus Experts

After struggling with limited success to obtain a reliable share of the available project water, farmers in Chekereni decided to 'go it alone' at the end of the project and to exploit groundwater resources within their village. The idea of using water from such sources is not new to the project: it was recommended by the Kilimanjaro Integrated Plan of 1977, but later discouraged in the Feasibility Report as being uneconomic. Drilling groundwater came up again in one of the meetings of the regional development committee. The regional water engineer in connection with the water-right application also repeatedly recommended it. Although most of these suggestions were unknown to the paddy cultivators in

Chekereni, on the basis of their local knowledge and experience they were convinced that there was enough water and that it would be feasible for them as farmers to exploit it.

Most of the farmers interviewed refer to the three trial sites excavated during the implementation of the project as evidence that there was enough ground water. They said that when the trial drilling was done, a lot of water fountained out. More reliable evidence is the borehole around the bus stand in Chekereni, which has been supplying water for domestic use since 1969 as well as for irrigation on the project's trial farm since 1982. On the basis of that evidence, and from villagers' own experience of drilling shallow wells within the residential area for private use, they were convinced that there was a large amount of groundwater worth exploiting. As the story below shows, they were committed to implementing the idea.

However, it seems that the project management did not support the idea. One of the Japanese experts still working on the project[15] agreed with the need expressed by farmers to find additional water sources. According to the expert, the most feasible source was rainwater harvesting. However, its exploitation required the construction of reservoirs and small-scale dams demanding large investments amounting to billions of shillings. The expert did not support groundwater drilling and argued that:

> The required investment in terms of equipment is enormous. The technology is available, but drilling water from underground is normally a hundred or say fifty years' life project, in other words, the source to be exploited should be able to provide water reliably for fifty years. Otherwise it is not worth the cost involved in drilling, pumping, installing the distribution system and maintaining it.

> In addition to capital investments, ground sources require to be recharged. In my experience, recharging ground sources requires a chain of mountains covered with snow like the Himalayas. In Lower Moshi there is only one mountain covered with snow, Kilimanjaro - and we are not sure of the volume that can be recharged into the ground from that snow.

> Maybe when drilling starts, it will not last more than three to five years; then we shall face the problem of investment recovery and recharging, which, of course, is impossible to handle.

> There is also another potential problem. If drilling is carried out in one village, the farmers may decide to drill down to 80 metres. In other areas, the depth may be 100 or 150 metres, and so on. If this happens, very soon all the springs will dry up. This has occurred in other countries, including Japan, where drilling was carried out rampantly. It is therefore the policy of the

Kilimanjaro Agricultural Development Project not to allow or encourage drilling in the Lower Moshi area. We have discussed this issue with the regional development director. He understood and agreed to our position that is why he is no longer talking about drilling groundwater.[16]

From this interview, it appears that the expert has persuaded the regional development director to change his mind about an idea, which was approved and budgeted for by the regional development committee in the 1989/90 annual regional plan. The project manager, unlike the Japanese expert, favored drilling. He was aware of the regional development committee's budget in 1989 and the test drilling that was carried out by the regional water engineer's office. But unlike the villagers, the manager claimed that the water yield from the test drills was very poor and that the whole project was considered uneconomic for irrigation.

Villagers, on the other hand, did not change their minds. In the interview with the Japanese expert, the plan by Chekereni farmers' to drill water in the village was evaluated. He was not surprised by the villager's plan, and had this to say:

> I do not believe what the farmers say. Frankly, your farmers are not mature: I am very sorry to say so, but they talk and talk good words, but one-sided talk. Sometimes I do not listen to them. For you, a researcher, you should observe, not only listen.[17]

After that serious observation and warning, the expert looked at me and gave the following questions as his criteria for showing that the farmers are not really serious and might not be able to carry out their intentions:

> Are the farmers, i.e. those planning to drill ground water, aware of the cost of the water per litre? If they drill water, what about equipment, machines for pumping, maintenance, electricity or diesel. That is not sustainable in this country where farmers are not willing to pay. They believe in free services from the government. All donors are saying, 'Stop!' - they have to pay.[18]

The expert was correct in saying that it is very costly to drill ground water. However, villagers are at least aware of the financial costs involved, though not so much the environmental implications or the length of time the borehole is likely to last.

As regards the question of payment, several claims have been made that farmers are willing to pay. Mzee Makishingo, the former Chekereni village chairman, did not agree with the Japanese experts that farmers were not willing to pay:

> Villagers are ready to contribute a lot of money to improve the water supply in this area. What we are now lacking is the appropriate expertise.[19]

147

According to the present village leaders, farmers were willing to finance the groundwater-drilling project. Although there has not been a public meeting where the idea has been fully discussed, the village leaders' assumption that farmers are willing to pay was the basis on which they decided to proceed with the drilling project.

In fact, a decision to proceed was made back in 1993. Following my discussion with the village chairman and village executive secretary, the village leaders carried out the following steps in pursuing the project:

The village council started by requesting the regional water engineer's office for assistance. A water expert was sent to Chekereni. After carrying out investigations, he confirmed to the village leaders that there was water, which could be exploited and utilized and seven potential drilling points were identified.

Most of them were located in the northern part of the village, which would simplify pumping into its main canal and therefore distribution by gravity. A drilling point close to the paddy-processing factory and the canal were identified as a priority point, on the basis of which costs were also worked out.

Subsequently, the regional water engineer's assistant advised the village council to obtain a drilling permit. The permit has yet to be applied for. Following the engineer's recommendations, the village chairman decided to proceed as follows:

> We wrote a short paper, which we presented to the irrigation project management. It did not receive the attention we had anticipated. At the same time, farmers' complaints were increasing. We then said, we know that our neighbours, the TPC sugar estate, irrigate 7000.6 ha of sugar cane by means of twelve boreholes supplemented by surface water from the Karanga River. And since the estate was established in the 1940s, it has never had any water shortage. I remember that it was at a village council meeting that we decided I should visit TPC sugar estate to find out how their boreholes were performing and to request their assistance in designing and making a cost estimate for one borehole. I visited TPC, and they agreed to help because some of their workers live in our village and others have paddy farms in Chekereni. They may also have private interests connected with the drilling project.[20]

After visiting the TPC estate, the village chairman made a report, which was presented to a village council meeting on 16th November 1994. Important points from the chairman's report include the following:

> One borehole is sufficient to irrigate 45 ha. of paddy or 100 ha. in the case of other crops which are less water-demanding. For the 243 ha. of paddy in

Chekereni, at least 2 boreholes should be constructed to cover 90 ha. per season, and the rest of the water from the Project should be used in the other three villages.

The cost of drilling one borehole (in Chekereni village), pumping and directing the water to the main canal in the village, which will later flow by gravity to the paddy farms, was estimated at about Tshs 115,286,000/=. The report also considers the mathematics of how to raise the funds and how much is likely to be required from each farmer. Considering the 768 paddy plots in Chekereni, each plot will be required to contribute Tshs 150,000 to cover the initial costs. Considering costs in running the boreholes, which include electricity, diesel in case of failure and attendant and watchmen, still a farmer can make a profit of Tshs. 80,000/= from one standard paddy plot.[21]

Although they are important issues, the questions of the environment and the length of time the boreholes can supply water were not taken up in the village chairman's report. In my view, the village council assumed that once a borehole has been drilled it would provide water for a very long period, so that the duration was not an issue. The village chairman was more concerned with how to raise a loan to carry out the project.

In order to obtain the support of the regional authority, which is necessary in order to approach potential donors like OXFAM and the FAO, the village chairman's report was submitted to the regional commissioner together with the village chairman's verbal assurance that the villagers would be ready to repay a soft loan. According to the village chairman, the village council still ha to approach OXFAM, who once assisted farmers in a neighbouring village, with a similar project. The village chairman is aware that OXFAM normally gives loans for a period of from ten to twenty years and charges a three percent interest rate.

The village chairman, on his part, is pursuing the project vigorously and is convinced that he will be successful and that the water situation will improve. Most of the villagers interviewed are aware of the plan but admit that they have not had a chance to discuss it at a public meeting. Discussion is important, because the plan commits the villagers to putting up a substantial amount of money. We do not know how the villagers will respond to the project and its implications, nor whether the village chairman will able to obtain the support of the Regional Commissioner and therefore a loan. These are some of the questions that will have to be resolved if the village council's drilling project is to be carried out.

The Japanese experts are not happy with the water situation in the project either. However, because they do not support the village council's drilling project, they have come up with an alternative plan, to draw water from Kikuletwa River at an intake located about twenty kilometres away in Hai district, on the western side of Moshi Town.

This project has reached a more advanced stage than the village council's project. A water-rights application has already been received. In one feedback session, the Acting Principle Water Officer told me that a feasibility study had been carried out, on the basis of which an application to draw 9000 litres per day from the Kikuletwa River had been submitted. According to the Water Officer, the amount applied for is all that is available in the river. It is likely that a water right will be issued, with the condition that 'storage dams are built to ensure the minimum flow condition, so as to maintain aquatic life in the river'. It is not yet clear whether these conditions will matter in the application or in the actual exploitation of the water source. Events will tell. Most villagers in Chekereni are aware of the Kikuletwa water project. They argue that even if the water is made available, if there is no proper and strict management there is no guarantee that farmers in places through which the canal will pass will not open up farms and use the water. Given their location at the end of the distribution system, they do not expect much from the Kikuletwa project.

Nevertheless, the land-use intensification process in Chekereni has reached a stage where the different actors are not happy with the situation they have jointly produced.

The project experts are not happy and now have to make another big investment in a water supply, even from a distant intake, to rescue irrigated paddy cultivation which has won them jobs, fame, and power over water allocation in the Lower Moshi area. Without paddy cultivation, it will be difficult to ask the farmers to continue servicing the loan. The project has to ensure access to water, which may lead to another struggle and may be a similar tragedy for the Kikuletwa River.

CHAWAMPU is also busy trying to manage the water situation in the project. Mobilizing other inputs, like tractors and fertilizer, is another important and delicate issue that the paddy cultivators have to cope with. Bylaws were in place by early 1995, and the Association acquired more powers and responsibilities after 28th April 1995, when Water Rights numbers 4807 and 4808 were formally transferred from the regional development director to CHAWAMPU.

The village council, most of whose members are paddy cultivators, has taken up groundwater drilling seriously. They show knowledge in their pursuit of the issue, but they do not seem concerned with the possible long-term consequences. Most important is the non-involvement of the other villagers, who are expected to contribute enormous amounts of money to finance the drilling.

The fact that Chekereni village leaders decided to pursue the project to drill groundwater and thus commit the other villagers to such an expensive venture without discussing its implications and seeking the villagers' consent is an example of a lack of participation and involvement by stakeholders in decision-making, even in the current political-administrative context in Tanzania, in which decisions are supposed to be more open.

Farmers with land in the irrigation project are not at all decided whether to continue with paddy in a situation of unreliable water or change to less water-demanding but less profitable crops. The profit potential from paddy is tempting, but the threat of hunger is also increasing. Given village economic conditions, the cash earned from paddy can hardly support the household to the next harvest.

There is therefore a conflict between the subsistence economy and the monoculture farming system introduced by the irrigation project. Traditional mixed farming supplies households with income and food in low quantities, but continuously, almost throughout the year. With this farming system, it was possible to ensure an overlap by seasons and the continuous use of land. Most farmers in Chekereni who were used to the traditional mixed farming system have not yet adjusted to a single-income situation requiring high discipline in managing household income. They complained bitterly to me about the situation in which they received just one single, small income. The habit of buying food for a considerable period of the year is still foreign to some households. Since the 1991 drought, the food situation in Chekereni has deteriorated to the extent that villagers rely on the maize given as food aid by church organizations.

The other 1298 ha of land in Chekereni, which is not included in the irrigation project, where 64 per cent[22] of households have farms, continue to rely on the low rainfall. Following the implementation of the project, it has not been found possible to extend irrigation to that area through the project canals. And since the village council's plan to drill groundwater will also be structured by the project canals, there is not much hope for extending the irrigated area beyond the project area. From a land-use point of view, the physical changes in the paddy fields are not easily predictable. A farming system is developing which mixes paddy when water is available with other crops in the dry season. To start with, this farming system may be considered a temporary practice until the water problem is solved.

It is interesting to note, however, that the main actors in the struggle to keep modernized irrigated paddy cultivation alive are still working in a decision-making system, which excludes other actors. There is not much interest in either the small project staff, CHAWAMPU or the village council in involving or sharing plans with one another or with the farmers who will be required to pay, whether water is taken from far away, from the Kikuletwa River, or from within their village. How the different actors will handle the issues that will arise in the land-use intensification process will show the extent to which they have learned from their past and present practices. But that is a matter for another investigation. One could go on observing these actors to see how they will pursue the projects they have initiated. But for now our account of Chekereni ends here, at a point, which is not only another beginning but may be a more interesting and active one.

Chapter Fourteen

Lessons for Policy Makers and Practising Planners

Introduction

We have heard the story. In this chapter we shall try to draw lessons from the Chekereni narrative. We shall look at the lessons relevant to policy makers and practising planners, particularly focusing on how to make planning more effective in managing changes in land use.

Plans Made and Implemented by Leaders in Collaboration with Community Members Have Higher Chances of Realizing Objectives

During the pre-Ujamaa period, the Chekereni settlement was established. This change took place between the 1940s and the early 1960s, the main factor behind the changes being the establishment of the Sisal Estates in the area. These estates attracted laborers who then decided to set up homes and farms in Chekereni to supplement their incomes. In the southern part of the village, the process of land acquisition, clearing and farming was carried out spontaneously, with very limited influence from the community or traditional leaders. In the northern part, individuals pursued the same process directly supervised by community leaders. In both situations, customary land rights were closely followed. The clearing and consolidation of the settlement was enhanced later in 1968 by the decision by the local government Officer to resettle flood victims in Chekereni. The land-use change events outlined above produced a settlement organized according to the traditional pattern, with farm and home located together and thus depicting a sparse pattern of homes and fairly open settlement. On average a family had more than ten acres of land in one location. Common resources, including grazing, firewood and water were, obtained outside the Chekereni settlement.

During the 1950s and 1960s, Mangi Sabas organized land-acquisition in the northern part of Chekereni. The community's objectives in that acquisition were to minimize threat of hunger and deal with the problem of shortage of land for inheritance in the villages in the highlands. In the land-acquisition processes, individual actors and community leaders were not guided by any formal plan but observed customary land-acquisition procedures. Decisions made by individuals like Mzee Mbindyo were justified through negotiations.

It was seldom that decisions made by community leaders had to be justified to their subjects. Mzee Ngowi, who described the process by which villagers acquired land in the northern part of Chekereni, told us that Mangi Sabas did justify his decision by referring to land shortage, the threat of hunger in the highlands and the lack of land for inheritance as the reason for urging his people to agree with his decision. It was not a difficult decision to justify, because both parties would gain: individuals received additional land and the Mangi gained more respect and power. There was therefore no possible conflict of interest. However, the practice of traditional leaders developing plans and ideas in their 'minds' on behalf of their subjects was common during the pre-Ujamaa period, and probably this was the Chief's constitutional right. An important lesson for planners here is that, in the 1930s and 1940s, decision-making under the traditional system of land use-change was hierarchically clear. Individuals knew where power lay, and the Chief's decisions were in most cases final.

Respecting Customary Land Rights and Compensation are Important Tools for Realizing Planning Decisions

Traditional leaders' authority in land administration and land use planning was abolished in 1963 by the Independence government. A new system of representation was introduced whereby government officials and politicians made land use planning decisions on behalf of individual landowners. In this arrangement, individual landowners could complain if they felt that their interests were not adequately considered.

Mzee Mbindyo's story about a meeting with the District Commissioner is one illustration of such complaints. From the story we learn that through representative decision-making, Mzee Mbindyo's interests were not taken into account in the decision to establish a large-scale farm on his land. But as he resisted moving, he was allowed to participate in the meeting where negotiations were held and the conflict resolved. Mzee Mbindyo won his case by referring to customary rights. He was thus entitled to compensation.

A point to note here is that Mzee Mbindyo's disagreement with the district authorities did not concern the type of land use to be introduced on the land but rather his land rights. Thus once Mzee Mbindyo had been compensated, the proposed activity could take place. It is also worth pointing out that Mzee Mbindyo's argument was based on customary rules, which were respected at the formal meeting in the District Commissioner's office.

Plans May Have Many Uses and Also Users

In the Chekereni story we experienced a situation where the District Council decided to build a canal to facilitate irrigation in Chekereni and other nearby villages. A plan drawn up by the Regional Water Engineer was used to determine the alignment of the canal, the location of the village communal and private farms, the location of the first residential area. The same plan was used to guide the detailed subdivision of the residential area into building plots for the Ujamaa migrants.

Both irrigation engineers and the village leaders used the plan. For the engineers, it was a technical guide in aligning and constructing the canal. To the Ujamaa Village Council, the plan was first used as a tool in determining the spatial organization of the housing area, and secondly as a political instrument for the Ujamaa migrants' struggles for land in Chekereni.

The plan was used as evidence that the District Council had sanctioned the area designated in the plan for the Ujamaa migrants. The village leaders probably enforced its proposals because they supported their own views and the interests of the Ujamaa migrants. For example, the Village Lands Allocation Committee closely enforced restrictions attached to plot development. The condition that construction of a house was necessary before one could qualify for a private farm made the Ujamaa migrants who had come to Chekereni for land work very hard towards that goal.

To the irrigation engineers and the Ujamaa Village Council, the plan performed very well. It was a success. Their objectives were achieved. But to the original migrants who lost their lands the plan was not a success, because it was implemented against their wishes. It is important to note that it was possible for the Village Council to use the plan against the wishes of the original migrants because of the decision-making system, which in most cases excluded the original migrants. The plan was used to facilitate the expropriation of land rather than to open up a discussion on land-use options among different land users. The expropriation of land, in which compensation was not considered, produced land conflicts, which were difficult to resolve.

For a considerable period during the implementation of Ujamaa, the Village Council referred to the engineer's plan in a number of land-use decisions. The spatial pattern it illustrated was tried out, and by and large achieved in the residential area.

It is clear that the village council's zoning idea as guided by the water engineer's plan of 1970, produced a spatial pattern in which there is a clear system of roads and paths and farms are separated from homes.

In general, the Village Council's 'plan', which was kept in the Village Chairman's mind, was closely observed all through the Ujamaa period, mainly by the Village Land Allocation Committee in carrying out their duty of regulating land-use change within the village.

We can therefore conclude that the Chekereni Village Council was able to transform land use from the traditional scattered form to the Ujamaa pattern by using the water engineer's plan, without direct support from either the spatial planning system at either regional or district level. However, in the 1990s the separation of farms from homes became impossible because of the shortage of land in the residential area, which compelled new households to create homes in the areas set aside for farms. Although this reduced the densities in the residential area, it lead to problems of distance to available community services.

When Decisions are Made without Records, It is Difficult to Ensure Accountability

In Chekereni, the practice of participation by representation was not as clear as outlined in the administrative structure. The Village Council, under the leadership of the Village Chairman and the Village Executive Officer, assumed powers over decision-making. The decision-making arena shifted from the influence of government officials in the ward and district to the Village Council, with little or no influence from the Village Assembly.

A classic example of a decision made by the Village Council without involving the Village Assembly is the 1976 decision to extend the village communal farm. This decision lead to the forceful acquiring of individual private lands into public ownership. The decision was presumably carried out by the Village Council. When the minutes were required by the Customary Lands Tribunal, the Village Council could not produce them. No minutes were kept of such an important meeting.

The lack of minutes is not only a violation of administrative procedures but is also against land-acquisition procedures as outlined in the 1975 Villagization Act, which was in operation by that time. The situation in which public decisions were made without proper records being kept made accountability on the part of decision-makers difficult. For instance, we cannot tell who really decided to expand the village communal farm.

Administrative procedures beyond the village level were also violated. The story shows incidences of lack of authority and of clarity in respect of duties and responsibilities. For example, judging from the letters exchanged among the different actors and institutions involved in Mzee Wetundwa's case, as narrated in chapter six, one cannot tell who was really answerable to whom. In this situation, one that was typical of the Ujamaa period, laws were consciously ignored, thus giving room to corruption and undermining the goals of fairness, equity and openness in decision-making. This leads to another lesson: the existence of a village constitution and other national level legislation provided no guarantee of equality, fairness or democratic practice. Practice was very much different from rules and in cases of violation there were very limited possibilities to question and punish violators. Checks and balances did not work.

Concepts May Be Useful for Planning but Should Not Replace Reality

In the early 1980s, about 850 ha. of land in Chekereni village was converted from traditional irrigated mixed farming to modernized irrigated paddy cultivation. The main actors in executing this change in land use were the Chekereni Village Council and foreign and local experts, with the occasional involvement of politicians and administrators at regional level.

The land-use change described above was proposed in the Kilimanjaro Integrated Plan of 1977 prepared by, foreign and local experts. The planners justified their proposal to invest in agricultural development in the plains by saying that, density was very low and that by using high technology from Japan, it would be possible to make the plains productive. The plan was approved by the Regional Development Committee, again under the system of participation through representation. The plan was also justified at the feasibility stage, but in a technically more advanced way.

Two concepts were applied. The 'Reservoir Simulation Model' was used to argue that there was sufficient water in the Rau River. The 'Internal Rate of Return' was used to prove that, investing in the Irrigation Project in the four villages was profitable, and that the investment would be recovered within fifty years.

Members of the Regional Development Committee did not question the proposal to introduce irrigated paddy in the plains. Instead they questioned the general concept of 'integrated planning'. Subsequently, the substance of the proposal, which was concerned with changing the farming system in the four villages, as well as changing the traditional irrigation system and most importantly the sharing of the Rau river water resources, was not discussed.

The plan was approved and its implementation endorsed. This was an instance where experts applied technical rationality and took over decision-making from individuals and from their leaders. The real water situation was not sufficiently taken into consideration

After the irrigation project had been approved, it acquired "national-level status", which was very instrumental in implementing the project, and especially in justifying the acquisition of land from Chekereni villagers. However, the approval could also be interpreted as a violation of the 1974 Water Utilization Act. In this instance, the Members of Parliament in the Regional Development Committee decided against legislation enacted by the same Parliament. Thus, in pursuing modern technology and the intensification of agriculture, laws were ignored at a regional level.

Implementing the irrigation project before applying for water rights made it possible to avoid discussions where other water users' interests might have surfaced and probably led to changes in the project plans or possibly to the abandonment of the project altogether. It was therefore a way of excluding other interests. It was also a strategy, which gave the irrigation project a stronger argument in the negotiations in processing the application. The project manager argued that the investment had already been made and that stopping the project might jeopardize the "interests of foreign donors" in other projects. Nowhere in the communication is the issue raised of why the law was ignored. The strategy worked, and water rights were granted. At national level, the result was that the Central Water Board was put into a situation where it could not really control access to water use in the Rau river as one of the national water bodies.

In other words the water office could not perform. That strategy made it legitimate for the Lower Moshi Irrigation Project to withdraw already allocated statutory and traditional water rights from other users of the project area, ignoring reality and thus creating a life-long conflict over water use between the project and cultivators both downstream and upstream. The assumption that community interests - in this case those of downstream water-users - would be defended by the leaders who attended meetings on behalf of their communities did not work.

The practice of communicating and deciding through official letters excludes the actual water and land users in the decision-making arena. Since the lack of involvement of stakeholders in decision-making had a significant implication in land- and water-use management in Chekereni, we shall discuss the issue in more detail here. I shall use knowledge about the water-rights application process to illustrate one form of the stakeholders' exclusion from the decision-making.

The application process initiated a dialogue between the main actors in the decision, the Project Manager, the Regional Water Engineer, the Acting Principal Water Officer and eventually the Central Water Board. All are government officials and experts representing their institutions and are therefore not necessarily answerable to the different water-use groups in the Rau river catchment area. The three experts communicated through official letters. The rest of the public was excluded from this arena. The dialogue and eventually the decision were confined to the experts. Water users as individuals or as groups had no access to the negotiations on how the water should be used. In addition, and probably because of this confidentiality, the experts were able to use their information selectively to favor their interests. For example they sorted out the type of information, which was made available to the Central Water Board, where the final decision was made. Thus in the application forms, the Project Manager tailored his information in such a way that the area to be irrigated was exaggerated and water-users downstream who were already affected were not mentioned. It appears that the information made available to the Central Water Board was adapted to facilitate a decision in favor of the application. That was probably possible because the other stakeholders were excluded.

But despite the granting of a formal water right to the irrigation project, the Water Allocation Authority, both nationally and locally, was unable to allocate water in accordance with the formal system, as the traditional system was not yet integrated with the formal system. It seems that the two systems of access were operating independently of each other and were both recognized nationally and locally. As a result, access to reliable water use in the Rau River depends not only on the rights held by users but also on the users' location. In the Chekereni case, control of water seems to lie with the upstream irrigators, and not with the Central Water Board through the water legislation.

Public Meetings May Be Useful to Villagers If They Are Able to Utilize Opportunities Offered by the Meetings

At village level, the irrigation project was introduced in such a way that farmers could not discuss the advantages and disadvantages of modernized irrigated paddy farming. The Village Council was excluded from the decision to locate the project facilities in Chekereni. Probably because of the village leaders' affiliation to higher authorities, the Village

Council did not question that decision. The public meeting, in which the Lower Moshi Irrigation Project was officially announced, six years after project implementation had started, provided an opportunity for farmers to ask questions. That public meeting became a place for dialogue between the project officials and the farmers. Although the discussion was limited to the villagers being informed about the project, the meeting also helped clarify the status of land rights within the project area. One of the councilors who attended the meeting in which land was allocated to the project declared that it was a matter of being informed about a decision that had already been made by the regional authority. He said:

> We were already used to receiving and accepting orders from above. Who will question orders from above? The region to us is like our father; we have to say, 'Amen'. If the Chairman and Secretary agree, then it has to be accepted. *'Mwenyekiti na Katibu wakikubali basi lazima ipite'*. [1]

The allocation of private lands to the project without any consideration being given to individual property rights is an instance of the use of vertical networks, in which the Village Council considered allegiance to the regional authorities as more important than affinity with the villagers, especially those who lost their land. We can conclude that in Chekereni, vertical networks were stronger than horizontal ones.

The Village Council's decision to accept the project proposals led to the following outcomes with respect to landownership and use rights.

The first group of villagers to be affected was the landowners whose land was allocated to the project's facilities. They lost their land rights without any compensation. The second group of actors who were affected was the farmers whose land was incorporated into the irrigation project. They lost their freedom to decide land use, since they had to adapt to mono-crop paddy cultivation, which, as we saw, gave them short-term gains but later became problematic, and that is the situation to date. The majority of farmers in the irrigation project obtained a single income from paddy harvests, which had to last for between twelve and eighteen months. It has been difficult for the farmers to get used to the change, as it requires great discipline in managing the household budget.

Having powers to decide without involving the other villagers, the Village Council acquired and allocated public lands for private ownership. Part of the village communal farm and the primary school were privatized on the basis of a Village Council decision. Some villagers are aware of the threat to public lands, discuss it, and given an opportunity may request an explanation.

Multi-party politics have produced other political groups with the formal right to organize meetings and question village council decisions, or simply to require that decisions concerning village resources be decided in public meetings. However, this potential has not yet been fully exploited.

Practising Irrigation in a Sustainable Manner Requires Effective Institutional Arrangement

Farmers within the project have been tied up to a much greater dependence on the availability of water and have therefore been open to risks from, say, changes in climate as well as changes in irrigation practices and water consumption upstream. From a land-use point of view the village community has become less in control of the necessary inputs for their cultivation. Moreover, the smallholders do not have reliable and effective institutional arrangements through which they can influence water-use in the upstream settlements.

As water shortage in the paddy fields became more severe, some farmers were not able to use their land. Others fought or paid heavily to obtain access to water. In Chekereni violence, occasional fighting and illegal payments to watermen were among the strategies used. Water-use schedules and cultivation plans are unreliable, and farmers were not able to use their land as frequently and intensively as they wished. In early 1995, project management allowed farmers to cultivate maize and other crops in the paddy fields.

That decision, which was also the result of pressure from farmers, reduced the monopoly of paddy in the irrigation project, which meant the emergence of a different farming system, which might lead to new land-use altogether. If the Village Council's plan to drill groundwater sources is realized, this may also have a substantial impact on land-use as well as environmental consequences for Chekereni and for the Kilimanjaro area as a whole.

A significant change in the institutional arrangement is that the central government, regional authorities and project management have to a large extent withdrawn from project management activities. This change has given room for the District Council, CHAWAMPU and the Village Council to become more active in decision-making in the irrigation project area.

At village level, this institutional change did not stop the practice of decision-making by excluding other stakeholders. A decision to drill groundwater sources in Chekereni was made by the Village Council, and a number of steps towards that end have been taken without consent having been sought from the rest of the villagers, who will be required to pay for the project. If the Village Chairman secures funds and drilling is done in Chekereni, a serious social conflict is likely to emerge if the villagers refuse to contribute for repayment of the loan.

At community level, CHAWAMPU, with the support of the District Commissioner, has attempted to initiate a process to control water-use within the Lower Moshi area. Suggestions have been made, but they lack relevant institutional support at village as well as at catchment area level. CHAWAMPU and the District Council seem to favour the use of the law and police in enforcing water use regulations than negotiating with water-users.

There is more notable affinity between CHAWAMPU leaders and the District Council than between CHAWAMPU and its grassroots members, which reflects the continuation of the strong vertical network left over from the Ujamaa period. At the district level, the Council has adopted a more active position in assisting CHAWAMPU to manage the irrigation project. But the district seems to lack the experience and capacity to co-ordinate the different actors: individuals, project experts, water user groups, village councils etc.

So far, the attempts made by different government institutions to cope with land- and water-use problems reflect the top-down approach, which is not different from the strategy that was used in implementing Ujamaa. The current land-use planning experts do not seem to have the skills and capacity to support the District Council. As a result, the different actors continue to pursue their decision-making independently of one another.

As a conclusion, the political, administrative and social transformation which was carried out in Chekereni in line with the wish to intensify land use has eroded social trust among villagers and their leaders. Social sanctions like the *masale* concept, which worked during the pre-Ujamaa period and was fundamental in enforcing local-level agreements, no longer works in Chekereni. The Village Council relies instead on its vertical networks, for instance, the District Commissioner, the police etc., to enforce land- and water-use decisions. On the other hand the police do not seem to have enough motivation to enforce penalties.

Throughout the three and half decades of land-use intensification in Chekereni, the arena for decision-making at local level was (and still is) occupied with the struggle over rights of land-use and ownership. Following the introduction of Ujamaa in Chekereni, the security of private rights in land depended on how rights-holders could negotiate and fight rather than the rule under which land rights were held. The struggle for property rights is likely to continue pushing aside land-use issues - for instance environmental aspects - from the village-level development agenda.

Local interests and local knowledge in land-and water-use do not surface sufficiently at higher decision-making levels. The structure for decision-making is such that decisions are mainly made on behalf of villagers as directives from above. The Lower Moshi Irrigation Project has brought changes that are not only physical. Mono-crop cultivation has exposed smallholders and their institutions to social, economic and environmental risks, which require more skills, and expertise in comprehensive resource planning than those being offered by the current land-use planning practice.

Coordination of different actors and the control of access to and use of natural resources require laws and procedures to be put in place and to be observed. But the existence of laws and formal institutions has not guaranteed that laws are observed during the decision-making process itself. Given the possibility of ignoring laws and excluding other stakeholders, the state is not, for instance, able to guarantee actual control of an individual's access to national or public resources. As a result of this situation, the declared planning intentions of enhancing equity and fairness and of preserving the environment are not achieved.

The point is that policies, legislation and plans can be important as a starting point and can provide a yardstick for decision-makers to evaluate their practice. But for legislation to work, a decision-making system, which acts to achieve the goals of the legislation, is required. I would therefore argue that a priority issue in land- and water-use management in Chekereni and in most parts of rural Tanzania is that of stakeholders' involvement and access to the sphere in which decisions on access to land- and water-use are made. In the following chapter we shall therefore use the Chekereni narrative to learn about participation and stakeholders involvement.

Chapter Fifteen
Politics in Land and Water Use Management

Introduction

In this chapter the focus is on the issue of politics and stakeholders' involvement in land-use change decisions. By examining the issue we shall be able to contribute to the current discussion in planning literature on transparency, openness and how to increase stakeholders' access to the forum where decisions are made.

In addressing the issue we shall use knowledge generated by the case and dialogue with other researchers dealing with land-use planning and stakeholders' involvement.

Chekereni: A Case of Top-down Land-use Planning

Centralized top-down land-use planning is the main type of decision-making in Chekereni and in rural Tanzania, mainly because of the way the state relates to the rural people.

The relationship, especially during and after the implementation of Ujamaa, seems to have been driven by several beliefs. The state is able to provide experts and funds and to carry out planning at village level. Secondly, the state is the only agent that can bring modernization and development to the rural people.[1] This belief is also associated with an even stronger notion that the state is able to define public interests and pursue them for the benefit of all. Land-use planning was therefore instituted as a strategy through which public interests in land development could be guaranteed. These notions crumble in the face of the Chekereni evidence.

Through the Chekereni story, we experienced the state in different ways, first in the intentions to intensify land use in the area through the transformation programme, and later in the objectives to improve the standard of living of the villagers through the Ujamaa idea and also through the irrigation project. On the other hand, through the mechanism of the state some groups benefited more than others. It was the leaders or experts and the few powerful individuals whose interests were primarily served by the state, through top-down land-use planning initiatives. Instances are also observed from the case study where laws were ignored and decisions made without the involvement of stakeholders, even those with administrative or legal rights to participate. At a detailed level we saw an incident where the top-down approach was used by the Village Council to acquire land for the leaders, their friends and relatives.

Problems of top-down land-use planning in Tanzania are not limited to Chekereni. Researchers like Oppen[2] and Fosbrooke[3] have emphasized the need to change to a more participatory approach. An evaluation of the land-use planning system in Tanzania was carried out in 1996 by the National Land-Use Planning Commission. The Commission reported that:

> The main mistake made by the government is that it tried to impose land-use planning as a top-down solution without really having the capacity for good planning nor the means of enforcement. Land-use planning has always been seen in Tanzania as a 'scientific' discipline and therefore the business of technical experts, with the land-users at best in the role of information providers.... The fact was ignored that in reality land-use planning is as much or even more about land suitability, and therefore more the business of the land-users themselves than of technical experts. [4]

Wood associates the practice of top-down planning with the failure to enhance local management capacities. In supporting the re-orientation of land-use planning towards a more participatory approach, he argues:

> Top-down village land-use planning tends to increase dependency on external intervention, skills and solutions, and fails to develop local capacity to analyse problems and develop locally relevant innovations. [5]

Wood's argument is valid in Chekereni, where the land-use intensification process was dominated and supported by interventions from central government and donors. The formation of CHAWAMPU (association of paddy farmers) was also initiated and carried out by the central government. Both the Village Council and CHAWAMPU seem to rely on the District Council more than on local grassroots. This affinity with central government institutions may limit local-level initiatives in the village. We can therefore interpret the Chekereni case as one in which top-down land-use planning has been practiced, producing limited institutional capacity at community level.

In addition to exposing the practical problems that appear to result from top-down land-use planning practice, the Chekereni case also illustrates the way land-use planning is perceived in Tanzania. In my view, land-use planning is better perceived by examining its practice. In the Chekereni case land-use change decisions have been carried out by experts in government institutions. The experts made plans, which were supposed to be implemented by other institutions, as it was believed that by executing the plans the villagers would benefit.

A direct example is the 1977 Kilimanjaro Integrated Development Plan. This was formulated by Japanese and government experts and carried out by a private company. The farmers in the four villages where irrigated paddy cultivation was introduced were supposed to be the beneficiaries. This approach to planning, one could argue, perceives it as a technical activity that should be confined to the state and its experts. The same belief seems to be held by the land-use planning system of the Ministry of Lands, Housing and Urban Development.

But in the Chekereni case land use planning was more than a technical activity. We saw that often experts and decision-makers used plans to legitimize their decisions and interests in land and the determination of access to water-use rights. Planning in Chekereni, it could be argued, was practiced politically.

Critical planning theorists have argued strongly against perception of planning as a technical activity. Cloke, for example, referring to several theorists, argues that:

> ...(T)he view of rural land-use planning as some kind of neutral and almost apolitical arbitration service between competing rural resource bidders is both artificially simple and politically naive.[6]

Planning theory literature has increasingly argued in support of perceiving phenomenon like the practice witnessed in Chekereni, as a complex political activity. It is a process, which involves bargaining among conflicting interests, and in most cases amounts to power games, that may ignore established regulations.[7]

It is probably interesting to make a short but an important note that the system of decision-making, where stakeholders cannot influence issues, is practiced not only in Chekereni and Tanzania but also in other countries of the world, for instance in Aalborg Municipality in Denmark, where democratic practices have a longer tradition than in Tanzania. Flyvbjerg reports that:

> Citizen participation has actually operated in Aalborg, and in many other instances of politics and planning in Scandinavia, it is little more than superficial hearings without any significant effect on either consensus creation or decisions. Decisions are made in a manner inaccessible not only to citizens but also to politicians outside the exclusive club of aldermen, mayors and ministers.[8]

We can therefore argue that the Chekereni case provides some evidence which supports critical planning theory in arguing for reorientation of the perception of land-use planning as a political process, never a purely technical activity. Within this re-conceptualization, the views as well as experiences of stakeholders and experts should be combined in the process of land-use planning.

Stakeholder Involvement in Planning Decisions

The idea of participation or stakeholder involvement is neither new in planning literature nor in planning practice in Tanzania. Section 29 of the 1956 Town Planning Ordinance (as revised in 1961 and in 1993) makes provision for individuals and local authorities to inspect and make written objections to schemes before the Minister approves them. Similarly, the 1975 Model Village Planning Handbook indicates that:

> "The site selection committee ought to involve the villagers fully in the selection of the sites for their villages". [9]

The 1993 Village Land-Use Planning and Implementation Guidelines also show a great awareness of the need for villager's involvement in plan making and implementation.[10]

Despite the available legislation and directives, participation has taken the form we saw in Chekereni, where leaders are supposed to represent the rest of the community. Judging from the Chekereni case neither all nor most of the different groups seem to have been represented.

After realizing the problem of representative participation, the Government, mainly through donor-supported rural development projects, has attempted to include direct participation in planning and the implementation of rural development. Projects such as these, which are driven by donors' interests in soil and environmental conservation, land productivity and minimization of social conflicts and poverty alleviation, are being tried out in almost all districts in Tanzania.

Let us look at the Soil Erosion Control/Agro forestry Project SECAP in Lushoto district in Tanga region north of Tanzania,[11] as an example of an attempt to involve stakeholders in planning. The project process, as outlined by Massaro, is as follows:

> - Once (project) staff selected villages, they asked leaders to call, publicise and convene meetings, not to convince villagers to adopt pre-set measures derived from research or mandate erosion control as earlier efforts had, but to initiate discussions and dialogue.
>
> - For about a year the staff met with villagers to discuss erosion and other problems, elicit village priorities, explore the advantages and disadvantages

of possible project measures and reach consensus on problems causes and on types of and amounts of participation needed for solutions.

- (Implementing the activities identified) led villagers and staff to create another structure under the village council, a Project Committee of six elected members to monitor participation, organize activities and maintain dialogue with project staff...

- One policy also agreed on by consensus was to introduce no inputs unless participation was assured and to withdraw from villages that no longer met participation standards. [12]

By examining the steps outlined above, it appears that the way the project was introduced did not reflect a real change of attitude away from the top-down approach. It was rather a strategy to ensure that the ideas and solutions developed above are carried out at local level. In the pre-participatory period, say in the Ujamaa period, central government policies were issued to village councils for implementation.

In the Lushoto example and in other projects, central government and donor interests in conservation were camouflaged by the idea of participation. Experts promised financial or other material support to villagers in return for village labour, attending meetings, or a financial contribution to the specific project. There were actually very limited opportunities for the villagers to negotiate and change the agenda developed by project experts which in my view, is not real involvement. This type of participation, which is also practiced in projects in other districts in Tanzania, has been described by Johansson and Mlenge as:

Participation to seek peoples participation in (experts' and government) projects instead of participating themselves in peoples' 'projects'.[13]

This approach to participation, which is also common in other countries, seems to be based on the idea that the desire of public leaders, experts and planners to achieve the common good is possible by following certain procedures. The process therefore becomes one of participation engineering. But the problem with this approach is not only caused by the unfounded belief that there is a defined and general technology and tools for the 'how' of participation, but also, it is enhanced by the problems associated with the notion that it is possible to define a common good to which all villagers will aspire. For instance, the different groups in Chekereni have different interests. Each individual or household or group is likely to participate for different purposes.

Nonetheless, compared to the Chekereni decision-making approach, the SECAP strategy appears more participative in the sense that at least the goal of involving villagers is declared by the experts, and initiatives are made in a year of meetings. We have no knowledge about how meetings were conducted in the SECAP project. We cannot therefore rule out the possibility that the meetings were carried out like the ones we saw in Chekereni, where they turned out to be arenas for announcing top-down decisions rather than a forum to encourage dialogue and empowerment of the stakeholders.

Chekereni: A Case of Empowerment

Empowerment, or how to change planning practice from a top-down technical activity to a more open political activity in which different groups of stakeholders are involved, is a central issue in current planning theory literature. A number of suggestions have been put forward. The latest, according to my knowledge, is the concept developed by thirteen European and American critical planning theorists. The concept, which the planners refer to as 'Argumentative or Communicative Planning', is based on the idea that planning decisions should also be guided or justified through practical reasoning in open discussion or debate.

Among the articles arguing for communicative planning is the one by Patsy Healey,[14] who uses a British planning background and has developed a concept she calls 'planning through debate'. Although she clearly states that the article is based on British planning, it may have something to offer to the Chekereni problem of how to carry out real participatory meetings with different groups of stakeholders. We shall now discuss the concept of planning through debates with the intention of finding out what contribution the concept may make to discussions about rural land use planning in Tanzania.

According to Healey, the idea behind the concept of 'planning through debate' is:

> The challenge of finding ways in which citizens, through acting together, can manage their collective concerns with respect to the sharing of space and time.[15]

From the 1940s, when the first settlers cleared the land in Chekereni, to the present day, farmers as individuals and as groups, as well as experts and the state, have struggled to find a way of managing land and water use. Rural land-use planning in Tanzania is facing a similar challenge, and therefore planners and decision-makers who wish to pursue decision-making in a more democratic way will have the same concerns as those expressed in the article.

Let us first be clear with regard to the basics of the concept of 'planning through debate'. The central difference between this concept and other concepts in planning, for instance, the top-down approach is that:

> Knowledge claims, upon which action possibilities are proposed, are validated in this conception of reasoning through discursively establishing principles of validity, rather than through appeal to logic or science, although both may well be considered as possibilities within the communicative context.[16]

The main idea is that neither the substance nor the process of land-use planning is pre-determined in legislation or in directives, but rather is identified and developed through and in debate. In this way, scientific calculations, like those applied in the planning of the irrigation project in Chekereni, are likely to be accorded less weight, and more room is created for common-sense practical reasoning.

In other words, the concept might be considered as one way of minimizing the influence of technical arguments in decisions and, borrowing a phrase from Flyvbjerg, 'In order for the power of reasoned argument to play a role in society...'[17]. What does this mean in the Chekereni context?

In principle it would mean, for instance, that different land-use intensification options would have to be debated by different groups of farmers and experts moving towards a decision on which option to pursue. The Ujamaa and irrigation project strategies would also have been debated in Chekereni as well as in the district. The reasons and justifications put forward by leaders, such as 'It's a national project', 'It's an order from the District Commissioner' or ' it's a party directive' and others, would not have been so easily accepted as the only justification for adopting a particular decision. Smallholders would also have had a greater say in planning decisions.

Ideas on what should be the agenda for planning, how to deliberate on it and make a plan out of the issues, how should it be used and so on, would have to come out of the debates and should not be predetermined by officials or experts.

This suggestion provides the potential to address the problem of static plans that do not deal with current and pressing problems. According to the concept of planning through debates, plans are likely to take a new dynamic form and to include issues of immediate priority to both the state and the stakeholders. For example, land-use planning discussions in Chekereni and the district would have focused on land-use intensification and on the availability of water for irrigation.

Under the new concept, debates acquire a central role in land-use planning meetings. While conducting this study, we observed several meetings in the region, district and Chekereni offices. Important decisions like establishing an Ujamaa village in Chekereni, implementing the irrigation project and re-allocating land were made in meetings. However they were organized not to debate openly and reconstruct the interests of the different participants, but to bless the views of the leaders or of strong participants with the well-known Swahili phrase -*kikao kimeamua* - 'the meeting has decided'.

In most of them, village leaders were not ready to accept criticism or open accusation. There were not only situations where decision-makers thought and acted as if 'We are right and you are wrong', but also, 'we are right, you are wrong and we should punish you straightaway'. Their words and decisions were final, probably because they lacked what Healey refers to as a 'reflexive and critical capacity, which should be kept alive in the process of argumentation'.[18]

There are two points to emphasize here. First, the mere fact that planning decisions take place in meetings in Chekereni does not automatically lead to more participatory decision-making. In most cases, meetings were used to justify rather than to deliberate on decisions and for that reason should be considered as a possible limitation on adopting the concept of planning through debates in Chekereni and in Tanzania.

Secondly, the fact that information is mainly kept by government officials in the region and in the district, and by the Village Executive Officer and the Chairman, means that other villagers who attend meetings are less informed. The practice of bureaucracy and confidentiality in handling information in public offices is likely to play a part in limiting the information available to other villagers and therefore to constrict their capacity to participate vigorously in debates. Thus in a way there is a big risk that during planning debates, leaders in association with experts may continue consciously to 'hijack' debates through different strategies or to do so unconsciously, because they are more knowledgeable and better informed than the rest.

In short, meetings in Chekereni might have limited rather than encouraged 'argumentation and debate'. We cannot, therefore, adopt the new concept without reforming the ways in which meetings are organized and how issues are raised and debated upon. If we adopt the new concept before we have developed ways in which meetings can really foster communicative debates in a free atmosphere, we may fall into problems similar to those created by the technical scientific rationality concept, where experts have taken over the power of decision-making from individuals and from the society.

To illustrate this point, we return to the participatory Project - SECAP in Tanga north of Tanzania. According to Massaro, the financiers of the project stated that:

> The impetus for participation had taken root and was spreading on its own...villages have adopted tree-planting, contouring and other methods without project aid...[19]

In this quote, it appears that participation is evaluated as a success by the financier because the implementation of project activities can take place without project funds. But later, Massaro tells a different story, namely that, 'full village support has not yet been secured', and he refers to an example where project activities were stopped because of a lack of villagers' support. He also reports court cases and fighting over grazing rights. The conflict concerned a decision made by project staff to restrict the use of a given grazing area without offering compensation or an alternative option to the owner of the resource. Such incidences suggest that the one-year meetings probably did not achieve as much consensus as reported. Otherwise one would expect the conflicts over resource ownership and use rights to have been dealt with in the meetings and not by fighting and court cases, as was the case in Chekereni. Massaro is therefore reporting a case where experts have assumed the role of decision-makers and pursued project activities, despite the declared objective of involving the villagers. The issue is, then, how situations where planning meetings are hijacked by experts or leaders can be avoided?

Kaiser and Godschalk[20] suggest that the role of ensuring that debates are open and participatory should be assumed by planners (experts). This means that they should not take sides with the state or with individuals or interest groups and should be expected to be neutral. The authors call upon planners to pay attention to the problem of un-participatory meetings.

They have listed the following as the skills that are needed by the new planner:

- Skills to foster participation by different interest groups;
- Skills in consensus building and in managing conflicts;
- Skills in information management and communication; and
- Skills in analysing and seeking creative solutions to complex and interdependent problems. [21]

Although the skills listed above were tailored for the American city-planning context, they seem to have some relevance to the debate on how to reform rural land-use planning in Tanzania. We shall therefore examine them further.

From an overall point of view, Kaiser's and Godschalk's assumption, which appears important for the case of Chekereni, is that future planners are supposed to be responsible in ensuring that planning takes place in debate and that stakeholders and the government participate. In other words, the different water users would have been involved in the negotiations for the water rights application. The new planners, unlike those we experienced in Chekereni, would have been less experts and decision-makers and more organizers. Future planners should participate actively in providing information and at the same time producing creative solutions to complex issues during debates. Therefore the planner has to master the procedures for carrying out communicative and participatory planning, as well as being knowledgeable about the substance of the planning issues being discussed. Procedural and substantive theories have to be brought together and integrated in the proposed planner's new toolbox.

If this new planner had been present in our story, he or she would have organized several meetings in Chekereni as part of the planning and implementation of the irrigation project. A meeting of farmers in the villages involved in the irrigation project would have been organized to provide an opportunity for smallholders to discuss, for example, land-use potentials and the limitations of the irrigation project and thereby chart out solutions.

A water-sharing meeting among the different water-users would have taken place and a sustainable process of negotiations initiated. Planners would have been active in managing the land-rights conflicts and assisting the dry-land cultivators outside of the project area on the complex issue of how to intensify land use without irrigation. The list of what we think Kaiser's and Godschalk's breed of planners and decision-makers ought to have done could go on but this is meaningless, because we know that they did other things. Why? There could be many reasons. First the planners and decision-makers were not neutral, and the context in which they did what they did might be an important factor.

We cannot, on the basis of the evidence at hand, argue that planners from, say, the Regional Town Planning Office would have been able to convince the Regional Development Committee or the expert donors to postpone implementation of the irrigation project until several water-user meetings or debates had been held to agree on how to share the water available. The planner would have been faced with arguments such as 'it is in the national interest to reduce food imports'. Probably the planner would have been ignored just like the Regional Land Development Officer was during the implementation of Ujamaa in Chekereni. We may therefore say that the socio-economic and political contexts did condition the way the planners and decision-makers acted in this case. Apparently the context in rural Tanzania has not changed sufficiently to warrant the introduction and practice of real participatory land-use planning.

A consideration of the context in which 'planning through debate' and the proposed new type of planner is to operate is an important issue that has not been taken good care of, either in the various participatory planning projects in rural Tanzania, or in the discussions of how to reform land-use planning. This is so probably because of a lack of detailed research showing the contextual elements that may influence the performance of planning approaches in different ways. The evidence from Chekereni may be used as one such piece of research, which warns that the culture of debates organized by government experts in rural Tanzania, does not as yet encourage openness. It is unrealistic to rely on experts (as planners) because they are yet to be seen as occupying a neutral position as organizers and actors.

Planners and other experts are individuals. They are also political and may decide to use some room for maneuver. They may either put their personal interests up front, or take sides with the state or with one or several stakeholders. They may also decide to adopt a role for the sake of the society or the environment. In reality, the planner in the present context in rural Tanzania has many choices.

We saw how the experts (planners) used their skills to make sure that the irrigation project was implemented. We also saw how village leaders (decision-makers) used Ujamaa to favour themselves and their friends. We cannot therefore rely on the assumption put forward by Kaiser and Goldschalk and many other researchers, like Feraro,[22] who believe that if planning theorists wrote a book of ethics and good conduct, then planners would follow it.

Let us leave the American planners and re-join Healey to continue our earlier discussion of British planning in Chekereni and the problem of actors' interests in (mis)directing planning debates. On the question of how to cope with the problem of individual experts' private interests in decision-making debates, Healey resorts to 'moral consciousness' as a means of suppressing personal interests. In one of the ten propositions for operating the concept of 'planning through debate', Healey argues:

> This in-built critique, a morality for interaction, serves the project of democratic pluralism by according 'voice', 'ear' and 'respect' to all those with an interest in the issue at stake. The important point is that the morality and the dilemmas are addressed inter-discursively, forming thereby both the process and the arenas of debate.[23]

In principle the 'in-built critique' may make planners behave morally. We take this as a point of departure in examining this quotation. In reality, the question is, what will evoke such criticism? Probably a feeling of respect towards other stakeholders.

Respect as such is an interesting concept in the Chekereni context in particular and in rural Tanzania in general. Traditionally respect in the Tanzanian context is a virtue that goes with the age of a person, i.e. the older one is, the more the respect she or he is given, and is supposed to show and give to social relations in the community. An elder or, in Swahili, *Mzee* is called upon for advice and asked for solutions when problems arise. The idea of respecting elders was mentioned several times in the narrative, but as in Mzee Wetundwa's case it was neither honoured nor applied. According to what we saw in the story, respect based on age has decreased tremendously over the years. Sources of respect today are either money or political power or both. In most instances, respect in rural Tanzania is accorded to donors (*wafadhili*), politicians, (*wajumbe*) and experts (*wataalamu*), rarely to elders.

It seems in Tanzania the criteria for respect are no longer based in the culture. Nor are they based on the principles of democratic pluralism, where the members of a society, rich, poor, old, young, men, women, etc., ought to be heard and respected. If the morality of interaction is based on respect and respect is based on administrative, technical and political powers, then we are back where we started- planning debates which are un-participatory and alienating on the part of the weaker groups.

Despite the limitations created by contextual factors in Tanzania, the concept of planning through debate has the following advantages for planning practice and in discussions on planning reforms in Tanzania. First, it provides an optimistic vision for guiding planners and decision-makers who wish to practice democracy. Secondly, the idea can be used to evaluate the performance of planning practice towards greater openness, inclusion and general democratic practices in society. Thirdly, by relating the concept to our knowledge of Chekereni, we have been able to penetrate the case further and developed a deeper understanding on the issue of stakeholder involvement in decision-making. In my view, this understanding might be an important step towards finding the right direction out of the plan-reality problem, which has continuously constrained the land use intensification attempts in Chekereni and in rural Tanzania.

For instance, after the dialogue with the concept of planning through debate and with other researchers, the problem of Chekereni can be redefined as that of decision-making practice where laws are not followed, ethics do not hold, respect is lacking and accountability is lost. I would then argue that without these basic conditions for a democratic process, it is unlikely that real stakeholder involvement in decision-making can occur in the land development processes in rural Tanzania.

The question then becomes one of how to re-introduce these elements in the Tanzanian villages. To guide and probably simplify our discussion, we shall break down the 'problem of Chekereni' as follows:

- how to insert laws, ethics, respect and accountability into communities similar to those found in Chekereni;
- how to ensure that 'tribal groups' (leaders, experts, etc.) do not continue making decisions for the rest to follow;
- how to ensure that the average farmer has access to decision-making and participates in the struggle over access to resource ownership and use; and
- how to strengthen civil society in Chekereni.

Flyvbjerg referring from four other authors suggests that, problems of excluding marginal groups from decision-making have been addressed with success:

> Feminist and environmental initiatives, now so crucial to the political life of many societies, succeeded in placing their issues on the public agenda, not simply by rational consensus, but through the power struggles and conflicts characteristic of activism and social change.[24]

The success reported above did not come from 'participatory engineering', i.e. top-down participatory initiatives from government experts or planners, but rather from power struggles and conflicts. Schon, describing a probably similar phenomenon, where marginal groups empowered themselves from within, hints at the forces behind such a process of empowerment in American society. In order to be able to experience an example of a successful empowerment process, we quote Schon in length.

> By the mid-1960s, the apparent consensus about the content of the public

interest - perhaps even about the feasibility of establishing such a consensus - faded away. As the harmful consequences of centralist planning and governmental action were discovered, special interest groups formed around issues of injustice, hazard, and neglect. By the late 1970s, it was clear that there was no national consensus about public interest. There was rather a field of special interests.... The (different) constituencies had learned to organize themselves, enter into public debate and take political action in order to bring their concerns to legislative and judicial reality. [25]

We also noted in the land and water use struggles in Chekereni, a number of individuals and groups who realized that there was no 'Chekereni consensus'. They organized themselves and fought for their rights and interests. Some managed, others did not.

The role of the legislature and the judiciary was very decisive in the success stories of the different interest groups described by Schon. We do not have any example where we saw the courts of law operating and making a judgment over the different court cases from Chekereni. Mzee Wetundwa's case and several other cases from Mama Tabu's group have been known to the Customary Lands Tribunal for years, but they have not been judged. It could be argued that, the groups in Schon's story, empowered themselves and brought their cases to an alternative decision-making system after the planning and administrative system failed them. From the evidence of Chekereni, we cannot yet talk of judicial reality.

What we can say is that Chekereni is a case of empowerment. An empowerment process was observed and has been narrated. Different interest groups struggled to find their own ways of accessing the decision-making arena and making their interests a reality. One might associate the low rate of success among different groups to the fact that since the adoption of socialism and single-party politics in Tanzania, it appears that, the legislature, judiciary and executive have been almost one and the same institution. In some instances, it could be the same person who heads the party institution and administrative office in the region or district. However, this may not be a sufficient explanation, because there are also cases where landowners in the highlands were able to fight successfully for their land rights against the Ujamaa Village Council within the same legal and institutional set up.

The concept of the 'strength of the civil society' or social capital, may help us understand the Chekereni empowerment process better.

Robert Putnam[26] studied two regions in Italy, comparing the strength of civil society in Seveso in the north and Pietrapertosa in the south. His main finding in relation to our discussion is that in the northern region, where the civil society was stronger, there were more democratic practices and empowerment processes than in the south, which he argued was backward not only politically, but also in its economic and infrastructure development. Putnam applied the concept of social capital to put together the different social relations and institutions, which enhance the civil strength of the society. According to him, the main elements, which constitute social capital, are trust, norms and networks. Elaborating on this, Putnam writes:

> The social contract that sustains such collaboration in the civic community is not legal but moral. The sanction for violating it is not penal, but exclusion from the network of solidarity and co-operation. Norms and expectations play an important role.... Ways of life are made viable by classifying certain behaviors worthy of praise and others as undesirable, or even unthinkable.[27]

By using the social capital concept in evaluating society in Chekereni, we see that there is a very limited amount of it. Sanctions are enforced by the police rather than by social ties. Solidarity and expectations seem to reside within limited groups formed for a particular interest, such as water, land rights or livestock security. This solidarity is not extended to other areas of normal life in Chekereni.

Vertical interactions are stronger and tend to undermine horizontal networks. Local leaders are inclined to foster vertical arrangements rather than horizontal ones. They feel themselves to be more part of the central government or the party office in town, than members of the local community. That feeling may be justified by the fact that they draw most of their powers from above, and hardly from the grass roots.

The notion of morality raised earlier in discussing 'planning through debates' is also central in the social capital concept, where it is associated with social sanctions established by the community to enforce moral behaviour. In the social capital argumentation, it is not just hoped that members will be moral but there are social sanctions and possibly tangible consequences for those who do what the society considers undesirable or unthinkable. But the situation in Chekereni is such that the network of solidarity and co-operation is very weak, especially between the leaders and the other community members.

As a result, social sanctions are weakened. The definition of what is undesirable or unthinkable varies between groups. Taking away individual land rights without negotiations or compensation is one form of behaviour, which is likely to be interpreted differently among different groups in Chekereni. Favouritism, including corruption, is not desirable but is practiced almost openly. What does this mean for the empowerment process in the village?

According to Putnam, social capital provides society with the opportunities and incentives to develop civic traditions leading to a strong civil society. In other words, social capital is a necessary input or driving force in a successful process of empowerment. The mere existence of different small groups in the Chekereni society may not be a sufficient factor to sustain a successful empowerment process. The groups need fertile ground on which to develop.

Earlier we argued, using the illustration of an empowerment process reported from America, that probably one way out of the Chekereni problem is through an empowerment process, which grows from within and through continuous struggles and conflict. Therefore planners and decision-makers who are keen to see more democratic practices will be concerned with how to provide fertile ground for the empowerment process to grow. We are therefore talking about providing that ground. However, Putnam cautions that it takes generations to develop social capital:

> Where institution building (and not mere constitution-writing) is concerned, time is measured in decades. This was true of the German Lander, it has been true of the Italian regions (he studied) and of the communal republics before then, and it will be true of the ex-Communist states of Eurasia, even in the most optimistic scenarios.[28]

Given the institutional problems we have examined in Chekereni, certainly there is a stronger need for institution building than there is for constitution writing, both in Chekereni society and within the planning system. It is likely that the pre-conditions for success as set out in the quotation will apply to Chekereni and to Tanzania.

Apparently decades of time is not the only input required in that type of a project. According to John Friedmann, the empowerment process, which he refers to as alternative development, requires more than time:

> ...It requires a strong state to implement its policies. A strong state, however, is not top-heavy, with an arrogant and cumbersome bureaucracy; it is, rather, an agile and responsive state, accountable to its citizens. It is a state that rests on the strong support of an inclusive democracy.[29]

With the idea of social capital and the need for a responsive state, we

180

can make the following comment on the problem of empowerment in Chekereni. The bureaucratic state, which is also top-heavy, may have contributed in limiting the process of empowerment in Chekereni. This is because although empowerment, as described by John Friedmann,[30] who offers examples from Latin American countries in the 1980s, and by Schon,[31] and in Chekereni, is caused by poor performance of the state institutions in fostering certain interests in a society, the same empowerment relies on the nature of the state. In most instances, the state provides the environment for individuals to (or not to) form associations that then grow into empowerment interest groups. In addition, the state maintains institutions like a judiciary, through which the groups can pursue their struggles. It is, however, a recent phenomenon in Tanzania for groups formed outside either village council or the CCM Party to be formerly recognized.

This condition may explain why the group of villagers behind Mzee Wetundwa's case does not want to appear in public. Instead they relied on Mzee Wetundwa. We remember that the Divisional Secretary accused Mzee Wetundwa of inciting villagers against Ujamaa because he had organized the group without the consent of the Village Council. In my view, the fact that the group did not come out into the open, like that of the farmers from villages in the highlands, might have contributed to both the Village Council and other officers in the District not taking the conflict seriously.

However there are signs that the nature of the state in Tanzania is changing. Since the 1980s, Tanzania has initiated a process of ideological reforms and has changed from being a single-party regime to having a more liberal multiparty politics. The nature of the state is likely to require more openness and transparency in decision-making than what was practiced in Chekereni. The new political context which is emerging, albeit slowly, is likely to encourage individuals and households to form groups and take a more active role in decision-making and development issues at local level. Individual households or groups of households have shown a capacity to initiate and pursue their own empowerment processes. It is worth noting that, smallholder collaboration is not only important for achieving political influence over decision-making. It is also crucial to the management of the agricultural intensification process, which is vital for rural development in Tanzania.

The intensification of rural land-use requires technological and other input, which individual smallholders alone can hardly acquire. We argue that it is through land users' initiatives that sufficient trust, norms and networks will be created among the villagers. It is these things that make up the social capital needed to foster group formation, maintenance of civic traditions, thus facilitating collaboration by which they are likely to improve their access to the needed political power, technologies and input.

We have seen that individuals, households and groups initiated a collaboration and empowerment process because of their interests. Kobia, writing on the basis of experience of Kenya, argues,

> It is as much the responsibility of individuals to press for their rights to participate in decisions that affect them directly (or even indirectly, e.g. environmental aspects) as it is the responsibility of the government to create and enlarge space for citizens' participation. Failure to let people participate robs the government its legitimacy and credibility.[32]

If, by becoming more liberal, the state adopts the role of being responsive and accountable to its citizens, as suggested by Friedmann in the quote above, and if the state wishes to govern with legitimacy and credibility, as suggested by Kobia, then it will wish to create more space for the involvement of stakeholders in decision-making. Without that change of attitude within the state, it is unrealistic to expect significant changes in the way land use planning is carried out. On the other hand, the day-to-day struggles of different stakeholders are likely to contribute in influencing the state to move towards a more democratic practice. As the state is changing, so will the land use planning system.

It is, therefore, within the changing nature of the state that we re-emphasize the role of land-use planning as that of creating more room and space for stakeholders' negotiations and contributions in land-use change decisions, not only because there are moral obligations involved, but also because this will enhance the credibility and legitimacy of the state.

Organizing planning debates in which stakeholders negotiate their interests is therefore a central role of planners. Planners who wish to encourage and sustain a real empowerment process must work towards democracy. There are no ready-made procedures on how to work towards democratic practice. The task is complex. The planner 'must take sides with open communication, in other words with participatory and discursive democracy'.[33] In the more democratic planning practice, credibility will no longer be based on the number of plans produced, but rather on the way different actors are enabled to resolve their disagreements in the most efficient and socially acceptable ways, given their differences.

Notes

Notes to Chapter One

[1] The National Land Use Planning Commission (NLUPC); *Guidelines for Village Land-use Planning and Implementation in Tanzania.* Unpublished report, 1993.

Notes to Chapter Two

[1] John Forester refers to a phrase, 'Don't ask, 'What's the problem?' ask, 'What's the story?' - That way you'll find out what the problem really is,' as a practical rule of conduct, recommended by Richard Newstadt and Ernest May, to planning and policy analysts. See Forester J., *Learning from Practice Stories: The Priority of Practical Judgment.* p. 186 - 209. In Fischer and Forester, J. (eds.) *The Argumentative Turn in Policy Analysis and Planning,* UCL Press, 1993. p.186,

[2] In 1918 the Germans lost Tanganyika to Britain and in 1923 The Imperial Ordinance was renamed The Land Ordinance, which facilitated land alienation under British rule. Later it was adopted by the independence government as the principal legislation in land administration in Tanzania, and was referred to as The Land Ordinance. According to Okoth-Ogendo, 'The ordinance extinguished the superiority title of landowners, both individually and collectively. The ordinance also gave the government powers to resume possession of land granted under any right or interest, should public purposes or interest so require, and to prescribe conditions under which rights granted by it could be enjoyed. See Okoth-Ogendo H.W.O., *Final Report on Reform of Land Tenure and Land-use Legislation in Tanzania.* Technical Annex 1. Technical Support Services Project URT/94/02T, FAO, Rome (1995) pp. 4-5.

[3] Mangi is the Chagga word for the subchief of a sub-area within the Chagga native administration. Below the sub chief are headmen, in Chagga language, Mchili. In this narrative, Mangi will mean Chief and Mchili headman (plural Wachili).

[4] In-depth interview with Mzee Mbindyo in his home in Oria village in September 1994. Mzee Mbindyo is a famous hunter, pastoralist and farmer who lived in Chekereni until 1975, when he moved to the neighbouring village of Oria, because socialism or Ujamaa was introduced in Chekereni.

[5] Already in 1950s, the Chagga traditional administration, i.e. the native administration under the Mangi system, was among the most advanced in the country. The native administration had established a local council as the supreme institution headed by a Paramount Chief locally referred to as Mangi Mkuu. For more information on the Chagga Council of that period, see, for example, Whitlam Smith, Esq., *Recent Trends in Chagga Constitutional Development:* A Report to the British Governor, May 1957.

[6] Figgis, T. F., '*A Report on the Present State of Chagga Land Tenure* (1958). p. 20: 'Unpublished report for the Governor, to be used by the Lands and Mines Department towards the implementation of recommendations made in the 1956 Arusha Land Tenure Conference.' Among the objectives of the conference was to evolve a territorial

land-tenure policy. Figgis was engaged as a consultant to examine the land-tenure customs of the Chagga in order to make suggestions towards a common tenure structure.

[7] *Mtaa* is the lowest level of the administrative hierarchy under the Mangi System. Each *mtaa* or street was administered by a Mchili. The *mtaa* were in 1970s, converted into villages under the Ujamaa villagization programme in Tanzania.

[8] In-depth interview with Mzee Linus Ngowi, Chekereni, March 1995.

[9] Johansen, T., *Small Holder Adaptation to Technological and Economic Change: Implications for Local Level Implementation of Development Plans-A Chagga case*. Department of Social Anthropology, University of Bergen, 1973, pp. 10-11.

[10] In-depth interview with Mzee Linus Ngowi, Chekereni, March 1995.

[11] Ibid.

[12] The first feedback session took place in Chekereni village on 30th November 1995. In attendance were four resourceful villagers: Mzee Bundala Masesa, Mhoja's relative; Mzee Athmani Bahari, a village councilor before Ujamaa; Mzee Mazwili who came from Kenya and knows Mzee Mbindyo; and, representing the Uru migrants was Mama Elizabeth.

[13] The 1923 land Ordinance was repealed by the Land Acts, number 4 and 5 of 1999, which, also recognize customary land tenure systems, and provide for registration of such rights.

[14] The Government of Tanganyika, Land Regulations, Government Notice number 232 of 1948. The regulations require rights owners to observe the following conditions:

1) to ensure that a given amount of money is spent in developing allocated land for agricultural use;

2) to reside on the land;

3) to use the land subject to the right of occupancy;

4) not to sub-let the land;

5) during the first year of the term, to cultivate one-eighth of the total arable land subject to the right of occupancy;

6) during each of the next five years, to fully cultivate a further one-eighth as aforesaid;

7) to have, at all times under the contract, the land fully cultivated to the satisfaction of the Governor.

[15] On average, the Lower Moshi area, including Chekereni, receives about 590 mm of rainfall annually, which falls mainly from March to May. Villages in the highlands receive more reliable rainfall of well above 750 mm annually.

[16] Anne Outwaters, 'Nature Notebook on the History of Kilimanjaro', *Daily News*, 24th September 1994.

[17] Usagara is one of the Sugar cane Estates established in Lower Moshi following

the construction of the Moshi-Tanga railway. Being a private estate, it had water-right number 198 issued in 1956, by which it was allowed to draw water from the Rau River through an open canal. The request by the Uru farmers was to share that right.

[18] *Sale*, plural *masale*, is a common plant in Kilimanjaro, frequently mentioned in Chagga culture. It has many functions, including land-use control. It acts as a traditional beacon as well as a hedge because it grows fast and has beautiful deep green leaves. It is also used as a sign of peace and reconciliation. When planted in the middle of an open field, it restricts access to it, and grazing on that field is not allowed. It is probably because of its many uses that the Chagga brought it with them to the new area in order to extend their land-use planning system to their new homes. Because free grazing livestock have continuously grazed on the *masale*, the plant is very rare in Chekereni, where farmers have opted for sisal plants as boundary markers instead.

[19] In-depth interview with Mzee Masanja Mhoja, Chekereni, September 1994.

Notes to Chapter Three

[1] United Republic of Tanzania, Land Ordinance, Cap 113 of the Laws. Under the provisions in this Ordinance, the Government can acquire lands, which are not being properly utilised and compensate the owners for the cost of unexhausted improvements on that land. That provision has been revised by Acts number 4 and 5 of 1999 which recognize that land has a value and thus compensation shall be much more comprehensive.

[2] During the interview, Mzee Mbindyo could remember neither the date nor the year when the tractor came to his land, nor the name of the Extension Officer.

[3] In-depth interview with Mzee Mbindyo, Oria village, September 1994.

[4] TANU, the Tanganyika African National Union, was the political party, which won the country's independence. It became the only political party. In 1977, it merged with the Zanzibar Afro Shirazi Party and become Chama cha Mapinduzi (CCM), which is still in power.

[5] In-depth interview with Mzee Mbindyo, Oria village, September 1994.

[6] According to the 1961 Land Ordinance and also section 53 and 54 of the Town and Country Planning Act of 1961, Mzee Mbindyo was entitled to compensation for clearing the original vegetation and for his crops since clearing contributes to the value of the land.

[7] In-depth interview with Mzee Hamis Mpangalala in Oria, December 1994.

[8] The Act was an extension of the development conditions made by the 1948 Lands Regulations into the lands held under right of occupancy conditions.

[9] In-depth interview with Mzee Hamis Mpangalala in Oria, December 1994.

[10] This issue is discussed in The United Republic of Tanzania, The Ministry of Lands Housing and Urban Development, *Report of the Presidential Commission of Inquiry into Land Matters; Vol. 1: Land Policy and Land Tenure structure*, Uppsala 1994, p. 11.

[11] In 1963, the role of traditional leaders in local administration, including land allocation, was abolished. The Native Authorities were then placed directly under the central government with appointed officials. However, traditional leaders continued to receive respect and commanded powers locally. They continued to be consulted either to provide advice on land allocation matters or evidence in cases of conflicts.

[12] The Arusha Declaration is known as a policy blueprint, which spelt out the intentions of the government in building a socialist state with priority in rural development. Under the Declaration, the state acquired greater powers to direct economic development through nationalization of land and other means of production, including factories. By vesting such powers in the state, TANU, as the only political party, also acquired more powers itself.

[13] The local administration structure in Tanzania consists of several villages making up a ward, which is administered by a ward development comittee with a secretary as executive officer while teh ward councilor is the chairperson. Above the ward is the divisional secretary answerable to the district commissioner.

[14] With the abolition of the traditional institutions, the lowest unit of administration was the village, within which a development committee was established, its chairman also being the chairman of the village.

[15] In-depth Interview with Mangi Joas in Kahe, December 1994.

[16] In-depth Interview with Mzee Wetundwa, Chekereni, September 1994.

[17] Neither Mzee Mbindyo nor Wetundwa could make the letter available to the author.

[18] In-depth interview with Mzee Mbindyo, Oria village, September 1994.

[19] According to Whitlam Smith, 'The British administrators from the early days endeavoured to establish a unified government for the whole tribe, and the means adopted to this end was the establishment of teh Chagga Council, consisting of all the Chiefs of the separete areas. Each chief took it in turn to preside, as a 'Primus inter Pares' over the council.... There was no popular representation.' See Whitlam Smith, Esq., *Recent trends in Chagga Constitutional Development,* May 1956, p. 7.

[20] The bylaws were meant to regulate land use in respect of lands held under customary rights. The focus was on the conservation of land; matching livestock numbers with available grazing lands, pest control, the enforcement of minimum acreage on compulsory cultivation and general improvements in agricultural methods. Land-use control schemes and conservation measures were formulated and implemented under the bylaws. Breach of these laws resulted in criminal sanctions.

For further discussion of this issue, see, for example, P. Brandstrom, *The Agro-pastoral Dilemma: Underutilization or Over-exploitation of Land among the Sukuma of Tanzania,* Uppsala, Department of Cultural Anthropology, Working Papers in African Studies, No. 8, 1985.

[21] Under German rule, cultivation near riverbanks was discouraged and tree felling on steep slopes other than of specially planted species forbidden. Later, under the British Administration, agricultural orders were issued by the Native Authorities throughout the mountain, prohibiting cultivation near riverbeds. The owners of the adjoining (land parcels) were content to regard the riverbanks as communal grazing

lands (see, for instance, T.F. Figgis, *A Report on The Present State of Chagga Land Tenure Practice 1958,* Unpublished Report for the Office of the Member for Lands and Mines, 1958, p. 39).

Through such conservation-based land-use measures, villages in the highlands were able to support a relatively high population density; about half an acre a head, with 3.5 acres to the average household.

See also T. Johansen, *Small Holder Adaptation to Technological and Economic Change: Implications for Local Level Implementation of Development Plans-A Chagga Case,* Department of Social Anthropology, University of Bergen, 1973, p. 11.

[22] Section 26, (pp. 43-46) of the 1961 Town and Country Planning Ordinance defines the contents of planning schemes to include the following provisions, which mainly focus on urban land-use aspects:

1) Preparation and execution of schemes for orderly development of land;

2) In the course of preparing plans, the following are matters in respect of which provisions may be made:

a) Reservation of areas, zones, and sites for various land uses with respect to public health regulations

b) Provision for location, widening, closure or diversion of roads

c) Allocation of sites and reserve lands for public services including playgrounds, water supply, sewerage, and refuse disposal and other physical infrastructure

d) Provision for the preservation of views, amenities of places, features of natural beauty, forests, woods etc

e) Regulating and controlling the density of development in any area...or by limiting the number and size of plots in any area

3) Redistribution of land; and

4) Adjustment of boundaries of holdings in different ownership.

[23] Similar planned resettlement programmes were implemented by the British government in the 1940s and 1950s; see, for example, A.S. Kauzeni et. al., *Land Use Planning and Resource Assessment in Tanzania: A Case Study,* IIED Environmental Planning Issues No. 3; IRA Research Paper no. 35, Dec. 1993, p. 23.

[24] For further details of the resettlement programme, see United Republic of Tanzania, Ministry of Lands, Settlement and Water Development, *A Report on the Village Settlement Programme from the Inception of the Rural Settlement Commission (in 1961) to December 1965,* which outlines the following spatial planning guidelines for the schemes:

1) Land within the scheme should be laid out and developed in accordance with a comprehensive land-use plan;

2) Each scheme should accommodate 250 families, each family to be allocated three acres of land for private use;

3) A village center of about 10 ha. for a primary school, water points, markets, a dispensary and other central services should be surrounded by homestead plots

187

measuring 2000m2 each. Private farms for food crops should be located behind the residential area. Villagers were supposed to work in the nearby sisal estates, as most of the schemes were, like the Chekereni one, planned for sites close to estates.

Notes to Chapter Four

[1] In-depth interview with Mzee Mhoja, Chekereni, September 1994.

[2] In-depth interview with Mzee Makishingo, Chekereni, October 1993.

[3] Ibid.

[4] Ibid.

[5] Letter from District Executive Officer to TANU Branch Chairmen in Samanga/Mtakuja, 22.07.1968. By then, Chekereni village was part of Mtakuja village and therefore administered by the same TANU Chairman.

[6] In-depth interview with Mzee Makishingo, Chekereni, October 1993.

[7] This officer is the representative of the Ministry of Lands, Housing and Urban Development, the ministry responsible for land matters, including land rights and land-use planning.

[8] Letter, ref. no. MS/5165/21, from the Regional Land Officer to the Administrative Secretary, Kilimanjaro, 17.03.71.

[9] This officer was responsible for assisting the formation of Ujamaa village councils and developing them into producer co-operatives.

[10] In-depth interview with Mzee Wetundwa, Chekereni, September 1994.

[11] 'Village Assembly' was the term used to describe a meeting of all adults in the village who were eligible to vote. Later in 1975, the Villages and Ujamaa Villages Act defined the Village Assembly as consisting of 'every person who is an ordinary resident in the country and who has attained the apparent age of eighteen years' (part iii section 5 sub section 2.).

[12] The amount includes a contribution for the primary school building, Tshs. 25/=; a contribution towards communal projects (mafungu), Tshs. 20/=; entry fee, Tshs. 2/=; and identity card, Tshs. 2/=. At that time, one US $ was worth Tshs 5/= .

Notes to Chapter Five

[1] Most of those who have received a loan have not been able to complete the repayments, and with the deteriorating paddy harvests they are worried that they will not be able to pay. Also, interest rates are rising. For instance, Mzee Sindato, who took out a loan, still has 25,000 Tshs. to pay back Villagers like Mzee Sindato, who have not completed repayments, are given priority in obtaining access to rented paddy plots on the pilot farm. But with the water shortage, even that cannot guarantee that the loans are finally repaid.

[2] In-depth interview with Mama Ontoneta Kahumba, Chekereni, October 1994.

[3] In-depth interview with Mzee Justin Ngowi, Chekereni, October 1994.

[4] In-depth interview with Mama Ontoneta Kahumba, Chekereni, October 1994.

[5] In-depth interview with Mzee Musa Chami, Chekereni, September 1994.

[6] The data was obtained from a physical survey conducted in Chekereni in June 1994, in which a house-to-house registration had resulted in a total of 1007 residential plots.

[7] In-depth interview with Mzee Musa Chami, Chekereni, September 1994.

[8] In-depth interview with Mzee Wetundwa, Chekereni, September 1994.

[9] Cattle were important to the Chagga. Milk, blood, meat and manure were of major significance in their domestic economy and their ritual life'. See Sally Falk Moore, *Social Facts and Fabrications: Customary Law on Kilimanjaro, 1880 - 1980,* Cambridge University Press (1986), p. 24.

[10] In-depth interview with Nasib Msuya, Chekereni, October 1994.

[11] Notes from feedback session in Chekereni.

[12] Ibid.

Notes to Chapter Six

[1] In-depth interview with Mzee Mbindyo, September 1994.

[2] Nyong'o, P. A. 'Africa: The Failure of One- Party Rule', *Journal of Democracy*, Vol. 31, no. 1, 1992. p. 90.

[3] In-depth interview with Mzee Wetundwa, September 1994.

[4] In-depth interview with Mzee Wetundwa, September 1994.

[5] For a detailed analysis of Tanzania's socio-economic characteristics of that period, see, for instance, Maliyamkono, T.L. and Bagachwa,, M.S.D., *The Second Economy in Tanzania*, James Currey Ltd., London 1990. (pp. 1 to 8).

[6] The increase in conflicts over land and cases reported in the courts of Law and to the President's office led to the creation of the Presidential Commission of Inquiry into Land Matters in 1991, set up to advice the government on minimizing land conflicts. See The United Republic of Tanzania, *Report of the Presidential Commission of Inquiry into Land Matters*, Uppsala, Sweden, 1994.

[7] In-depth interview with Mzee Wetundwa, September 1994

[8] In Tanzania, district administration is organized in such a way that below the district commissioner is the divisional secretary, who "administers" the ward executive officers in the respective division. Each administrative district is subdivided into divisions, which are further subdivided into wards covering a number of villages. In this case, the district administrative officer was trying to use the authority directly below him to pressurize the lower level administration in the ward and the village.

[9] It is a local African custom for younger people to greet elder people, even if the former have a higher official position. Mzee Wetundwa was accordingly right to expect greetings from the secretary, who is much younger than him, especially when she had met him not so long ago. The lack of greetings might have undermined the environment for discussion.

[10]In-depth interview with Mzee Wetundwa, Chekereni, September 1994.

[11] TANU is an abbreviation for The Tanganyika African National Union, which is the political party which gained independence in Tanzania until 1977 when it joined with the Afro Shiraz Party of Zanzibar and became CCM, the current ruling party in Tanzania.

[12] We should remember that the two witnesses are the former leaders who allocated the disputed land to Wetundwa and his group from Mkonga.

[13]The defendants were the village secretary and a member of the village lands allocation committee, who were seen by Mzee Wetundwa as being responsible for the decision to acquire his land.

[14]That was the second site inspection. The first was made in 1988 for the district administrative officer, but the information was not used.

[15] Report by the ward executive secretary to the Regional Customary Lands Tribunal, 16th February 1990, case file number 14 of 1990.

[16] Letter from the Moshi Rural member of Parliament to the Lands Tribunal Secretary, dated March 21st, 1991.

[17] Act number 22 of 9th November 1992 an act regulating land tenure in villages established pursuant to Operation Vijiji, which provided for the settlement of land disputes and associated purposes-in short, the Regulation of Land Tenure (Established Villages) Act, 1992.

[18] The *Guardian,* 6th April 1996.

Notes to Chapter Seven

[1] David Buuck, Foucault and Post colonialism: An Investigation, Perspectives on Postmodernism Spring/Summer 1996, Vol. 2 No.1.

[2] The Regional Administration Act, 1997 under the Local Government Reform Programme in Tanzania, has proposed to replace the RDC with a Regional Consultative Committee which is composed as follows: The Regional Commissioner is the chair, the Regional Secretariat is its secretary, all Members of Parliament in the Region, and from all districts members are the District Commissioners, the District Executive Directors, and the Chairmen of district councils in the region.

[3] Castello, M.J. 'Market and State: Evaluating Tanzania's Programme of State-led Industrialization', *World Development,* Vol. 22, no. 10 (1994), p. 1517.

[4] For further discussion of this point see, for example, L. Birgegard, *A Review of Experiences with Integrated Rural Development IRD,* Swedish University of Agricultural Sciences, Uppsala 1987.

[5] The United Republic of Tanzania, *Kilimanjaro Integrated Development Plan 1977,* p. 11.

[6] Ibid., p. 10.

[7] Ibid., p. 12.

[8] Ibid., p. 110.

[9] The Community, which involved co-operation between Kenya, Tanzania and Uganda in economic projects, transport and industrial development, collapsed mainly due to differences in political developments in the three countries. A new form of co-operation was signed in March 1996.

[10] Morrissey, O., 'Political Commitment, Institutional Capacity and Tax Reform in Tanzania', *World Development*, Vol. 23, no. 4 (1995), pp. 637-49.

[11] The United Republic of Tanzania, *Feasibility Report on Lower Moshi Agricultural Development Project: Main report*, JICA 1980, p. 11.

[12] Personal communication with Mr Kivugo, Director of Planning, Ministry of Water, 13th March 1996. Also discussions with S. Mgana, Water Engineer, Dar es Salaam, August 1996.

[13] The United Republic of Tanzania, *Feasibility Report on Lower Moshi Agricultural Development Project: Main report*, JICA 1980, p. 11.

[14] Ibid., pp. 56, 70.

[15] Section 3 of the "Draft Bill for the Environmental Management Act 2004," defines an EIA as a systematic examination conducted to determine whether or not a programme, activity or project will have any adverse impacts on the environment. Section 79 (1) of the same draft, declares that it is obligatory to undertake EIA. Any person, being a proponent of a project or undertaking specified in the second schedule to this Act, shall be required to undertake or cause to be undertaken, at his own cost, an environmental impact assessment study.

[16] Interview with the District Agricultural Development Officer, Moshi, December 1994.

[17] Ibid.

[18] Jamhuri ya Muungano wa Tanzania, Programu ya Kutekeleza Sera ya Taifa ya Kilimo na Mifugo, Wizara ya Kilimo na Maendeleo ya Mifugo, 1985 (pp.4-7).

[19] Interview with the District Agricultural Development Officer, Moshi, December 1994.

[20] The National Land Use Planning Commission was created in 1984 to advise the government on matters related to land use and therefore contribute in implementing proposals made by the 1985 Agricultural Policy.

[21] Interview with the Kilimanjaro Regional Town-Planning Officer, December, 1994.

[22] Johanson, L. (1991), Land Use Planning and teh Titling Programme: The Case of Dirma Village in Hannang District. Unpublished Workshop Paper.

Notes to Chapter Eight

[1] In-depth interview with Mzee Makishingo, Chekereni, October 1993.

[2] Notes from a feedback session with cluster leaders in Chekereni, February 1996.

[3] Letter from Chekereni village chairman to the ward executive officer, dated 13th March 1984.

[4] Efforts to make an appointment for an interview with Mzee Elisadi failed. He is said to have left the village and villagers do not know exactly where he moved . The story from Mzee Makoko, who is one of Mr Elisadi's relatives and former neighbors, is used instead.

[5] In-depth interview with Mzee Joseph Makoko, Chekereni in, September 1994.

[6] Ibid.

[7] In-depth interview with Mama Kahumba, Chekereni, October 1994.

[8] In-depth interview with Mzee Edmund Kirumbuyo, Chekereni, October 1994.

[9] In-depth interview with a group including Mzee Athmani Bahari, Chekereni, October 1994.

[10] For further discussion of this point, see Ruth Ammerman Yabes, 'The Zanjeras and the Ilocos Norte Irrigation Project: Lessons of Environmental Sustainability from Philippine Traditional Resource Management Systems', in J. M. Vivian and D. Ghai (eds.), *Grassroots Environmental Action: People's Participation in Sustainable Development*, Routledge: London 1992.

Notes to Chapter Nine

[1] An informal talk with a surveying assistant from the Regional Lands Development Office, who was working on the project on a part time contract, revealed that the project experts had set a land loss of 25 per cent as the maximum.

[2] In-depth interview with Mzee Chami, Chekereni, November 1994.

[3] According to the list of 'strangers' who were allocated paddy plots in Block RS 4-1, obtained from the villagers in Chekereni, the District Commissioner's son is one of the beneficiaries in the name of Robert Ruben.

[4] By then, the six standard paddy plots created for training purposes on the pilot farm were handed over to the village council and were thus used as communal paddy plots for the village.

[5] In-depth interview with Mama Tabu, Chekereni, October 1994.

[6] Notes from a letter written on 10th May 1988 by the District Administrative Officer on behalf of the District Commissioner to the Central Water-users' Committee.

[7] In-depth interview with Mama Tabu, Chekereni, October 1994.

[8] The two villagers sued by Mama Tabu were Mzee Alfonsi Sindato and Mzee Abdi Mfinanga, both members of the village lands allocation committee and involved in the re-allocation. During fieldwork, I made several attempts to talk with them, but whenever I made an appointment they never honoured it, and I could not compel them to be interviewed.

[9] Letter dated 14th July 1993 from the ward executive officer to the Chekereni village chairman.

[10] The Water-users' Association was the institution set up for water management, replacing the traditional institution by the name of *Wameeku wa Mfongo*.

[11] Letter dated 26th August 1993 (in Swahili) from the village executive Officer to the

District Commissioner.

[12] See also J. C. Scot, *Dominations and the Art of Resistance*... 1990, quoted in L. Fortmann, 'Talking Claims: Discursive Strategies in Contesting Property', *World Development*, Vol. 23, no. 6 (1995), p. 1056.

Notes to Chapter Ten

[1] Japanese International Cooperation Agency (JICA), *Expert Final Report for the Kilimanjaro Agricultural Development Project*, October 1991, p. 128.

[2] Ibid., p. 112.

[3] Minutes of a meeting between the Central Water-Users Committee and the Project Experts in Chekereni, 19th March 1988.

[4] In-depth interview with Mzee Chami, Chekereni, November 1994.

[5] *United Republic of Tanzania, Kilimanjaro Agricultural Development Project, Expert Final Report,* Japanese International Co-operation Agency, October 1991, p. 128.

[6] Letter dated 18th July 1987, Regional Water Engineer to the Lower Moshi Irrigation Project Manager.

[7] Letter dated 11th September 1987, from the Lower Moshi Irrigation Project Manager to the Regional Development Director.

[8] Letter dated 24th September 1987, from the Moshi District Executive Director to the Regional Development Director.

[9] The team comprised the Lower Moshi Project Manager, the Lower Moshi Project Agronomist, the District Irrigation Officer and one engineer from the Regional Water Engineer's office.

10 *Report of the Technical Team for the Regional Project Implementation Committee,* October 1987.

[11] Ibid.

[12] Ibid.

[13] Minutes of a meeting held on 14th November 1987, between the Central Water-Users Committee, Project Experts and district officials.

[14] Minutes of a meeting of the Regional Project Implementation Committee, 18th April 1988.

[15] Regional water advisory boards were established under the 1972 Decentralisation Act, their main duty being to grant water rights to applications from regional rivers.

[16] In the traditional furrows system, control points do not have gates. Instead, water is controlled locally by the duration of flow rather than by volume. Since the *Wameeku Wa Mfongo* were respected and the water allocation schedule known, there was no need of strong control gates. Social sanctions worked in place of a control gate.

[17] Minutes of a meeting of the Regional Project Implementation Committee, 18th April 1988.

[18] *Mzalendo* Chama Cha Mapinduzi (CCM Party) Newspaper, 13th February 1994.

Notes to Chapter Eleven

[1] Letter dated 8th August 1986; From the Lower Moshi Project Manager to Principal Secretary, Ministry of Lands, Water, Housing and Urban Development.

[2] By then the Ministry of Water no longer existed independently. Water administration had been incorporated into the Ministry of Lands, Water, Housing and Urban Development.

[3] The Water Utilization (Control and Regulation) Act no. 42 of 1974 focuses on the administration of water-use rights allocation from national water sources, for instance the Rau river. The Act was amended in 1981 by the Water Utilization (Control and Regulation) (Amendment) Act no. 10 of 1981, which established a Central Water Board to replace the existing Central Water Advisory Board. Since then, national water supply sources have been subject to the control of the National Central Water Board.

[4] Letter dated 10th April 1986 from the Regional Commissioner's Office, Kilimanjaro Agricultural Development Project, which the Lower Moshi is part of. The regional irrigation engineer signed the letter.

[5] Letter dated 8th August 1986, from the Lower Moshi Project Manager to the Principal Secretary, Ministry of Lands, Water, Housing and Urban Development.

[6] Ibid.

[7] Ibid.

[8] See Hydrographic Report from the Regional Water Engineer to the Water Law Officer, 3rd November 1986.

[9] Ibid.

[10] Ibid.

[11] Letter dated 31st October 1986, Acting Principal Water Officer to Regional Water Engineer.

[12] Ibid.

[13] Letter dated 12th November 1986, from the Regional Water Engineer to Acting Principal Water Officer

[14] Ibid.

[15] Letter dated 25th June 1987, Water Law Officer, Ministry of Water, to Regional Development Director, concerning three applications for water rights for Rau and Njoro rivers.

[16] Letter dated 16th July1987, Lower Moshi Project Manager to Regional Water Engineer.

[17] Ibid.

[18] Letter dated 18th July 1987, Regional Water Engineer to Regional Development Director.

[19] Letter dated 9th August 1988, Regional Water Engineer to Acting Principal Water Officer.

[20] Letter dated 28th August 1988, Acting Principal Water Officer to Regional Development Director.

[21] Letter dated 28th October 1988, Lower Moshi Irrigation Project Manager to Principal Water Officer as a covering letter for the second application.

[22] According to the administrative structure of the irrigation unit of the Ministry of Agriculture, the country is divided into irrigation units, which cover several administrative regions. The Zonal Irrigation Office in Moshi deals with irrigation activities in the three regions of Tanga, Arusha and Kilimanjaro regions.

[23] Feedback from the Acting Principal Water Officer, in his office in Dar es Salaam, 13th August 1996.

[24] Pangani Basin is one of the five river catchment basins within the Indian Ocean drainage system. It covers a catchment area of 56,303 square kilometres and controls most of the rivers originating from Kilimanjaro region, including the Rau River. The basin comes under the Pangani Basin Water Authority, the first authority among the other basins to be established in 1991. See also M. M. Kivugo, *Water Resources in Relation to Land Use Planning and Land Tenure in Tanzania,* FAO 1995.

[25] Feedback from the Acting Principal Water Officer, in his office in Dar es Salaam, 13th August 1996.

Notes to Chapter Twelve

[1] In-depth interview with Mzee Musa Chami, Chekereni, September 1994, and again in November 1994.

[2] In-depth interview with Mama Kahumba, Chekereni, October 1994.

[3] Japanese International Cooperation Agency (JICA) 1991, *Expert Final Report for the Kilimanjaro Agricultural Development Project.* See p. 118, under project impacts.

[4] In-depth interview with Mzee Musa Chami, Chekereni, September 1994, and again in November 1994.

[5] In-depth interview with Mama Kahumba, Chekereni, October 1994.

[6] In-depth interview with Mzee Edmund Kirumbuyo, Chekereni, October 1994.

[7] Ibid.

Notes to Chapter Thirteen

[1] Committee members included the zonal irrigation engineer and one of his officers, the district irrigation officer, one irrigation engineer from the Lower Moshi Project, the village chairmen of Mandaka Mnono, Kisangesangeni, Kahe and Mabogini villages, ward executive officers and the divisional secretary.

[2] In-depth interview with Mzee Minja, a retired lawyer with a farm in Chekereni, December 1994. He was also a leader in CHAWAMPU during the fieldwork period and lives in Moshi Town.

[3] Report of the Technical Committee to the District Commissioner, 1994.

[4] Bylaws for the management of the Lower Moshi Project were drafted in 1986 and approved by the Moshi District Council on 27th June1986. On 11th March 1994, *The Moshi District Council (Lower Moshi Agricultural Development Project, Operation and Maintenance of Project Facilities) Bylaws 1994* were submitted to the Minister for Local Government for approval. Among its provisions is the protection of irrigation facilities so that Moshi District Council can prosecute people for vandalism. The bylaws were fully approved in early 1995, nine years after the process started.

[5] In-depth interview with Mzee Kamuu, Chekereni, 1994.

[6] In-depth interview with Mzee Justin Ngowi, Chekereni, October 1994.

[7] In-depth interview with Mama Kahumba, Chekereni, October 1994.

[8] In-depth interview with Mzee Joseph Makoko, Chekereni, September 1994.

[9] Minutes of a meeting of the Moshi Rural District Development Committee, held on 4th February, 1991.

[10] In-depth interviews with Mzee Chami in Chekereni, September and November 1994.

[11] In-depth interview with Mzee Minja, a retired lawyer with a farm in Chekereni, December 1994. He was also a leader in CHAWAMPU during the fieldwork period and lives in Moshi Town.

[12] In-depth interview with Mama Kahumba, Chekereni, October 1994.

[13] In-depth interview with Mama Kahumba's neighbours, Chekereni, October 1994.

[14] In-depth interview with the Project Manager in his office in Moshi town, December 1994.

[15] After the Government of Japan's official contract in Lower Moshi expired, two experts were employed under what is called 'post-project support'. One assists CHAWAMPU in management, especially in finance and in collecting service charges from farmers so that it can finance its own activities and service the project loan. The other has more to do with the technical aspects of the project, such the tractor workshop and the water supply system. These are in principle the two main experts involved running the project behind CHAWAMPU.

[16] In-depth interview with the Japanese expert in his office in Moshi Town, December 1994.

[17] Ibid.

[18] Ibid.

[19] In-depth interview with Mzee Makishingo, Chekereni, October 1993.

[20] In-depth interview with the village chairman and village executive officer, Chekereni, February 1996.

[21] Ibid.

[22] According to the household survey carried out in Chekereni in June 1994, of the 213 households interviewed (out of an estimated 1003 in total), only 80 said that their farms were included in the irrigation project. 106 said that their farms were not included. The rest had farms located in areas which could not be irrigated by the canal because of gravity.

Notes to Chapter Fourteen

[1] Notes from a feedback session with cluster leaders in Chekereni, February 1996.

Notes to Chapter Fifteen

[1] See for example,

1) Ingle, C., *From Village to State in Tanzania. The Politics of Rural Development,* Cornell University Press, London 1972,

2) Shivji, I., *Class Struggles in Tanzania:* Tanzania Publishing House, Dar es Salaam 1975, Hyden, G., *Beyond Ujamaa in Tanzania: Underdevelopment and Uncaptured Peasantry.* London 1980.

3) Stein, H.M Theories of State in Tanzania: A Critical Assessment. *The Journal of Modern African Studies* vol. 23 no.1, 1985, pp. 105-123.

[2] Oppen Von A., *The Importance of Traditional rights of land use and rehabilitation of degraded areas for the conservation of Tropical Forests- Case Study Tanzania.* Aide Memoir on short Term consultancy study to GTZ - Tanzania 1991.

[3] Fosbrooke, H. *The Utilisation of Indigenous Institutions in Formulating and Implementing Land Use Systems.* Paper for the HADO Seminar, 5 March 1984.

[4] De Pauw E., *Development of Land Use Planning and Land Tenure in Tanzania.* Main Report - Technical Support Services Project TSS1-URT/94/02T (April 1996), p. 56.

[5] Wood, A., Re-orienting Land Use Planning: Towards A Community Participatory Approach *Proceedings of the Local Level Adaptive Planning Workshop.* London, IIED. May 1991. p. 26.

[6] Cloke, P.J.(Ed.) *Rural Land Use Planning in Developed Nations.* London, Unwin Hyman. 1988. p. 7.

[7] For further discussion on this point, see for example,

1) Forester, J., *Critical Theory and Planning Practice,* APA Journal, July 1980,

2) Healey, P., McDougall, G. and Thomas, M.J., *Planning Theory: Prospects for the 1980s,* Oxford Pergamon. 1982.

3) Flyvbjerg, B., *Rationality and Power: Planning and Democracy in Practice.* Translated by Steven Sampson. (Draft 4.0) Forthcoming.

[8] Flyvbjerg, B., Empowering Civil Society: Habermas, Foucault and the Question of Conflict. Paper for symposium of John Friedmann, University of California, Los Angeles, April 11 - 13, 1996, p. 6.

[9] Urban Planning Division, Ministry of Lands Housing and Urban Development, *Model Village Plan Handbook*, 1975, p. 4.

[10] National Land Use Planning Commission, Ministry of Lands Housing and Urban Development, *Village Land Use Planning and Implementation Guidelines for Tanzania.* 1993. Section 2.9.1 of the guidelines require planners to mobilize people, including villagers, for implementation of the plan. The guidelines criticize top-down land-use planning and outline steps for practicing 'Community Based Village Land Use Planning', as a new approach developed to 'displace the authoritarian system which has developed in most undemocratic societies'. See pp. 18 - 19, and Appendix. 4-1

[11] SECAP is one of the projects proposed by the 1975 Tanga Region Integrated Rural Development Programme (TRIDEP) financed and carried out under the German government through GTZ. SECAP as a project was initiated in 1984.

[12] Massaro R. J., *Beyond Participation: Empowerment for environmental Action in Tanzania's West Usambara Mountains,* in Friedmann J., and Rangan H., (eds.) *In Defense of Livelihood, Comparative Studies on Environmental Action.* Kumarian Press, 1993. pp. 38 - 39.

[13] Johansson, L., and Mlenge, W., *Empowering customary community institutions to manage natural resources in Tanzania. Case study from Bariadi District.* Forest Trees and People Newsletter No. 22, 1992 p. 42.

[14] Healey, P., Planning through Debate. The Communicative turn in planning theory. *TPR* vol. 63. (2) 1992, p. 145.

[15] Ibid.

[16] Ibid.

[17] Flyvbjerg, B., Op. Cit., Forthcoming. (draft 4.0p. 181)

[18] Healey, P., 1992, Op. Cit. p. 155.

[19] Massaro R. J., 1993, Op. Cit. p. 42.

[20] Kaiser, E.J., and Godschalk, D. R., Twentieth Century Land Use Planning, A Stalwart Family Tree *Journal of the American Planning Association.* Vol. 61 no. 3. Summer 1995

[21] Ibid., p. 365.

[22] Feraro, G., Planning as a Creative Interpretation, in Seymour, M., Mazza, L., and Burchell, R., (eds.) *Planning Theory in the 1990s.* New Brunswick, NJ. CUPR Press, (forthcoming)

[23] Healey, P., 1992. Op. cit., p. 155.

[24] Flyvbjerg, B., Op. Cit., Forthcoming (p.172 of draft 4.0)

[25] Schon, D. A., *The Reflective Practitioner, How Professionals Think in Action,* Basic Books, United States, 1983. p. 207.

[26] Putnam R., *Making Democracy Work, Civic Traditions in Modern Italy.* Princeton University Press, 1993.

[27] Ibid., p. 183

[28] Ibid., p. 184

[29] Friedmann, J., *Empowerment: The Politics of Alternative Development.* Blackwell Cambridge. 1992 p. 35

[30] Ibid., p. 142 - 146.

[31] Schon, D. A., 1983, Op. Cit.

[32] Kobia S., *The Quest for Democracy in Africa,* National Council of Churches of Kenya, 1993, p. 3.

[33] Dryzek, J. S. Policy Analysis and Planning: From Science to Argument, in Forester, J., and Fischer F., (eds.) *The Argumentative Turn in Policy Analysis and Planning.* Duke University Press, 1993. p. 228.

Richardson, L. *Footprints in the Brain of Cambridge Thompson*. Blackwell, Cambridge 1999, p. 15.

Ibid., pp. 147, 350.

Schon, D. A. 1983, *Op. Cit.*

Penrose, *The Logic of Scientific Discovery*, National Council of Business Studies, 1992.

Harvey, P., *Key Analysis and Predictions from Scenario Assignment and Coping, L. and Brehmer, W., eds. The Keyword from View to Essay. Methodology and Coping. Data.* Lawrence, Associates, p. 239.